# HEALTH PROBLEMS
# PROBLEMS
## in the Classroom 6-12

# Advisory Board

**Laura Abraham, B.A.,** elementary and special education educator, Villa Park, IL

**Linda Adamczyk, M.S.,** family and consumer science educator, St. John, IN

**John P. Allegrante, Ph.D.,** professor of health education, Teachers College, Columbia University, New York, NY

**Kathy Brown, M.A.,** visiting instructor, School of Education, Purdue University Calumet, Hammond, IN

**Karen Carroll, R.N., Ph.D.,** Children's Memorial Hospital, Chicago, IL

**Simone R. Fontaine-Hampton, M.D.,** family practice, University of Illinois Carle Hospital, Urbana, IL

**Laura G. Gilliland, M.A., Educational Specialist,** in-school suspension presider, Baton Rouge, LA

**Lisa Gold, M.D.,** North Point Pediatrics, Crown Point, IN

**Virginia Bresnahan Graves, R.N., M.S.,** Double Sunrise Inc., Beverly, MA

**Daphne Northrop,** managing editor, Education Development Center, Newton, MA

**Lisa S. Pearlman, R.N., M.N., A.C.N.P.,** Hospital for Sick Children, Toronto, Ontario

**Katherine Robinson, R.N., M.S.N.,** supervisor of health services, Hammond Schools, Hammond, IN

**June Taylor, R.N., M.S.,** Indian River School District, Millsboro, DE

**Leanna M. Withrow, B.S.,** inclusion staff for community special recreation association, Lansing, IL

**Susan F. Wooley, Ph.D., C.H.E.S.,** executive director, American School Health Association, Kent, OH

# HEALTH PROBLEMS

## in the Classroom 6-12

## An A-Z Reference Guide for Educators

Dolores M. Huffman, RN, PhD
Karen Lee Fontaine, RN, MSN
Bernadette K. Price, RN, MSN, CMM

**CORWIN PRESS, INC.**
A Sage Publications Company
Thousand Oaks, California

*For information:*

Corwin Press, Inc.
A Sage Publications Company
2455 Teller Road
Thousand Oaks, California 91320
E-mail: order@corwinpress.com

Sage Publications Ltd.
6 Bonhill Street
London EC2A 4PU
United Kingdom

Sage Publications India Pvt. Ltd.
B-42, Panchsheel Enclave
New Delhi 110 017  India

Printed in the United States of America

**Library of Congress Cataloging-in-Publication Data**

Health problems in the classroom 6–12: An A–Z reference guide for educators/
Dolores M. Huffman, Karen Lee Fontaine, Bernadette K. Price.
 p. cm.
Includes bibliographical references and index.
ISBN 0-7619-4563-6 (cloth)—ISBN 0-7619-4564-4 (pbk.)
 1.  School children—Health and hygiene—United States—Handbooks, manuals, etc.
2.  School health services—United States—Handbooks, manuals, etc. 3.  Health
education (Middle school)—United States—Handbooks, manuals, etc. 4.  Health
education (Secondary)—United States—Handbooks, manuals, etc.
I.  Fontaine, Karen Lee, 1943- II.  Price, Bernadette K. III.  Title.
LB3409.U5H83
2003 373.17′1—dc21

                                                    2003004330

This book is printed on acid-free paper.

03   04   05   06   10   9   8   7   6   5   4   3   2   1

| | |
|---|---|
| *Acquisitions Editor:* | Faye Zucker |
| *Consulting Editor:* | Patti Cleary |
| *Editorial Assistant:* | Stacy Wagner |
| *Copy Editor:* | D. J. Peck |
| *Production Editor:* | Diane S. Foster |
| *Typesetter:* | C&M Digitals (P) Ltd. |
| *Proofreader:* | Sally M. Scott |
| *Indexer:* | Molly Hall |
| *Cover Designer:* | Michael Dubowe |

# Contents

# Preface

Adolescent children with a variety of common health problems, chronic illnesses, and disabilities are present in virtually every school system across the United States. Because these adolescents are now included in the regular classroom environment, it is important for teachers, coaches, classroom aides, and school administrators to be familiar with their unique health care needs.

The classroom teacher is often at the forefront in responding to classroom emergencies, recognizing a potential health problem, or providing support to children living with chronic illness or disability. *Health Problems in the Classroom 6–12: An A–Z Handbook for Educators* will be a valuable and easy-to-use resource for teachers and others in learning about various health problems and the appropriate classroom management. The goal of this text is to provide concise and practical information about health problems that teachers are likely to encounter in their classrooms. It is not, however, within the scope of this book to address every health problem known to adolescents or to include every known situation that can occur in the classroom environment.

## How This Book Is Organized

*Health Problems in the Classroom 6–12* begins with an overview in Part I. Chapter 1 covers common health problems, accidental injuries, chronic illness, disability, and the effects of hospitalization on adolescents as well as their impact on the classroom milieu. Chapter 2 discusses family and community issues influencing adolescents and offers strategies for promoting positive development of these young people. Chapter 3 focuses on stigmatizing issues associated with adolescents and teens. This chapter specifically addresses the concerns of labeling and the importance of promoting self-esteem. Relationships with peers, gender identity issues, and sexual identity also are discussed.

Part II is an alphabetical reference guide to 150 health problems that affect adolescents. Arranged for convenient "at-a-glance" review, each topic identifies a common health problem, chronic disease, or disability and then offers the following coverage of the topic:

- Provides other names by which the problem/illness is known or referred to
- Gives a brief description of the problem/illness written in language appropriate for laypersons
- Identifies primary groups affected by the health problem
- Offers associated signs and symptoms
- Presents suggested classroom guidelines with cross-references to appropriate health policies and procedures as well as to other related health problems
- Recommends attendance guidelines
- Indicates medications that the affected students may be taking
- Suggests communication topics to be discussed with parents/caregivers or others
- Lists authoritative resources such as national organizations associated with the specific health problem/illness and Web sites where teachers might be able to obtain further information

Part III covers a variety of useful procedures and guidelines. Here the teacher will learn about the appropriate method of hand washing as the most effective way in which to decrease the spread of infectious disease in adolescents. Also in this section is a pictorial guide for administering epinephrine in emergency situations; procedures for providing for the needs of adolescents with casts, tracheostomies, or feeding tubes; the Centers for Disease Control and Prevention's guidelines for the prevention of skin cancer; medical emergencies that warrant immediate response; guidelines for handling bleeding, cuts, and abrasions; the procedure for conducting a testicular self-exam; the recommended schedule of immunizations; and a table of infectious diseases related to pets and reptiles that may be found in the classroom. It is the hope of the authors to adequately address the concerns of teachers regarding appropriate management of health issues in the classroom.

## How to Use This Book

The intent of this book is to provide an easy reference for school personnel to access in the event of encountering students in the classroom who are experiencing health problems or concerns. Teachers who just want to increase their knowledge in assisting students with a myriad of health concerns may also find this book of value. In addition, this book provides suggested guidelines for managing specific health problems in the most effective and least disruptive manner. The teacher can refer to the alphabetical listing of each health problem. Health problems are identified by both their common name and their medical nomenclature. A bold **911** label has been assigned to selected signs and symptoms. This **911** designation serves as an alert that this selected sign or symptom may be indicating a medical emergency or life-threatening situation and that the teacher might want to elicit immediate medical assistance for the child. Classroom guidelines are intended to suggest certain strategies or techniques in planning for the health needs of children present in the classroom. The teacher can refer to the communication section for identifying key questions to be addressed so that the adolescent experiencing health problems can be successfully integrated into the classroom environment. The teacher who desires to further his or her knowledge beyond the scope of this text may find the selected resources valuable in enhancing understanding of the adolescent's health issues.

# Acknowledgments

The authors gratefully acknowledge the comments and support we received from our Advisory Board and from the many individuals who offered us substantive textual contributions:

Judith Conedera, R.N., M.S.N., P.N.P./C., associate professor, School of Nursing, Purdue University Calumet, Hammond, IN

Dennis R. Cullen, D.D.S., private practice, Munster, IN

Renée Fife, R.N., M.S.N., assistant professor, School of Nursing, Purdue University Calumet, Hammond, IN

Deborah Kark, R.N., M.S.N., C.S./F.N.P., associate professor, School of Nursing, Purdue University Calumet, Hammond, IN

Ellen M. Moore, R.N., M.H.S.N., C.S./F.N.P., associate professor, School of Nursing, Purdue University Calumet, Hammond, IN

Chris Reid, R.N., M.S.N., associate professor, School of Nursing, Purdue University Calumet, Hammond, IN

Leslie Rittenmeyer, R.N., Psy.D., associate professor, School of Nursing, Purdue University Calumet, Hammond, IN

Susan Swinski-Heibel, R.N., M.S.N., clinical faculty, Indiana University Northwest School of Nursing, Gary, IN

Joy Whitman, Ph.D., associate professor, School of Education, DePaul University, Chicago, IL

Nan Yancy, R.N., M.S.N., associate professor, College of Nursing and Health Professionals, Lewis University, Romeoville, IL

Corwin Press gratefully acknowledges the contributions of the following reviewers:

Michelle Barnea, educational consultant, Early Childhood Consulting and Training, Millburn, NJ

Dottie Bauer, assistant professor of education, Keene State College, Keene, NH

Anita Davis, chair, Charles A. Dana professor of education and director of elementary education, Converse College, Spartanburg, SC

Neil Izenberg, M.D., director, kidshealth.org; director, Nemours Foundation Center for Children's Health Media, Alfred I. duPont Hospital for Children, Wilmington, DE

Dianne Koontz Lowman, assistant professor of occupational therapy, Virginia Commonwealth University, Richmond, VA

# About
# the Authors

**Dolores M. Huffman,** R.N., Ph.D., is Associate Professor of Nursing at Purdue University Calumet. She has been a nursing educator for more than 30 years. In her academic career, she has taught classroom health issues for elementary teachers. In addition, she has been employed as a community health nurse. In that capacity, she has worked with families of school-age children living with disability and has previously served as a camp nurse for special needs children. Her interest covers the health needs of persons across the life span. She may be reached by e-mail at huffman@calumet.purdue.edu.

**Karen Lee Fontaine,** R.N., M.S.N., is Professor of Nursing at Purdue University Calumet, where she has been teaching for 20 years. She is also a certified sex therapist and maintains a private practice counseling individuals and couples. Her publishing awards include the American Journal of Nursing Book of the Year Award (2000) for *Healing Practices: Alternative Therapies for Nursing* and the Annual Nursing Book Review Sigma Theta Tau (2000) for *Mental Health Nursing* (fourth edition). Her distinguishing academic honors include the Luther Christman Excellence in Published Writing Award, Gamma Phi Chapter, Sigma Theta Tau, Rush University (1997) and Distinguished Lecturer, Sigma Theta Tau International (1994–1995). She has also served on the Editorial Advisory Board of the *Journal of Couple and Relationship Therapy* since 2000.

**Bernadette K. Price,** R.N., M.S.N., C.M.M., is a nurse midwife in private practice. Previously, she was Associate Professor of Nursing at Purdue University Calumet for 15 years. During her years in education, she taught maternity and pediatrics courses as well as a course for elementary education students about health problems in the classroom. During her three decades in nursing, she has worked with infants, school-age children, and adolescents in many different settings, including staff nursing in maternity, clinic, and office settings; home visits with new families; Healthy Start and Head Start programs; and many community education programs. She can be reached by e-mail at bprice@comnetcom.net.

# PART I

## Health Issues in the Classroom

# 1

# Health, Illness, and Disability During Adolescence

Adolescence is a time that represents profound physical, cognitive, emotional, and social change. For some adolescents, this period in their development is exciting and happy; for others, it is a roller-coaster ride of ups and downs; and yet for others, it is tumultuous and confusing. One thing is certain: As adolescents move through this developmental period, the adults in their lives are often caught in the wind of their sails, making it necessary for both adolescents and adults to change the way in which they relate to each other. During this time, adolescents prepare and practice for the coming role of young adulthood.

Teachers might spend more time with adolescents than do even their own parents. Adolescents are a captive audience throughout a long school day, leaving the school and the people who work there partly responsible for dealing with the multitude of potential and real problems that are inherent in this age group. Many of the health problems for this age group are directly related to adolescents' behaviors. For instance, adolescents who are depressed may be vulnerable to sleep disorders, eating disorders, and accidents. Adolescents who are active in sports may be more prone to orthopedic injuries.

Adolescents who have a chronic disease such as diabetes may rebel against doing those things that are necessary to keep them healthy. In part, understanding adolescent growth and development is akin to understanding the health-related issues of adolescence. More than ever before, the literature is rich with research about this developmental period and provides us with a glimpse into the adolescent world.

This chapter provides an overview of adolescent growth and development. In addition, it provides an introduction to common health care problems and addresses the impact of chronic illness and disability on the developmental stage as well as the effects of hospitalization.

# Adolescent Growth and Development

## Physical Development

After infancy, adolescence is the second greatest growing period in a person's life. Many of the physical changes can be attributed to the gradual but considerable increases in the various hormones. These hormonal changes produce the manifestations of puberty, leading to the development of primary and secondary sex characteristics. The primary sex characteristics are those related to reproduction, and the secondary sex characteristics are those related to the distribution of muscle and fat tissue, the development of breasts and hips in girls, and the voice changes and growth of facial hair in boys. For girls, the onset of menarche occurs during this time. The onset of a girl's period is a complex biological and psychosocial process but seems to occur earlier in age than ever before, with the average age being approximately 13 years. Sex hormones increase gradually throughout adolescence. The sex drive is triggered by these hormones, which are higher during adolescence than during any other time of life. It seems that boys are more aroused by external sexual stimuli than are girls, who seem to often connect sex with love.

Often, adolescents will experiment with their sexual selves. Masturbation is common in both sexes during the middle adolescent years and is considered a normal behavior. It is also not uncommon for some adolescents to question their own sexual orientation and consider the possibility that they are homosexual. In some cases, these are transient thoughts, feelings, and behaviors; in others, the adolescents' sexual orientation is already predetermined. It is very important that if adolescents ask for support while experiencing these feelings, they get a calm and well-balanced perspective.

Although most of the physical changes that occur during this developmental period seem to be taken in stride, it is important for adults to understand that these changes are sometimes psychologically uncomfortable for growing adolescents. Body image is strongly affected by puberty. When adolescents deviate from what they consider the norm, they often feel unhappy and lose their confidence. The rapid skeletal growth during this period often leads to clumsiness, and adolescents sometimes feel outside of their own bodies. Actions that are sometimes viewed as carelessness by adults are frequently the result of adolescents becoming accustomed to their own bodily changes. A calm noncritical response is more helpful to maintaining self-confidence than is criticism. A sense of humor also helps.

## Cognitive Development

Cognitive development during adolescence marks a time when there are significant changes in how adolescents are able to think and problem solve. During this time, adolescents develop important new skills. Piaget viewed adolescents as moving to a qualitatively new level of cognitive development. Adolescents are able to apply logical thought to more complex problems. They are able to look beyond the present and into the future and begin to explore the possibilities of what might be, not just what is. Piaget called this hypothetico-deductive reasoning. This means that adolescents can think of hypothetical solutions to problems and choose which solutions best fit the problems. Adolescents' ability to think more logically and systematically simultaneously gives them the ability to construct logical arguments themselves and to question the illogical arguments of others. This is difficult for adults who are often used to dealing with the more concrete thinking of school-age children.

Adolescents are also able to begin to see the connections between abstract concepts. This is one reason why they are able to learn advanced mathematical skills. Because of this ability, adolescents are able to start developing a philosophy or ideology of life. They start to develop their own ideas about life, morality, relationships, fairness, love, good, and evil. It is not unusual to see adolescents become very passionate about a particular issue. They no longer depend on others to define their views on certain things. This is not to say adolescents are not influenced by others; rather, it means they are capable of independent thought.

An additional aspect of cognitive development is that adolescents develop an egocentrism, believing that they are unique and that no one else has experienced the thoughts and feelings that they have. They believe that this is particularly true of adults; therefore, they do not share these thought with adults. In part, this might explain the secretiveness of adolescents, but consequently, it deprives them of an alternative perspective. This is frustrating for adults but is consistent with the task of adolescents forming independent self-identities.

## Emotional Development

The major task of adolescence is to develop a secure sense of self. This involves the process of understanding self, understanding one's relationships with others, and understanding one's roles in society. Eventually, adolescents must synthesize all of their past experiences into integrated, well-formed, personal identities. As adolescents move through this developmental stage, their sense of self is at first very fragile but grows with maturity. It is postulated that one of the reasons why adolescents do not share things with adults is because their emerging self-identities are fragile and so adolescents feel a need to protect it. Young adolescents often believe that if they share too much information, adults will be able to see through them, leaving their self-concepts vulnerable to attack. It is further thought that adolescents' tendency to view themselves as indestructible is actually a defense of their fragile but emerging self-concepts. Older adolescents have a more developed sense of self than do younger adolescents and are also better at viewing others as unique.

Some adolescents have a more difficult time than others in resolving the identity crisis that is part of adolescent development. Adolescents are said to be in a state of identity diffusion when they are not engaged in exploring their own identities. Many times, these teens find the thought of moving forward in life as overwhelming. These feelings are sometimes exhibited as behaviors that focus on the here and now, that is, a focus on the immediate with no emphasis on future goals and plans. Identity diffusion is normal during early adolescence but should resolve itself as adolescents move toward young adulthood.

All adolescents need ample opportunity to develop their self-identities. According to Erikson, adolescents need two things to develop a well-integrated sense of identity. First, adolescents must carry forward from their earlier developmental years a sense of confidence, competence, autonomy, trust of others, and initiative. Second, adolescents need time to practice and experiment with new roles and need to receive support from parents and others while they do this. A warm and supportive environment leads to increased opportunity for identity development.

## Social Development

Peer group relationships are extremely important to developing adolescents. Being a member of a peer group also contributes to identity formation. Due to adolescents' greater cognitive abilities, peer relationships become more complex and relationships grow deeper. There is a movement away from the same-sex relationships of middle childhood toward having to coordinate same-sex relationships with opposite-sex relationships.

The school environment in one sense fosters a separation from family. In many families, the home provides the base of operation but most activities occur in the school environment, with peers becoming the most important relationship. As adolescents move to separate from parents, they often become more dependent on peers. Adults sometimes feel frustrated by the notion that peers have more influence on their adolescent children than they do. The truth is probably somewhere in the middle. Adolescents tend to rely on their peers for advice and support, but this does not negate their need for involved families and adults in their lives that buffer the outside world.

# Common Health Problems During Adolescence

In the absence of chronic disease and disability, the problems that adolescents face are usually directly related to their developmental stage and related behaviors. Adolescent health issues are typically of the crisis type such as pregnancy testing, birth control information, testing for sexually transmitted diseases, sports injuries, and injuries resulting from accidents.

## Risky Behaviors

Despite good parenting techniques and role-modeling by adults, adolescence is frequently a time for experimenting with risky behavior. The reasons for risk-taking behavior can include poor self-esteem, identity crisis, group dynamics (e.g., peer pressure), and the perception of adolescents that they are invulnerable to harm. Teenagers can also be faced with an array of family problems, such as domestic violence, child abuse, separation, and divorce, that can contribute to this

problem. Adolescent depression places adolescents at risk for an array
of serious problems, including suicide.

## Substance Abuse

Substance abuse remains a serious adolescent problem. Alcohol is
one of the most widely used substances by this age group. Although
the use of cocaine is declining, marijuana is still the most popular
adolescent drug. Many adolescents do not view marijuana as a drug.
Designer drugs such as ecstasy are also problematic and sometimes
life-threatening. In addition, despite media campaigns, tobacco use is
still prevalent among teens. Substance abuse is associated with an
array of health risks such as unsafe sex, unwanted pregnancy, driving
under the influence, automobile accidents, and criminal activity.

## Sexual Experimentation

Sexual experimentation can also lead to an array of health
problems for adolescents. The sexually active teenager is a reality.
Teenagers need access to information that is honest and frank. Each
year, approximately 1 million girls get pregnant in the United States.
Adolescents are vulnerable to sexually transmitted diseases, including AIDS. Information about "safe sex" practices, contraception, sexually transmitted diseases, peer pressure, and cultural definitions of
gender roles needs to be disseminated to the adolescent population in
a factual and nonjudgmental way.

## Body Image and Eating Disorders

Body image and the associated problems can lead to other serious
health risks. Behaviors such as crash dieting, the development of eating disorders, obesity, the use of diet pills, and the use of steroids all
have serious health consequences. Through media exposure, young
people are barraged with images of thin women and muscular men.
Beauty is associated with happiness, success, and affluence, causing
young people to judge their own body images against what they perceive as the ideal. Diseases such as anorexia nervosa and bulimia are
difficult to treat and can lead to serious health problems or even
death. Obesity is becoming a serious problem in our society; it leads
to the development of chronic diseases and is further correlated to
poor self-esteem. The use of diet pills and steroids also creates dangerous health risks. Programs that teach good nutrition, exercise,
stress reduction, and the health risks associated with artificial diet

aids are needed. Furthermore, providing opportunities for teens to explore their own identities and build self-esteem is essential.

## Depression and Suicide

One of the most serious problems of adolescence is depression. Depression is often difficult to identify in adolescents. It is generally thought that this is due to the fact that adolescents often self-medicate their own feelings of sadness. Learning to cope with the disappointments of life is part of adolescent development; unfortunately, some adolescents feel overwhelmed and are not able to cope. Suicide is the third leading cause of death among adolescents, and during the past 25 years there has been a 25% increase in suicides among adolescents. Because of the seriousness of this problem, both parents and teachers must be able to recognize the danger signs associated with severe depression and potential suicide. If you suspect that an adolescent is depressed and may be contemplating suicide, you should look for the following signs:

- Loss of interest in previously pleasurable activities
- Sudden and striking personality changes
- Neglect of appearance
- Withdrawal from family activities
- Isolation from friends and social activities
- Noticeable changes in eating and sleeping habits
- Physical complaints such as stomachache and headache
- Decline in school performance
- Drug and alcohol abuse
- Unusual rebellious behavior
- Angry and/or violent outbursts
- Giving away of prized possessions
- Talking or joking about suicide
- Writing notes, poems, or essays about suicide
- Creating artwork that depicts depressive scenes
- A previous suicide attempt

Suicide attempts can be prevented when the involved adults act quickly. If it is suspected that an adolescent might be suicidal, the following interventions are appropriate:

- Share your observations with the adolescent. Do not be afraid to say the word *suicide*. This brings the unspeakable out into the open and may help the teen to feel that someone has heard his or her cry for help.

- Ask the teen to talk about his or her feelings, listen carefully, and do not dismiss problems or get angry.
- Do not judge the severity of the problem from an adult perspective.
- Never agree to keep discussions of suicide secret.
- Acknowledge the adolescent's fear, despair, and sadness.
- Provide reassurance that problems can be handled, but do not dismiss the problem.
- Do not ignore the warning signs of suicide.
- Get professional help immediately.
- Do anything necessary to protect the safety of the adolescent.

## Accidents and Injuries

Despite stricter laws regarding automobile safety, 78% of all unintentional injuries among adolescents are due to motor vehicle accidents. Three-fourths of all motor vehicle fatalities are males. The death rate from motor vehicle accidents is the highest in youth age 19 years or under than in any other age group in the United States. The use of alcohol while driving a vehicle (*see* Alcohol Abuse) significantly contributes to these alarming statistics. Given the seriousness of this problem, extensive educational strategies, coupled with parental involvement that not only focuses on preventive information but also targets specific behaviors and underlying etiologies, need to be implemented in our school systems across the country.

The Centers for Disease Control and Prevention, in its 2001 report on *School Health Guidelines to Prevent Unintentional Injuries and Violence*, provides guidance for the prevention of accidental injuries in the school setting. Some of these guidelines include the following:

- Establish a social environment that promotes safety and prevention of unintentional injuries.
- Implement health curricula and instruction that advocate health and safety. Through this provision, students develop the knowledge, attitudes, behavioral skills, and confidence necessary to adopt and maintain safe lifestyles.
- Provide safe physical education and extracurricular physical activity programs.
- Arrange for programs that teach and encourage all school personnel ways in which to promote safety and prevent accidents.

These are just a few examples of health problems encountered by teachers in their day-to-day interactions with adolescents. Each day, teachers must understand the health concerns of these young people and often must make independent decisions regarding the management of these problems. In some instances, teachers play a vital role in reducing occurrences of health problems or even deaths of adolescents through preventive measures. In other situations, teachers initiate or follow through on strategies to manage health problems and bolster learning and academic success.

## Chronic Illness in the Inclusive Classroom

Federal mandates of laws of inclusion, advancing technology, and improved treatment regimens in the health care field have significantly increased the number of adolescents facing the challenges of living with a chronic illness while attending schools of learning.

Approximately 11 million adolescents live with chronic illness in the United States, representing about 31% of the population. Adolescents living with chronic illness have significantly more obstacles to overcome, and these barriers may severely interfere with the normal tasks of adolescents. These hurdles may include alterations in normal growth and development, exclusion from certain classrooms, social acceptance, a sense of being different from one's peers, overcoming feelings of dependency at a time when autonomy is valued, and excessive absences from school. Teachers who are knowledgeable about the unique health and educational challenges are able to respond sensitively and appropriately to students with chronic illness.

Not surprisingly, adolescents who have excessive absences from school face more challenges in meeting academic standards and outcomes. The school environment not only provides opportunities for learning but also encourages adolescents to interact, work together, resolve conflict, and solve problems. As a result of this process, adolescents develop a growing independence and a sense of the *who* that they are becoming. Any student who misses school due to chronic illness is deprived of these invaluable experiences.

Asthma, one example of a chronic illness, is the most common long-term respiratory illness for this age group (*see* Asthma). It is the leading cause of health-related absenteeism, with more than 10 million school days missed per year. When young people experience breathing difficulties, their attention is focused on their bodies and their anxiety levels increase. Inattention and anxiety interfere with the ability to learn. When this becomes a frequent or chronic situation, adolescents with asthma may be at increased risk for learning problems. Developmentally, adolescents do not want to be considered different from their peers, so they may refrain from using their medications in front of others or avoid informing teachers that they are in need of some assistance. Knowledgeable teachers are attuned to these problems and may be able to intervene before such situations worsen.

For adolescents with chronic illness, access to understanding teachers is critical for a positive school experience and academic success. For those students who do not experience any health problems, the sensitivity and role-modeling by teachers often makes the difference between acceptance and rejection of these vulnerable adolescents. Teachers can gain knowledge regarding health problems from school health personnel, communication with parents/caregivers/children, this text, and resources available on the Web. Knowledgeable teachers are less likely to act on the basis of their own bias and prejudices and are more likely to create a sensitive and caring school environment.

## Disabilities in the Inclusive Classroom

There are several labels that refer to the process of integrating young people with disabilities into the regular classroom. This concept has been identified by some school systems as "mainstreaming," "regular education initiative," "full inclusion," "partial inclusion," and/or "inclusion." Regardless of the selected terminology, current federal laws such as the Individuals with Disabilities Education Act (IDEA) mandate that any child with a disability has a right to attend free and appropriate public education in the least restrictive environment provided by his or her local school system. In a response to these legislative directives and considerable commitment of some school districts, tremendous strides have been made in overcoming challenges in providing disabled adolescents with access to education.

The U.S. Bureau of the Census indicates that 6.5 million children have some type of disability and that 96% of these students attend regular schools with their nondisabled classmates. Based on these statistical data, it is vital that all teachers have an understanding of adolescents' abilities and disabilities as well as the unique needs inherent in being disabled. A knowledgeable and sensitive teacher, who understands each student's individualized education program and meets the student's needs, will do much in creating a classroom environment where "inclusion" is a positive experience for children with and without disabilities.

Common disabilities seen in adolescents include learning problems and impairments of speech, hearing, and sight. In addition, some students have activity limitations and restrictions such as confinement to a wheelchair and use of a cane or walker. Regardless of the source of these disabilities, teachers working with these young people can significantly affect the adolescents' ability to achieve the developmental task of gaining a sense of identity. A focus on these adolescents' strengths or abilities, rather than on their disabilities, may give the adolescents a new perspective of what they believe they can accomplish and foster a sense of self-worth. Adolescents who attend school have the advantages of learning and socializing with a diverse group of peers as well as the disadvantage of confronting that they are "different" and may be the focus of ridicule and exclusion by their classmates. A knowledgeable teacher, who is sensitive to what it means to live with a disability, plans activities in which all adolescents can participate and models acceptance of differences that may have a significant impact on these adolescents' sense of belonging while enhancing nondisabled students' understanding of disability.

The adolescent living with disability brings to the classroom a vast array of concerns to be addressed by his or her school system. In addition to educational issues, these concerns include the following:

- Arranging for a safe exit from the classroom in case of an emergency situation
- Sensitizing nondisabled students to promote "inclusion" without embarrassing or breaching the confidentiality of the disabled adolescent
- Developing learning strategies that take into consideration the disabled adolescent's frequent absenteeism and energy level
- Planning a classroom schedule that meets the unique health needs of the adolescent

The teacher will need to communicate with parents/caregivers, school health and educational personnel, and the adolescent to better understand these concerns. Enhanced understanding will ensure appropriate planning for the disabled adolescent's successful integration into the classroom.

In addition to educational and safety concerns, teachers have identified fears related to appropriately responding to medical emergencies associated with specific disabilities in adolescents. Classroom emergencies such as seizures (*see* Epilepsy and Seizure Disorders), a sudden onset of flushed and sweating skin in a child with spinal cord injury (*see* Spinal Cord Injury: Long-Term Care), and difficulty in breathing in a child with cystic fibrosis (*see* Cystic Fibrosis) require knowledgeable teachers who understand both the significance and the urgency of responding to these situations. Access to information, training, and identification of resource personnel are crucial in addressing these issues and in decreasing the worries of teachers.

The importance of school in the lives of all children is well known. For adolescents living with disabilities, being in school serves to afford them a sense of normalcy and acceptance. Therefore, teachers play a significant role in enhancing disabled adolescents' self-esteem and assisting them with having a positive view about attaining an education.

The incorporation of a healthy lifestyle during adolescence will provide benefits not only during the teenage years but also during adulthood.

## Hospitalization

Hospitalization can be a difficult experience for adolescents. Adolescents who are hospitalized may experience a variety of feelings that are connected to their developmental stage. Because adolescents often see themselves as invulnerable to harm, hospitalization can be difficult for them to understand. Most adolescents do not believe that bad things can happen to them or their friends. When their belief is proven to be wrong, they sometimes need additional support to adapt.

Adolescents are not yet adults but are not still children. Because of their size, most people expect them to act like adults, forgetting that they have not yet developed the range of coping skills that adults have developed. During an episode of hospitalization, adults must remember that an adolescent might not be able to act as "adult" as they would expect. Psychosocial responses of the adolescent during hospitalization might include periods of rebelliousness where the adolescent will attempt to maintain his or her autonomy. Conversely, the adolescent might display signs of regression where he or she will display more childlike behaviors. Both responses are consistent with normal adolescent development. Adults need to meet the adolescent on his or her own terms and at his or her level of functioning at this time and place.

Additional psychosocial responses are typical of any person who is hospitalized. Feelings of anxiety, helplessness, frustration, and anger are normal responses to hospitalization. These feelings reflect a perception of threat to identity and body image, a sense of powerlessness, and a sense of loss of control. Anxiety related to environmental changes, pain, and special procedures is also common.

Adolescents need to be treated with respect and be involved in their own care. They need to be listened to and allowed to put their feelings into words. Positive coping mechanisms need to be reinforced and encouraged. Hospitalization constitutes a crisis that can serve to increase adolescents' coping repertoire for the future. As with adults, some adolescents have better coping skills than do others. Emphasizing positive experiences in coping may serve to increase adolescents' sense of well-being and may negate some of the unpleasant effects associated with the hospital experience.

# 2

# Family and Community Issues

Anumber of family and community issues affect the physical, emotional, cognitive, and academic development of adolescents. Because development occurs in the context of relationships, understanding children as a part of their families and communities provides a holistic perspective. This chapter overviews the impact on adolescent's development of familial conflict and abuse and adjustment problems within the community.

## Family Issues

For most of us, families are our earliest and most enduring social relationships. As the fabric of our day-to-day lives, families shape the quality of our lives by influencing our outlooks on life, our motivation and strategies for achievement, and our approach to coping with adversity. Within our families, we develop our sense of self and our capacity for intimacy. Through family interactions, we learn about relationships and roles and about our expectations of others and ourselves. As individuals and family members, we are simultaneously independent of and part of our families.

### Conflict and Anger

Anger and conflict are a normal part of living with others and a dimension of the family process. Conflict can be either constructive or destructive to individuals and the family system as a whole. Constructive conflict is issue focused and involves strategies of negotiating and mutual problem solving. Destructive conflict escalates beyond the initial issue and involves threats and coercion as strategies.

Expression of anger within the family is not necessarily harmful. In fact, it is healthy for children to observe anger in adults when conflicts are expressed constructively and perhaps resolved. It is through this family process that children find out how to work out disagreements and learn appropriate ways in which to handle interpersonal differences with friends, peers, and loved ones.

When anger is combined with criticism, contempt, defensiveness, or withdrawal, conflict becomes destructive to individuals and the family system. Children who witness unhealthy conflict show greater emotional and behavioral reactivity and often are inappropriately drawn into adult disputes. Adults who engage in repeated negative and hostile interactions are less able to parent their children effectively. Daily, intense, adult-adult conflict makes family life unpleasant, may cause a breakdown in discipline, and decreases adults' sensitivity to children's needs. The spillover effect of adult-adult destructive conflict is the transfer of negative mood, affect, or behavior to the adult-child relationship. Children react not so much to the fact that adults are fighting as to the impact of conflict on their sense of security. Children worry about possible divorce and what will happen to everyone in the family. If the themes of the adult conflict are child related, such as fighting over discipline, children experience greater shame and self-blame than if the themes are adult related.

Exposure to destructive conflict increases children's vulnerability to disorders such as depression and anxiety. Destructive conflict also increases the probability that children themselves will become aggressive with others and develop oppositional defiant disorder or conduct disorder. These disorders are presented in Part II of this text.

## Divorce

Divorce is a transitional crisis that interrupts children's developmental tasks. Divorce forces major practical and emotional readjustments, and short-term distress is normal. As in other family crises—job loss, serious illness, death—the key that determines whether the crisis is temporary or results in permanent impairment is the family's response and coping abilities. Even divorces that are handled well, both emotionally and financially, may contribute to temporary maladjustment in children. Studies show that after a period of time, children and teens who have experienced divorce differ very little from those who have not experienced divorce.

The transitional crisis consists of two overlapping phases: (a) separation and legal divorce and (b) settling in to the new family structure. When adults work at the transition in healthy ways, it takes 2 to 3 years for a family to adjust to its new structure. When emotional issues are not resolved or there is an angry and/or vengeful divorce, a family can remain stuck for years or perhaps even for generations.

The new family structure, referred to as the "binuclear family," consists of two households (the household of each parent) and both extended family networks. Ground rules are established for living separately, for example, where the children will reside, and how visitation is arranged.

## Blended Families

When parents remarry or form a new family unit, the new structure is referred to as a blended family. The two expected peaks of emotional tension are at the time of a parent's serious commitment to a new relationship and again at the time of actual formation of a blended family. If both parents blend families at about the same time, children may feel as though they are on an emotional roller-coaster. In addition, all children suffer when there is intense conflict between their biological parents, and all children benefit when parents maintain civil, cooperative, coparental relationships.

Adjustment to a new family structure seems to require a minimum of 2 to 3 years. New relationships are harder to negotiate because they do not develop gradually, as intact families do, but rather begin "midstream." Children cannot forget the relationships that went before and that might still be more powerful than the new relationships. Children rarely surrender their attachment to their first parents, no matter how negative the relationships. Family integration is harder when there are adolescents. Both girls and boys in early adolescence, beginning at age 11 or 12 years, seem to have a particularly difficult time adjusting to blended families. If they are concerned about distancing and individuating from their families of origin, teens especially will often resist learning new roles and relating to new family members.

One of the greatest challenges for parents is to allow children to experience and express the full range of negative and positive feelings toward both sets of parents and stepparents. Often, parents will subtly or directly demand children's complete allegiance. Children feel "caught"—afraid that if they do not express love for a new stepparent, they will anger one parent, but that if they do express such love, they are being disloyal and will lose the love of the other parent. Some attempt to resolve their divided loyalties by taking sides or by playing one side against the other.

Children's struggles with blended family issues may surface at school. If depressed or anxious, children may withdraw from teachers and peers. Or, they may engage in acting out or antisocial behaviors. Suggestions for classroom management of these problems can be found in Part II of this text.

## Chronic Illness and Disability of Family Members

Chronic illness or disability often places the family under significant levels of stress. Families must master the practical and emotional tasks of the immediate situation while trying to plan for the uncertainties of the future. Family burden is the overall level of distress experienced as a result of the illness or disability. This burden includes disruption in household functioning, restriction of social activities, and financial hardship due to medical bills and perhaps the loss of one income. Hospitalization for acute episodes leads to disruption of the family system as children suffer repeated separations and an unpredictable environment.

When chronic illness or disability of a parent occurs during the child-rearing phase in the family life cycle, it usually serves to prolong this period. Appropriate reallocation of roles and high levels of adaptability and problem solving may make the difference between successful and dysfunctional coping and adaptation. The new structure of the family may resemble a single-parent family with an added "dependent"—the ill or disabled adult. It is likely that the well parent will have to turn to the children to share responsibilities. In some cases, children may have to sacrifice their own developmental needs.

In general, illness and disability tend to push individual and family developmental processes toward transition and increased cohesion. Symptoms, loss of function, demands of new roles, and fear of loss through death all require the family to pull together. Relapsing illnesses alternate between periods of drawing the family inward and periods of release from the immediate demands of the disease.

## Death

Coming to terms with death is the most difficult task a family must confront in life. The death of a family member radically disrupts the family system. The first priority in managing the crisis of grief is to reestablish a stable equilibrium that is necessary to support ongoing family development. The fewer the family resources—extended family, friends, financial supports—the more the family system will be stressed. Family members need to be able to talk with one another about their emotions concerning the death and its circumstances. A family's ability to communicate about death is partially determined by its members' previous patterns of communication. When individuals are unable to talk about the death, any misconceptions about the cause or circumstances cannot be corrected. For example, in some families the cause of death is never told to children, who then grow up with questions or distorted ideas.

A teenager's reactions to the death of a parent depend in part on the degree of caretaking they have lost, the emotional state of the surviving parent, and the availability of other caretakers. It is important that adults do not underestimate the signficance of the loss, especially for those teens who verbalize few of their feelings.

Adolescents cognitively can understand death in adult terms. They may associate the tragedy with their age-appropriate search for independence. Some may feel guilty because they wished to be free of parental control prior to the death of a parent. If other family members over-idealize the deceased parent, some teens may feel alienated and not understood. Teens also worry about how well the surviving parent will care for them and what will happen to the family. Some teens may become closer to the family and might even feel responsible for the family's survival. Others may begin acting out as their attempts to become their own persons are complicated with grief. Boys tend to use acting-out behaviors to escape their pain. They may engage in anti-social behaviors such as fighting, stealing, and engaging in substance abuse. Some girls become sexually active in an attempt to escape their pain or may become pregnant to comfort themselves and replace their loss. These acting-out behaviors further stress the grieving family system.

When a child in a family dies, the needs of the surviving siblings are too often neglected. If the child who dies was ill for an extended period, the surviving siblings may have had less attention paid to their needs for some time. Normal sibling rivalry may contribute to intense survival guilt that can block normal growth and development. Complicating the loss is a sense of also losing the parents, who may be preoccupied with their own grief. Parents may also become overprotective of the surviving children, leading to difficulties with autonomy and separation.

All family members play roles both within and outside the family. Realignment of roles is a necessary function of grieving. Roles may be reassigned on the basis of achievement and interest or on the basis of gender and age. Individuals must adapt and adjust to the new roles and to the absence of the deceased family member. The more flexible family will typically be more successful. Like individuals, families are unique in their mourning processes. What is effective for one family might not be effective for another.

## Abuse, Neglect, and Family Violence

Abuse refers to a pattern of behavior that dominates, controls, lowers self-esteem, and/or takes away freedom of choice. It is systematic persecution of another individual, ranging from subtle words or actions to violent battering—acts of commission. Abuse also includes various types of neglect—acts of omission. In all 50 states, teachers are required by law to report suspected incidents of child abuse, and in all 50 states there is a penalty—civil, criminal, or both—for failure to report child abuse.

Each year, approximately 2.8 million American children experience at least one act of physical violence, and 1.4 million are otherwise abused or neglected. Children who live in homes where a parent is being abused are 1,500 times more likely to be abused than are children living in nonviolent homes. Physical abuse is often disguised as discipline. For many, hitting begins when they are infants and does not end until they leave home. Adolescents are more likely to be beaten up and to have a knife or gun used against them than are younger children. In the United States, homicide is one of the five leading causes of death before age 18 years.

Each year, more than 300 parents in the United States are killed by their children. In 90% of the cases, the teen had been severely abused and/or the mother was a victim of abuse, the teen's attempts to get help had failed, and the family situation had become increasingly intolerable prior to the murder.

Emotional abuse is often equally as damaging as physical abuse. Words can hit as hard as a fist, and the damage to self-esteem can last a lifetime. Emotional abuse involves one person shaming, embarrassing, ridiculing, or insulting another person either in private or in public. It may include destruction of personal property or the killing of pets in an effort to frighten or control the victim. Statements such as "You can't do anything right," "You're ugly and stupid—no one else would want you," and "I wish you had never been born" are devastating to self-esteem.

Neglect is the most frequently reported type of child maltreatment. It includes lack of adequate physical care, nutrition, and shelter.

It also includes unsanitary conditions that often contribute to health and developmental problems. Lack of human contact and nurturance is considered to be emotional neglect.

Victims develop low self-esteem as they begin to believe the abuse that they endure is evidence of personal worthlessness. The effect of living in a climate of fear and uncertainty contributes to an increased risk for several mental disorders, including depression, substance abuse, self-mutilation, and eating disorders. Fully 60% to 85% of abused children are at risk for posttraumatic stress disorder. Family violence has the worst mental health outcomes of any form of interpersonal violence because there is no safe and supportive place for retreat.

Childhood sexual abuse is a process, not just an event. Not all children become symptomatic following sexual abuse; some might not encounter difficulties until adulthood, and some might never experience symptoms. A single traumatic experience usually does not lead to mental disorders. To the extent that other life experiences are positive, children are likely to experience few long-term effects, if any. To the extent that other life experiences are also negative, the effects of the sexual abuse are amplified.

There is no identified "sexual abuse syndrome," and reactions vary greatly from one child to another. The effects of sex abuse are most severe when the incidents are frequent and occur over a long period of time, the activities are wide-ranging and extensive, there is more than one perpetrator, the relationship to the perpetrator is close, and sex abuse is combined with physical and emotional abuse. In these situations, behavioral, cognitive, and physical problems emerge along with difficulties with emotional stability and interpersonal relationships during childhood, adolescence, and adulthood.

Abuse disrupts the smooth progression of development in several ways. For some, there is an intensification and fixation of the current developmental stage. Others regress to an earlier stage. And some prematurely accelerate and develop pseudo-maturity. The general rule of thumb is that the earlier the abuse, the more profound the damage.

## Community Issues

### Homelessness

For the past 25 years, more than one-half million Americans have been left homeless, living on city streets, and (if they are lucky) sleeping in emergency shelters each night. The homeless include people of every race, ethnic background, and educational level. Families now constitute 37% of the homeless population. Many homeless families are headed by women who take their children and flee from abusive husbands or partners. One of the most profound effects of homelessness is that families may lose their sense of identity as a family, parents may lose their sense of competence, and children may lose their concept of home.

Many adolescents find themselves living on their own as a consequence of running away or being thrown out by their families. Some leave to escape physical or sexual abuse. In other situations, parents of acting-out adolescents may force the teens out of their homes as a way of gaining control in their own lives. Adolescents also become homeless because of family conflict, chaotic family systems, and unsuccessful foster care situations.

Homelessness has a significant impact on the education of children. The inability to prove residency for local school systems becomes an enrollment problem. Live-in shelters often have a time limit for residency, after which the family must seek a different shelter. This situation disrupts the educational process by forcing school changes every few months. Multiple new curricula, new teachers, and new peers make for poor educational outcomes.

## Community Violence and School Violence

Violence in the United States has reached epidemic proportions in urban, suburban, and rural areas. Although urban youth may experience higher levels of exposure than do others, children generally are exposed to a startling amount of violence. Those who are not direct victims or witnesses hear stories of violence told by family members, peers, and neighbors. The media also present many models of violence to which children are exposed. Some movies and television shows demonstrate that "good" people use force to achieve "good" ends. Many story lines make no attempt to justify the use of force for "good" ends; they simply portray endless senseless acts of cruelty by some humans on others. With these types of community and media examples, children develop values that tolerate, and even accept as normal, everyday violence between people.

Every 2 hours, a child dies from a gunshot wound and many more are seriously wounded. Armed assailants are becoming significantly younger, with nearly half being between ages 11 and 20 years. Males, the chief perpetrators and also the chief victims of violent acts, are twice as likely as females to be victimized by other males. Males also hurt themselves at a much higher rate, with a suicide rate four times that of teen girls.

Affective violence is the verbal expression of intense anger and emotions. It is the bullying, ugly taunts, disrespect, alienation, scapegoating, and physical threats that many children experience every day. Victims of affective violence are more likely to experience distress and depression than are children who are not subjected to it. More research is needed on how exposure to violence affects growth and development, intellectual growth, school performance, decision-making ability, and hope for the future.

Predatory violence includes hate crimes that are motivated by bias and hatred of minority groups. People are harassed, tortured, or even killed just because they are different. Hate crimes occur in rural, suburban, and urban communities alike, targeting racial or ethnic minorities, religious minorities, and gay, lesbian, bisexual, or transgendered (GLBT) people. African Americans are the most frequent target, GLBT individuals are the next most frequent target, and they are followed by European Americans and Jews. A large proportion—60%—of hate crime perpetrators are youthful thrill seekers who commit these crimes for the "thrill" associated with the act of victimizing.

Many teens live in a violent world. Some experience this "typical" violence plus an increased risk for violence unique to their minority status. Ideally, the school setting could offer a temporary haven where all students feel safe. The reality, however, is that hate crimes often occur during school hours. For example, 90% of GLBT youth report verbal abuse, and as many as half are physically harassed while at school.

There are four types of personal cause homicide: nonspecific homicide, revenge homicide, patricide/matricide homicide, and authority killing. In nonspecific homicides, only the perpetrator, who seems to want as many victims as possible, knows the motive. The crime often becomes a massacre with little regard for the value of human life. The crime, although planned, is often unorganized and includes no arrangements for escaping the police. On December 1, 1997, in West Paducah, Kentucky, Michael Carneal, age 14 years, entered his high school and opened fire on a prayer meeting, killing three and wounding five people. When another teen grabbed him to stop him, Carneal said, "Kill me please, I can't believe I did that."

Perpetrators of revenge homicides retaliate for real or imagined offenses brought on by the victim. Depending on the event that triggered the act of revenge, there may be multiple victims. The murder(s) is prearranged and organized, including plans for escaping the scene of the crime. A recent stressful event or the accumulation of chronic stress often motivates children who commit revenge killings.

On March 24, 1998, in Jonesboro, Arkansas, Andrew Golden, age 11 years, and Mitchell Johnson, age 13 years, sat on a hill 100 yards away from the school. As the children and teachers left the building in response to a false fire alarm, the two boys fired 22 rounds of ammunition, killing 5 and wounding 15 people.

Patricide and/or matricide may be a response to many years of physical and sexual abuse. Typically, children and teens who kill parents flee the scene, only to be captured fairly quickly. Juveniles who have killed parents are typically European American, middle-class boys who have had little contact with law enforcement. In October 1997, Luke Woodham, age 16 years, stabbed his mother to death and shot two classmates to death. At trial, he testified that his mother called him names and picked on him.

Those who kill authorities often do so in response to real or imagined offenses. The targets may be individuals or buildings or structures that symbolize the authorities. The killer may desire to commit suicide or die at the hands of police to attain martyrdom for the murders. On May 21, 1998, in Springfield, Oregon, Kipland Kindel, age 15 years, shot his parents to death at home. He then went to the local high school and opened fire, killing 2 students and wounding 20 others. He asked the police officer who led him away to shoot him.

Although the nation's schools actually are safer than ever before, the legacy of the killings at schools across the country looms large in the minds of Americans. In spite of the fact that 100,000 guns are brought to school each year, less that 1% of all violent deaths of children occur in or around school property. Teachers are also victims of school violence, with 6,250 threatened with bodily harm and 260 physically assaulted every year.

A nonscientific volunteer survey of 129,593 students in Grades 6 to 12 found that 25% of the students said they do not feel safe from violence in school, 30% said they have been threatened physically at school, 25% said they have been hit at school, and 20% said they have been robbed at school. Nearly half of the respondents reported that there was a gun in their home, and of those, more than half said that they had access to it. Another study of suburban high school students found that 20% believed it was okay to shoot someone who has stolen something from you and that 8% believed it was okay to shoot a person who has done something to offend or insult you. Those attitudes reflect the continuing potential for violence in our schools. The Gun Free Schools Act requires schools to expel for a least 1 year any student who brings a firearm to school as well as to refer the student to the criminal justice or juvenile justice system.

Victims, victimizers (bullies), and bystanders (observers) all need to be involved in antiviolence intervention. Schools should have zero tolerance for bullying, victimizing, and standing by during violent acts. The Centers for Disease Control and Prevention has developed a sourcebook titled *Best Practices for Youth Violence Prevention* to assist schools and communities in formulating and implementing appropriate interventions (www.cdc.gov/ncipc/dup/bestpractices.htm).

# 3

# Stigma and Self-Esteem

Being knowledgeable about diversity includes understanding the attitudes and perceptions that perpetuate social equality and inequality. Teachers must strive to be open-minded—learning what their biases are and changing those that prevent them from seeing and understanding the perspectives of other people.

## Stigmatizing Issues

Stigmas are created when individuals possess personal attributes and belong to social categories that make them different from others in such a way that they are perceived as tainted, discounted, and/or discredited. The effect of being seen as having a stigma leads people to being stigmatized and assigned labels according to their difference from the norm, with the norm depending on the environment or culture in which the individuals are immersed. These labels bring with them negative connotations that lead to disrespecting those individuals being stigmatized, creating barriers between people, and interrupting communication. At its worst, labeling results in fear and mistrust of others, prejudice, discrimination, and even violence.

When stigmas are being assigned to individuals, stereotypes are being used. Stereotypes are assessments and beliefs we create about groups of people based on characteristics of those groups. They limit us in that we look for those characteristics that agree with our preconceived ideas about a group and disregard the evidence that does not fit with our beliefs. When we use stereotypes to form opinions of individuals, we ignore the unique characteristics of the individuals and assign them characteristics we believe to be true of the groups to which the individuals may belong. For example, we may have stereotypes of gay men as effeminate, Asian Americans as smart, Jewish Americans as thrifty, and lesbians as masculine. When meeting someone who is lesbian, we may expect her to like to do "manly" things or to look like a man when in fact she does not. Engaging in these kinds of stereotyping behavior allows us to easily move to stigmatizing individuals, holding prejudices about them, and then discriminating against them.

Prejudice is similar to stigmatizing and stereotyping in that it is maintaining a negative feeling about people who are different from us. Prejudicial attitudes are based on limited knowledge, limited contact, and emotional responses rather than on careful observation and thoughts. They are beliefs, opinions, or points of view that are formed before the facts are known or in spite of them. They often operate as if they were the "truth," and this makes them difficult to change unless actively counteracted.

Discrimination is prejudice that is expressed behaviorally. When people discriminate against others, they are using prejudice, stereotypes, and stigma to justify their actions. These actions often include behaviors such as denial of access to resources (e.g., education, jobs), power (e.g., advancement in a career), and respect (e.g., assuming that women are not good at math and so expecting less of female students).

In addition, acts of racism, heterosexism, ageism, ethnocentrism, sexism, classism, and ableism are examples of discrimination. Each of these "isms" involves a tendency to judge others according to similarity to or dissimilarity from a standard considered to be ideal or normal and is shaped by personal or group judgments. In a society composed of multiple groups, we must counteract such biases, or isms, to prevent discrimination and injustice.

During preadolescence and adolescence, acts of discrimination in school are often committed between peers, although accounts of discrimination perpetrated by administrators and teachers have also been documented. Adolescents of these age groups have the cognitive abilities to understand which groups are discriminated against in their cultures and communities, how they themselves might fit into some of those categorical groups, and how discrimination is supported by subtle institutional policies and actions. They are also more aware of how this discrimination hurts them and others.

# Self-Esteem

The effect of discrimination and stigma on the self-esteem of adolescents is considerable. Adolescence is a time when individuals' self-esteem is quite unstable as they work toward defining themselves more clearly. When they define themselves based on stigmatizing issues, the likelihood of adolescents arriving at a healthy and consistently positive sense of self is decreased. It undermines their belief in themselves and their dignity.

Self-esteem consists of two major components: (a) how we realistically perceive ourselves and (b) the value (both cognitive and emotional) we put on that perception. For example, if adolescents are smart, see themselves as being smart, and value being smart, their self-esteem will be enhanced. When this process encompasses many core characteristics of adolescents, self-esteem will be high. Maintaining positive self-esteem includes having many of these kinds of feelings and experiences and being able to manage negative appraisal from others without it significantly damaging adolescents' positive perceptions of themselves.

## Self-Esteem During Childhood

The development of self-esteem begins during childhood when individuals experience being loved, accepted, and valued by important adults in their lives. The more they have positive experiences of being valued for themselves unconditionally, the greater their self-esteem. As children develop and move beyond the preschool years, they become more aware of their abilities and qualities as well as the criteria by which society will evaluate them. Their self-esteem now has conditions of worth, and children internalize the yardsticks imposed on them by outside influences. Repeated experiences of being valued by others for their behavior or characteristics lead children to value themselves and to increase their self-esteem. Important in this process is that children see themselves as doing something to cause these positive evaluations by reaching or maintaining the expected standard by which they are judged. Children with high self-esteem have more positive evaluations of themselves and have a sense of competence. They also know their good points, can take care of themselves, are able to accept failures, and can learn from mistakes.

In contrast, when children experience consistent and persistent negative social, emotional, verbal, physical, and educational experiences, they begin to evaluate themselves negatively and to develop low self-esteem. Many times, emotional and verbal neglect and abuse can be as damaging, if not more damaging, for children than is physical neglect or abuse. Being shamed, insulted, ridiculed, or embarrassed either privately or publicly is destructive and can have long-term effects. If children are told that they are "not good enough" because of their gender, nationality, or race, this too will negatively affect their self-esteem. What occurs as a result of these experiences is a process by which children begin to evaluate themselves negatively and then form damaging opinions about themselves. These experiences can result in feelings of social isolation, shame, and worthlessness that can lead to feelings of hopelessness, helplessness, anxiety, and/or depression.

## Self-Esteem During Adolescence

Although our self-esteem becomes fairly well established by middle childhood, it remains vulnerable throughout our lives. Adolescence brings with it the challenge of maintaining and developing positive self-esteem in light of the many comparisons adolescents make to an ideal self—a self often constructed by their peers and the media. This shift during adolescence from parental approval to peer approval makes this time particularly vulnerable for adolescents in terms of evaluating themselves favorably against the ideal set by other adolescents and the media. What comes with it is a self-consciousness that leaves adolescents prone to the approval or disapproval of friends. In the desire to be accepted by peers who mirror the ideal that adolescents set for themselves, adolescents' self-esteem, especially during early and middle adolescence, is susceptible to the opinions of others. For girls during this period, this is often observed in concern about body image and body size, leaving these young women open to developing an eating disorder. If adolescents are different in a significant way from members of their peer group, the stigma assigned to that difference could leave them even more vulnerable to feeling poorly about themselves. However, as adolescents take on different roles, integrate the various aspects of their personalities, and find others who can support their actual selves, they find during later adolescence that their self-esteem becomes more stable and impervious to the evaluation of others.

## Teachers and Adolescent Self-Esteem

During these years, as adolescents manage the myriad challenges to their growing identities and sense of self, teachers who help to build and solidify positive self-esteem in their students can have long-lasting effects. Because criteria for building self-esteem differ among and within cultures, communities, and societies, teachers who are mindful that there are varying criteria can support adolescents in continuing to develop their self-esteem within those students' worldviews. Ways in which to do so include the following:

- Provide students with compassion, caring, and patience. This will give them a sense of acceptance, belonging, and security.
- Encourage students to believe in themselves by helping them to develop confidence in their own judgment about their abilities.
- Facilitate opportunities for students to question their own and others' beliefs so that they can form their own opinions about issues and themselves.
- Foster in students a curiosity about themselves as wonderers, producers, initiators, problem solvers, explorers, and partners. Encouraging students to investigate phenomena worthy of their attention will help them to see how their actions resulted in outcomes that were meaningful to them and others.
- Promote cooperative learning strategies and help to establish cooperative goals so that self-evaluations created through competition and comparison with others is diminished. This is particularly important for girls because they tend to learn best in cooperative settings. All adolescents need to continue to learn how their efforts individually affected the whole. This builds their sense of self-efficacy and encourages feeling valued by the group.
- Teach adolescents positive self-talk. Much of our self-esteem has to do with what we tell ourselves. We all engage in self-talk that either praises or discourages ourselves. Helping students to tell themselves "I can do this in spite of what my friends think" and "I am worthwhile even if my friends don't approve of me" will be useful for the times when they are frustrated with their own abilities and the opinions of their peers.
- Acknowledge and celebrate students' varied talents and achievements. As adolescents consolidate their identities, all healthy facets of their personalities will need attention.
- Reframe failures as "successful failures" in that something can be learned by each attempt an adolescent makes at achievement. Doing so will communicate your support of students' persistence, competence, and overall ability to deal effectively with life's problems.

- Finally, encourage students to ask themselves the following questions:

  – What have I tried that was new today?
  – What have I done today better than before?
  – Who are the people I have helped today?
  – Who has helped me today?
  – What gave me the most pleasure today?
  – How do I feel about myself today?
  – What do I think about myself today?

## Gender Identity Issues

Gender is often thought of as a biologically determined, and therefore a fixed, component of a person's being. How a person conducts himself or herself as a boy or girl is thought to be influenced by the person's gender or sex. However, gender and sex are different concepts, even though they often are used interchangeably. A person's sex is the result of biology and chromosomal makeup. Gender has been defined as how a person expresses or performs his or her sex as prescribed by society. That is, how a person acts as male or female is the result of the messages he or she receives about what it means to be male or female in the society into which he or she is born and how to express that femaleness or maleness through behavior, attitude, and desires. These messages are pervasive and are present even before a child is born. These gender role expectations influence the gender identity a child is to adopt. As adolescents, girls are expected to be interested in makeup, fashion, their bodies, and boys and to see themselves as female when they engage in these activities or express these ideas, whereas boys are expected to like sports and cars, be interested in girls and sex, and be leaders and to see themselves as male when they do so.

Gender identity has great fluidity, however, given that it is a concept created by society. Unlike a person's sex, gender identity is not unalterable (although with recent advances in medicine, a person's sex can be altered as well). Yet Western societies tend to cast adolescents into categories of male and female and expect them to behave in ways that fit the society's positions of those categories as if these classifications were unalterable. Children learn early in life what the expectations are and how to perform their gender so as to not become marginalized. The messages about how to be a boy or girl are given to them by their parents, teachers, the media, and other children.

Nevertheless, not all girls and boys perform gender in the same way, agree with the impositions of societal messages, or feel that their biological sex fits their gender identity. As a result, a common route through which adolescents become stigmatized is gender identity issues. When adolescents blur the boundaries of traditional gender roles and engage in cross-gender identity behavior, they are often labeled, ostracized, and/or treated with suspicion by teachers and society; harassed, teased, and/or rejected by their peers; and misunderstood and embarrassed by their parents. This is most often observed with adolescent boys who wear makeup, paint their nails, or wear female clothing as well as with adolescent girls who show no interest in these "female" things.

The effect on the self-esteem of adolescents who claim gender identities that are unexpected of them is devastating. Because they do not have people with whom they can talk and who understand them, they feel isolated and angry, experience anxiety and depression, and socially withdraw. They may be classified as having a mental disorder called gender identity disorder and be treated for this through psychotherapy. This further stigmatizes and entrenches the shame they feel as a result of not fitting in and of being treated as different by their parents, peers, and teachers. Thoughts of suicide and running away are not uncommon. These adolescents are in need of people who can listen without judgment or fear and who can help them to understand themselves better. Teachers who find the time to notice children struggling with gender identity issues and to offer these adolescents the opportunity to talk about their feelings can normalize the adolescents' experiences. Doing so may also communicate to other students that crossing gender role boundaries is not a process that is to be stigmatized.

## Sexual Identity Issues

Related to the stigma associated with gender identity issues is the stigma associated with gay, lesbian, and bisexual sexual identities. Often thought of as a person's sexual orientation and behavior, sexual identity is most commonly classified as either homosexual, bisexual, or heterosexual. For adolescence, the concept of having a questioning sexual identity is a more recent phenomenon and one that needs to be acknowledged as well.

Just as the expectation for gender identity is that males and females will subscribe to traditional ideas of what it means to be male or female, the expectation of society is that adolescents will express their sexuality heterosexually. However, we know that although most adolescents do so, there is a percentage of adolescents who will be gay, lesbian, bisexual, or transgendered (GLBT). It is during this time in their lives that they begin to express their sexual identities publicly or at least to acknowledge them privately. Many adolescents keep their sexual identities private when their sexual orientation is GLBT because of the stigma associated with gay, lesbian, bisexual, and transgendered identities.

The result of attributing stigma to GLBT sexual identities has a long history of discrimination, hate crimes, and rejection. The 1999 report on anti-gay activity by the People for the American Way recorded more than 300 incidents of anti-gay discrimination, twice what was recorded in 1998. In the Federal Bureau of Investigation's *Uniform Crime Reports* for 1999 and 2000, hate crimes based on sexual orientation constituted the third highest category after race and religion. In high schools, GLBT adolescents face harassment and cruelty by their peers, as well as by teachers and administrators, on a daily basis. Jokes are often made, words such as "sissy," "fag," "gay," and "homo" are used freely, and boys' behavior that can be seen as "feminine" as well as girls' behavior that can be perceived as "masculine" is discouraged by peers and teachers out of fear that these children will "become gay." There have been lawsuits brought forward (and won) against school administrators for not protecting GLBT students against the violence they have endured while in school. Rejection by family, society, and educational systems due to individuals' sexual orientation occurs frequently and sometimes with violent or deadly outcomes. One needs only to remember the torture and crucifixion-style killing of Matthew Shepard, a gay college student in Wyoming.

The effect of these kinds of actions on the self-esteem of GLBT adolescents is devastating. Numerous studies have indicated that suicide rates among GLBT adolescents are disproportionately high given the occurrence of homosexuality in the population. Anxiety about others knowing about a person's GLBT sexual identity is also high. The fear among adolescents that parents might abandon them and leave them homeless and that peers might ostracize and harm them is not unrealistic or ungrounded. A decreased ability to concentrate in school, truancy due to the fear of coming to school and being harassed, promiscuity in reaction to "proving" one's heterosexuality, drug and alcohol abuse to escape from one's feelings, and aggressive behavior to manage internal confusion are common behaviors in which GLBT adolescents engage while wrestling with their sexual identities. These behaviors are not a product of being GLBT but rather are a product of managing the stigma attached to these sexual identities and the fear of others' responses.

The issue of GLBT sexual identities is also relevant when discussing the sexual identity of parents and the impact this has on adolescents in school. The number of families headed by same-sex parents is significant. Current estimates indicate that there are between 6 million and 14 million families with GLBT parents. Some of these homes have been created after children were raised with opposite-sex parents for a period of time and then transitioned into homes with parents of the same sex. These children will have multiple concerns as they adapt to homes that are different from their previous homes as well as to homes that are stigmatized by society.

Regardless of how GLBT families were created, children of GLBT parents will face certain challenges in school. When they hear jokes about GLBT people, hear derogatory names being used, and/or watch discriminatory behavior being conducted, they will feel the same kind of shame, anger, and hurt that people who are GLBT feel. Adolescents who have GLBT parents will go through their own "coming out" process as they make decisions about how and when to tell friends and teachers. These adolescents may be afraid of others' reactions to their parents, may be worried about the judgments others will make about their own sexual identities, and may feel confused about how to fit in with mainstream school discussions about parents. In the classroom, they may feel that their families are invisible when reading or hearing about issues that discuss "moms and dads" but not two moms or two dads. At school events, they may feel ashamed to have both parents attend or may feel protective of their parents if they do. They may encounter discrimination from parents of their friends who do not understand what it means to be GLBT and so are afraid to allow their children to interact with the adolescents of GLBT parents. This may cause friction at home and anger toward their GLBT parents. These adolescents may also wonder what it means for their own sexual identities to have GLBT parents.

All school personnel face the challenges of having adolescents who are GLBT or questioning or who are a part of GLBT families. As teachers, there are many things you can do to help these children feel more included and manage the stigma they are experiencing as well as to create safety for all students. Following are some ideas:

- For adolescents from GLBT homes, invite the parents to the school to talk about what they might need and how they would like to be included in school activities. This is particularly important when there are multiple caregivers such as biological and nonbiological parents.

- Include books that represent various kinds of families and relationships and that are either written by GLBT authors or address GLBT concerns. Doing so helps these adolescents to feel visible and included and educates other students about these issues as well.
- Find ways in which to incorporate issues of diverse sexualities and the contributions people who are GLBT have made to society. This can be done in any subject class given that GLBT people have contributed to the sciences, arts, and humanities.
- Display symbols in your classroom that represent the GLBT communities. These might include a rainbow flag, a pink triangle, or a double male or double female symbol. Adolescents who are GLBT or questioning will look for symbols that signal to them that they are welcome and safe in this environment.
- Use language that is inclusive. When describing relationships or families, use words that indicate that families and relationships can consist of same-sex partnering.
- When language that is derogatory is being used, jokes that are offensive are being told, or behavior that is discriminatory is being observed, stop the interaction and talk about the harm that such behavior causes. This will protect GLBT students and educate the others about these issues.
- If you notice an adolescent who talks about himself or herself as feeling "different" or "not fitting in" in some way, be aware that this may be an indication that the child has same-sex attractions and is "feeling you out" to see whether you are someone to whom it is safe to talk. Be sensitive to this language and talk to the adolescent about his or her feelings in a way that normalizes the student.
- Be aware of your own language that communicates information that traditional gender roles are the norm. Many GLBT adolescents do not ascribe to traditional gender roles and will feel excluded. In addition, those adolescents with GLBT parents will also feel excluded by your language because their parents will most likely cross gender roles.
- If you know of an "outed" GLBT teacher at your school, ask him or her if you can consult about these issues. That will decrease your own homophobia and lack of knowledge about these issues as well as help you to feel supported.
- Finally, use the ideas about how to increase self-esteem. Listening to these adolescents and taking their concerns seriously will ultimately help them to feel that they too belong in your classroom.

# PART II

## Health
## Problems A–Z

# Adjustment Disorder

Also known as: stress response

## Description

Adjustment disorder is a response to an identifiable stressor or stressors that results in significant emotional or behavioral symptoms. The associated distress is in excess of what would be the expected response to the stressor. If the symptoms last less than 6 months, the adjustment disorder is referred to as acute; if symptoms last 6 months or longer, it is referred to as chronic.

## Primary Groups Affected

- Between 2% and 8% of adolescents experience adjustment disorder.
- Adolescents from disadvantaged life circumstances experience a high rate of stressors and may be at increased risk for the disorder.

## Signs and Symptoms

- Decreased performance at school
- Temporary changes in social relationships
- Somatic (physical) complaints
- Depressed mood, tearfulness, or feelings of hopelessness
- Nervousness, worry, or fears of separation from primary caregivers
- Disturbed conduct such as violating age-appropriate social norms or engaging in truancy, vandalism, or reckless behavior

## Classroom Guidelines

- Provide support and reassurance to adolescent during times of stress.
- Encourage adolescent to verbalize concerns and worries.
- Ask adolescent what measures he or she has developed to manage anxiety or depression.
- Provide opportunities for success. Praise and reinforce behavior whenever possible, focusing on positive characteristics and behaviors.
- Encourage adolescent to help someone else. The end result is usually that the helper will feel better about himself or herself.
- Discuss and model the resolution of interpersonal conflict—compromising, negotiating, and dealing with frustration.
- Establish reasonable and meaningful consequences for both compliant and noncompliant behavior.

## Attendance Guideline

- Exclusion from school is not required.

## Medications

- Depending on symptoms, adolescent may be on antidepressant or antianxiety medications.

## Communication

- Ask how family has tried to resolve the problem.
- Discuss what has worked and what has not worked.
- Encourage participation in extracurricular activities.

## Resource

- Center for Mental Health Services
  (800) 789-2647
  www.mentalhealth.org

# Alcohol Abuse

Also known as: binge drinking, substance abuse

## Description

Alcohol abuse is defined as the purposeful use of alcohol, for at least 1 month, that results in adverse effects for oneself or for others. Alcohol dependence occurs when the use of alcohol is no longer under control and continues despite adverse effects. Adults may take from 2 to several years from the first use to full dependency. Preadolescents and adolescents often make this progression in 6 to 18 months.

## Primary Groups Affected

- Ages 10 to 14 years is a time of special risk for beginning to experiment with alcohol.
- If a biological parent/caregiver is an alcoholic, there may be a genetic influence as well as a modeling influence.

## Signs and Symptoms

- Mood changes: flare-ups of temper, irritability, defensiveness, family conflict
- "Nothing matters" attitude, sloppy appearance, lack of involvement in former interests, general low energy, intolerant of delayed gratification
- School problems: poor attendance, low grades, recent disciplinary action
- Switching to friends who are also abusing alcohol, impaired social skills
- Memory lapses, poor concentration
- Smell of alcohol on breath, bloodshot eyes

- Mild impairment: euphoria, impaired thinking and judgment, slurred speech, staggering gait
- Severe impairment: confusion, stupor, decreased respiration, coma

## Classroom Guidelines

- If you suspect alcohol abuse during school hours, confront the issue rather than ignore it.
- Be aware that if a student is moderately to severely impaired, emergency treatment might be necessary—**911.**
- Help student to develop problem-solving skills given that he or she has avoided problems through the use of alcohol.
- Encourage adolescent to improve fitness through regular exercise or by becoming involved in a sport.
- Check with administration to provide drug education classes for students.

## Attendance Guideline

- Students should not attend classes under the influence of alcohol.

## Medication

- Ondansetron (Zofran), an antinausea drug, helps to decrease alcohol craving.

## Communication

- Ask whether family conflict has recently escalated.
- Ask family whether there are signs that youth is abusing alcohol.
- Suggest that family contact the U.S. National Institutes of Health about the "Make a Difference: Talk to Your Child About Alcohol" program.

## Resources

- U.S. National Institute on Alcohol Abuse and Alcoholism
  U.S. National Institutes of Health
  www.niaaa.nih.gov

- Alcoholics Anonymous
  (212) 870-3400
  www.alcoholics-anonymous.org

- Children of Alcoholics Foundation
  164 West 74th Street
  New York, NY 10023
  (212) 595-5810
  www.coaf.org

- U.S. National Institutes of Health
  Make a Difference: Talk to Your Child About Alcohol
  (301) 443-3860
  www.health.nih.gov/result.asp

- Mothers Against Drunk Driving
  (800) 438-MADD
  www.madd.org

# Allergy: Drugs

Also known as: drug reactions

## Description

It is very difficult to distinguish among a drug allergy, a side effect of taking a particular drug, a bad reaction to a drug, and a reaction due to taking a combination of drugs that are incompatible. A health care provider's diagnosis is necessary to identify a true allergy. Any of these responses, however, can range from a mild one to a severe life-threatening allergic response that may develop within a few minutes after taking a particular medication. In a true drug allergy, antibodies in the body mistake a drug as a harmful substance and attack it, causing an allergic response. It is not known exactly how prevalent drug allergies are among adolescents. It is known that most drug allergy deaths from anaphylactic shock occur in persons with no medical history of allergic reactions. Medications that have been found to have a higher incidence of initiating allergic reactions include antibiotics and some heart medications. Atypically, drug reactions can be delayed, occurring up to 7 days after the last ingestion of the drug.

## Primary Groups Affected

- Any adolescent may experience a drug reaction; however, incidence increases with the number and amount of drugs taken.

## Signs and Symptoms

- Itching
- Stuffy nose
- Dizziness/headache/disorientation
- Anxiety/irritability/restlessness
- Red blotchy skin

- Puffiness around eyes
- Hives (red bumps)
- Swelling of face, neck, hands, legs—**911**
- Wheezing—**911**
- Difficulty in breathing—**911**
- Increased heart rate and irregular rhythm—**911**
- Decreased blood pressure—**911**
- Abdominal cramping
- Loss of consciousness—**911**

## Classroom Guidelines

- If adolescent exhibits *any* **911** identified signs/symptoms, activate local emergency medical system.
- If adolescent loses consciousness, establish an airway and prepare to start CPR if needed.
- Be aware that adolescents in severe distress might need epinephrine (*see* Procedure K, Part III).
- Keep adolescent warm and calm.
- Keep adolescent flat unless breathing is too difficult in this position.
- If adolescent shows any of the preceding signs and symptoms, observe carefully because reaction may progress from mild to severe in a very short period of time.

## Attendance Guideline

- Exclusion from school is not required.

## Medications

- EpiPen injectable might be necessary during a severe reaction.
- If EpiPen is used, still activate local emergency medical system. Secondary reactions do occur hours after the initial allergic response.

## Communication

- Notify parent/caregiver of any drug reactions immediately.
- Ask parent/caregiver/adolescent to identify drug allergy history on school forms so that record can be tagged as a Medic-Alert.
- Ask whether adolescent has an identifying bracelet or card to be worn.

## Resources

- www.allergic-reactions.com
- www.mayoclinic.org

# Allergy: Food

Also known as: adverse reaction to food, food intolerance, food anaphylaxis, food hypersensitivity

## Description

Food allergies are allergic or hypersensitivity reactions to specific foods as a result of eating, touching, or inhaling the scent of the food. Foods that most commonly cause a reaction are peanuts, milk, eggs (egg yolks are considered less allergenic than egg whites), seeds (sesame and caraway), soy, shellfish, fish, and wheat. Although rare, food-induced deaths do occur. In studies, adolescents who died from food-induced allergies usually ingested the offending food at school.

## Primary Groups Affected

- Adolescents of any age may be affected, but reactions may become more severe each time adolescents are exposed to the food.
- Adolescents living with asthma tend to experience serious reactions to food allergies.

## Signs and Symptoms

- Food reactions are unique to each person, varying from a relatively mild case of hives to life-threatening breathing problems.
- Most severe reactions to food occur within the first hour after ingestion.
- Never assume that just because an adolescent says a prior reaction was mild that the current reaction will be mild.
- Stomach reactions can include nausea, vomiting, gas, cramping, and diarrhea.

- Breathing (respiratory) reactions can include runny nose, stuffy nose, sneezing, coughing, itching or swelling of lips, tongue, throat, change in voice, difficulty in swallowing, tightness of chest, and shortness of breath—**911.**
- Skin reactions can include hives, itching, and a red flat skin rash.

## Classroom Guidelines

- Take all reactions seriously and treat promptly.
- Ensure strict avoidance of offending food.
- Be alert for foods brought in for school celebrations or assignments.
- When in doubt concerning a food, do not allow adolescent to eat it.
- Look for key words that warn of the presence of offending foods.
- Have parent/caregiver/adolescent provide foods adolescent can eat.
- Send adolescent to school nurse if symptoms occur after eating a certain food(s) or activate the emergency medical system.
- Be aware that epinephrine might need to be administered at first indication of any lip, tongue, mouth, or throat allergies (*see* Procedure K).
- Send adolescent to hospital after epinephrine injection because reaction can occur again for 6 to 9 hours.
- Remove offending food and activate local emergency medical system if there is a life-threatening reaction. Notify school health care provider or nurse.

## Attendance Guideline

- Exclusion from school varies depending on the severity of reaction.

## Medication

- Epinephrine may be used in severe emergencies (*see* Procedure K).

## Communication

- Ask parent/caregiver/adolescent what happens to adolescent when exposed to the allergic food.
- Ask whether the reaction occurs with eating or just smelling the scent of the offending food.

- Ask whether reaction seems to be getting worse with each exposure.
- Ask whether food allergy has been confirmed with testing.
- Ask whether adolescent wears a Medic-Alert bracelet regarding allergy.
- Ask what ingredient words should be identified regarding items brought into classroom by other students/parents.
- Ask what adolescent can have as alternative snack or treat.

## Resources

- American Academy of Allergy, Asthma, and Immunology
  611 E. Wells Street
  Milwaukee, WI 53202
  (414) 272-6071 or (800) 822-2762

- U.S. National Institutes of Health
  NIH Publication No. 91-2650
  *Managing Allergy and Asthma at School: Tips for Schoolteachers and Staff* (free booklet)
  http://allergy.mcg.edu

- Food Allergy Network
  4744 Holly Avenue
  Fairfax, VA 22030
  (703) 691-3179
  (Informative newsletter and sends out regular warnings about commercial food products containing unwanted food proteins)

# Allergy: Hay Fever

Also known as: allergic rhinitis, summer cold

## Description

Hay fever is the most common chronic condition of all allergic disorders. An adolescent with hay fever may react to one or more specific allergy-causing substances such as pollen, mold, dust mites, and pet dander. Inhaling one of these allergens causes the adolescent to release substances that inflame the linings of the nose, sinuses, eyelids, and eyes.

## Primary Groups Affected

- Any adolescent, with a higher incidence in adolescents with a family history of hay fever

## Signs and Symptoms

- Congestion
- Runny nose
- Frequent sneezing
- Watery eyes
- Itchy eyes, nose, roof of mouth or throat
- Cough
- Can trigger an asthma attack or cause wheezing or shortness of breath—**911**

## Classroom Guidelines

- Adhere to medication regimen as ordered by health care provider and school policy.

- Remove offending substance from room if possible.
- Keep windows and doors closed and use air-conditioning in classroom if available.
- Keep adolescent indoors as much as possible during pollen season and especially when grass is being cut.
- Keep classroom as free of dust as possible during pollen season to reduce levels of pollen and mold. Do not let adolescent be present during cleaning.
- Avoid chalk dust, room deodorizers, and cleaning solutions.
- Remind adolescent to bring tissues and a bag for disposal.
- Limit adolescent's exposure to classroom pets.

## Attendance Guideline

- Exclusion from school is not required.

## Medications

- As ordered by health care provider, oral medications, sprays, and/or eye drops may be used.
- Antihistamines may be prescribed, but be aware that they can cause drowsiness.
- Adolescents receiving allergy shots might not get relief for 6 months to 2 years.

## Communication

- Notify parent/caregiver if adolescent complains of any symptoms.
- Ask parent/caregiver/adolescent for information regarding allergies and any medication management.

## Resource

- www.mayoclinic.org

# Allergy: Latex

Also known as: NRL, IgE reaction

## Description

Latex allergy is an allergic or hypersensitivity reaction to natural latex. Reactions are unique to each person and vary from a skin reaction to severe breathing difficulties. The specific cause for reaction is unknown. Each exposure to latex may bring on a more serious reaction than the previous one. Latex can be found in numerous classroom items. Latex reactions may be in response to exposure to the following: erasers, rubber bands, carpet backings, rubber balls (e.g., koosh, tennis, rubber basketball), balloons, elastic in clothes, spandex swimwear, rubber sole shoes, insulation material, bicycle helmets, chewing gum, mouse pads for computers, racquet handles (e.g., table tennis, golf clubs, baseball bats), raincoats, rubber boots, modeling clay, socks with elastic, swimming goggles, caps, snorkels, bandages, and adhesive tape.

## Primary Groups Affected

- Any age group
- Adolescents with spina bifida
- Adolescents with bowel or bladder programs that require urinary catheters or latex instruments
- Adolescents with cerebral palsy
- Adolescents who have had multiple surgeries
- Adolescents experiencing allergic reactions to bananas, kiwis, avocados, potatoes, tomatoes, and/or chestnuts

## Signs and Symptoms

- May include skin reaction (allergic contact dermatitis)
- Sneezing, itching, redness resulting from contact with latex

- Wheezing, chest tightness, difficulty in breathing—**911**
- Facial swelling, lip swelling, tongue swelling, swelling of any body part—**911**
- Decreased level of consciousness—**911**

## Classroom Guidelines

- Observe adolescent if he or she is experiencing difficulty in breathing. Activate local emergency system.
- Modify latex exposure in the classroom.
- Keep low-protein, powder-free, non-latex gloves in the classroom.
- Keep a current list of latex-free items (can be obtained by contacting the Spina Bifida Association, (800) 621-3141.
- Notify parent/guardian if adolescent has local skin reaction after an exposure.
- Send adolescent to school nurse if symptoms occur after exposure or activate local emergency medical system in case of a severe reaction.
- Be aware that adolescent in severe distress might need epinephrine (*see* Procedure K) as ordered by health care provider. Another dose might be needed in 20 minutes if adolescent is not improving and local emergency medical system has not arrived.

## Medication

- Epinephrine may be used in severe emergencies (*see* Procedure K).

## Attendance Guideline

- Exclusion from school varies depending on the severity of the reaction.

## Communication

- If adolescent has a known allergy to latex, ask parent/caregiver/adolescent what a reaction looks like.
- Ask whether the reaction seems to be getting worse with each exposure.
- Ask whether adolescent had latex antibody testing and results.

- Ask whether adolescent wears a Medic-Alert bracelet regarding the allergy.
- Ask whether adolescent uses epinephrine for any latex reactions.

## Resources

- Spina Bifida Association of American (semiannual list of items that contain latex and alternatives)
  (800) 621-3141
  E-mail: sbaa@sbaa.org

- Latex Allergy Information Service (monthly newsletter)
  (860) 482-6869
  Compuserve: 76500.1452
  www.latexallergyhelp.com

# Anaphylaxis

Also known as: anaphylactic shock

## Description

Anaphylaxis is an extremely serious form of an allergic response to a specific allergen (something that causes an allergic response) that is life-threatening. Anaphylaxis can affect breathing and significantly decrease blood pressure as a result of an allergic response to certain foods, medications or immunizations, or insect stings or as a result of exposure to latex or other chemicals. Immediate action is needed to prevent death from occurring. It takes only 1 to 2 minutes for a mild reaction to go to anaphylaxis. In addition, the faster the onset of an anaphylactic reaction, the greater the chance the reaction will be severe. It should be noted that adolescents who have previously experienced only a mild reaction to one of the triggers are more likely to experience a more severe reaction with repeated exposures.

## Primary Groups Affected

- Any adolescent

## Signs and Symptoms

- Anxiety/irritability/restlessness
- Generalized flushing or red blotchy skin
- Puffiness around eyes
- Hives (red bumps)
- Abdominal cramping, nausea, vomiting, diarrhea
- Itching (may include itching in mouth)
- Tingling sensation around mouth or face
- Sudden feeling of weakness
- Sweating

- Change in quality of voice
- Stuffy nose
- Swelling of face, throat, lips, tongue, neck, hands, legs—**911**
- Wheezing—**911**
- Difficulty in breathing or swallowing—**911**
- Heart rate increases and irregular rhythm, weak rapid pulse—**911**
- Decreased blood pressure (and accompanying paleness)—**911**
- Collapse, loss of consciousness—**911**
- Dizziness/headache/disorientation—**911**

## Classroom Guidelines

- If adolescent exhibits identified signs/symptoms, activate local emergency medical system—**911.**
- If adolescent loses consciousness, establish an airway and prepare to start CPR if needed.
- Be aware that an adolescent in severe distress might need epinephrine (*see* Procedure K). Another dose might be needed in 20 minutes if adolescent is not improving and emergency medical system responders have not arrived.
- Keep adolescent warm and calm.
- Keep adolescent flat unless breathing is too difficult in this position.
- If adolescent shows any of the preceding signs and symptoms, observe carefully because reaction may progress from mild to severe in a very short period of time.
- Send adolescent's health record and empty EpiPen(s) with emergency medical system responders and write time when you gave medication.

## Attendance Guideline

- Exclusion from school is not required.

## Medications

- Epinephrine by injection may be used for severe reaction. Check expiration date (*see* Procedure K).
- If epinephrine is given, continue to activate local emergency system. Secondary reactions do occur hours after the initial allergic response.
- Antihistamines may be prescribed, but be aware that they can cause drowsiness.

## Communication

- If adolescent has a known severe allergic response, discuss with parent/caregiver/adolescent the necessity of having an EpiPen (check expiration date) and the technique for administration.
- Notify parent/caregiver immediately.
- Ask parent/caregiver/adolescent to identify allergy history on school forms so that record can be tagged as a Medic-Alert.
- Ask adolescent whether he or she has an identifying bracelet or card to be worn.
- Discuss with parent/caregiver/adolescent measures to avoid reoccurrence of exposure to triggers such as avoidance of certain foods, precautions when outdoors if adolescent experiences insect allergies.
- Ask for information about allergies and circumstances under which medication should be used as ordered by health care provider.

## Resources

- www.allergic-reactions.com
- www.mayoclinic.org
- www.schoolnurse.com

# Anemia

Also known as: iron deficiency anemia, low energy, poor blood, low blood

## Description

Iron deficiency anemia is a common type of anemia. As the name implies, the body does not have enough of the mineral iron. Iron is needed by the body to make hemoglobin in the red blood cells. The hemoglobin carries oxygen from the lungs to all of the cells and tissue of the body and carries away all of the carbon dioxide. Iron deficiency anemia may be caused by poor iron intake in the diet, blood loss, or inadequate absorption of iron. Anemia can be diagnosed by a blood test (complete blood count) and can usually be treated by dietary improvements and iron supplements. If iron deficiency anemia is left untreated, it can lead to serious health problems such as delayed growth in children, irregular heartbeat, and even heart damage.

## Primary Groups Affected

- Children of any age, but most common under age 2 years
- Adolescents, especially girls

## Signs and Symptoms

- Fatigue
- Pale skin color, nail beds
- Decreased pinkness of lips
- Brittle nails
- Cracks in sides of mouth
- Sores on tongue
- Cravings for non-nutritive substances such as ice, dirt, paint, clay, and starch

- Headaches
- Poor appetite
- Frequent infections
- Restless legs syndrome (uncomfortable tingling or crawling feeling in legs that is relieved by walking)

## Classroom Guidelines

- Dispense medication according to school regulations.
- Support adolescent in making good food choices: iron-fortified grains, pasta, and cereals; red meats and egg yolks; green and yellow vegetables; raisins, dried fruits, and seeds.
- Be aware that coffee and tea inhibit absorption of iron.
- Understand that vitamin C, such as that in citrus juices, increases absorption of iron.
- Be aware that iron supplements may cause constipation and will cause adolescent's stool to become black in color.

## Attendance Guideline

- Exclusion from school is not required.

## Medications

- Vitamin, iron, and folic acid supplements may be prescribed (usually oral form but sometimes by injection).
- Iron supplements are usually best absorbed on an empty stomach; however, if they cause stomach upset, taking them with food may help.

## Communication

- Ask parent/caregiver/adolescent about acceptable and unacceptable foods to eat.
- Ask about schedule of medications so as to support/monitor adolescent's compliance with treatment plan.

## Resource

- www.mayoclinic.org

# Anger

## Description

Anger serves a variety of adaptive functions. It signals that something is happening in the environment to which individuals must pay attention. Anger mobilizes and sustains energy at high levels of intensity so that individuals can respond to the situation. Individuals learn how to regulate their anger through socialization by caregivers, peers, and the larger society.

## Primary Groups Affected

- The first clear expressions of anger appear at about 4 months.
- By 7 months, anger is targeted to another individual.
- Anger remains a human emotion throughout life.

## Signs and Symptoms

- Some adolescents experience anger more intensely and have more difficulty in managing their anger than do other individuals.
- Older adolescents are able to mask their anger better than are younger ones.
- Adolescents who are able to manage their expressions of anger and have low-intensity emotions exhibit higher quality social functioning with peers and adults.
- The pattern of low self-regulation and high intensity of emotions is a risk factor for problem behaviors and rejection by peers and adults.
- Rejected adolescents exhibit more negative nonverbal behaviors such as banging books and banging keyboards.

## Classroom Guidelines

- Present adolescents with hypothetical anger-producing situations. Discuss how they would feel and what they would do in these situations.
- Discuss appropriate management behaviors for angry feelings by providing emotional coaching.
- Discuss consequences for both hostile and nonhostile responses to provocation.
- Facilitate empathetic and prosocial responses toward others.
- Encourage adolescents to shift gears—to spend some time doing things they like to do.
- Show confidence in adolescents' ability to manage anger and frustration.
- Look at how you handle your own anger. Are you setting a good example?

## Attendance Guideline

- Exclusion from school is not required.

## Medication

- No medication is required.

## Communication

- Discuss with parent/caregiver how anger is managed at home by all family members.
- Be aware that adolescent and family may benefit from psychotherapy for anger management and behavioral disorders related to expressions of anger.

## Resources

- Caring for Every Child's Mental Health
  www.mentalhealth.org/child

- Center for Mental Health Services
  U.S. Department of Health and Human Services
  (800) 789-2647

# Animal Bites

## Description

Any adolescent may be the victim of an animal bite from pets in the classroom or when encountering animals in outdoor areas. Dog bites are the most frequent source of all animal bites. Cat bites, however, are more likely to cause infection in adolescents. The incidence of rabies is more common in bites from raccoons, skunks, bats, and foxes. There are many instructional reasons for having animals in the classroom; however, it may be prudent to have all classroom pets examined by a veterinarian prior to boarding these animals in the school. Bites that break the skin have a greater likelihood of becoming infected. Serious injury, viral and bacterial infections, psychological trauma, and even death can be complications associated with animal bites (*see* Procedure G).

## Primary Groups Affected

- Boys more often than girls
- Any adolescents in contact with animals

## Signs and Symptoms

- Open area on the skin with surrounding teeth marks
- Significant crush injury—**911**

## Classroom Guidelines

- Understand that animal should be captured if this can be done safely.
- Call local animal warden/authority to capture animal.
- Speak calmly to adolescent to decrease his or her anxiety.

- Wash wound with soap and water. If antiseptic soap is available, use it. You might need to repeat this procedure three or four times to decrease animal's saliva in the bite site.
- For deeper bites, apply a sterile pressure bandage.
- Raise the affected part to decrease bleeding.
- Remember that ice may be applied to site to decrease swelling.
- Notify parent/caregiver and encourage to take adolescent to health care provider.
- Follow school guidelines in reporting bite to health department.
- Discuss with adolescents how to protect themselves from animal bites: Do not separate fighting animals, do not bother animals when they are eating, and avoid strange or sick animals.

## Attendance Guideline

- Exclusion from school is not required.

## Medications

- Antibiotics may be ordered and need to be given on schedule.
- Tetanus toxoid is given if adolescent is not sufficiently immunized. Tetanus shots are given every 10 years, and if adolescent's last tetanus shot was more than 5 years ago and the wound is dirty, a booster may be given. Boosters should be given within 48 hours of a bite injury.
- If animal is not found or shows evidence of rabies, adolescent will undergo a series of rabies vaccines and antiserum injections.

## Communication

- Notify parent/caregiver immediately and urge to see health care provider.
- Follow school policy in documenting incident.
- If adolescent is receiving series of rabies vaccine and antiserum injections, ask parent/caregiver/adolescent for information concerning reactions.

## Resources

- http://medicine.bu.edu/dshapiro/zoo1.htm
- www.mayoclinic.org

# Anxiety Disorder: Generalized

Also known as: overanxious, severe anxiety

## Description

Generalized anxiety disorder is extreme unrealistic worry that is unrelated to any recent events. These adolescents are so afraid or worried that they are unable to function normally and the routines of daily life are disrupted. They may also exhibit excessive conformity and a strong desire to please others. This disorder may be accompanied by panic attacks or social phobias (*see* Panic Disorder and Phobia: Social).

## Primary Groups Affected

- Usually begins during childhood or adolescence but may begin during one's 20s

## Signs and Symptoms

- Worry about a broad range of situations, strong need for reassurance
- Physical symptoms: restless, on edge, easily fatigued, muscle tension, stomach complaints, shortness of breath, headaches, dizziness
- Decreased concentration
- May have impaired relationships with peers
- In severe cases, may become preoccupied with catastrophic thoughts and visions

## Classroom Guidelines

- Encourage adolescent to verbalize fears.
- Draw on previous coping methods that have been successful.
- Help adolescent to identify alternative outlets for a moderate level of anxiety such as physical sporting activities, taking a walk, and talking to a friend.
- Guide individual in identifying his or her own desires in specific situations to minimize the need to please others.
- Help to identify interpersonal support systems.
- Encourage deep breathing during episodes of increased anxiety.

## Attendance Guideline

- Exclusion from school is not required.

## Medication

- Adolescent is unlikely to be on medication.

## Communication

- Ask youth about the usual symptoms of a moderate level of anxiety as well as of the panic level of anxiety.
- Discuss what measures adolescent has developed to manage anxiety.
- Suggest self-help support groups.

## Resources

- Anxiety Disorders Association of America
  11900 Parklawn Drive, Suite 100
  Rockville, MD 20852
  (301) 231-9350
  www.adaa.org

- National Mental Health Association
  1021 Prince Street
  Alexandria, VA 22314-2971
  (800) 969-NMHA
  www.nmha.org

# Appendicitis

## Description

The appendix is a small wormlike pouch that extends out from the colon on the right-hand side of the body. It has no known purpose. Appendicitis occurs when the appendix becomes inflamed and filled with pus. It is the most common cause of abdominal pain requiring surgery in children. Treatment is removal of the appendix (appendectomy) within 24 to 48 hours of the first symptoms.

## Primary Groups Affected

- Anyone can develop appendicitis.
- The highest risk group is between ages 10 and 30 years.

## Signs and Symptoms

### Early Symptoms

- Aching pain over the belly button
- Pain shifting to the lower right abdomen, halfway between the belly button and the hip bone
- Pain worsening if the person coughs, walks, or makes other sharp movements
- Pain decreasing if the person lies on his or her side and bends knees
- Nausea and sometimes vomiting
- A low-grade fever (99 to 102 degrees) that starts after the other symptoms appear

### Late Symptoms

- Rupture of the appendix, which is a medical emergency—**911**
- Pus from the appendix and contents of the small intestine being released into the abdominal cavity

- Sudden relief of pain immediately after the rupture, followed by intense pain throughout the abdomen—**911**
- Abdomen becoming distended and rigid—**911**
- Rapid heart rate and rapid shallow breathing—**911**

## Classroom Guidelines

- Be aware that because youth might not always have typical symptoms of appendicitis, it is best not to take abdominal pain lightly.
- If adolescent is in acute distress, have parent/caregiver notify primary health care provider.

## Attendance Guideline

- Youth will need to recover from surgery at home. Physician will determine when the individual may return to the classroom.

## Medication

- Antibiotics may be prescribed to prevent complications from surgery.

## Communication

- Because appendicitis is not uncommon in adolescents, all "stomachaches" should be reported to parent/caregiver.

## Resource

- www.mayoclinic.org

# Asperger's Disorder

Also known as: mild autism

## Description

Asperger's is a disorder of the brain characterized by severe impairment in social interactions as well as repetitive patterns of behavior and activities. The disorder can range from mild to severe.

## Primary Groups Affected

- Usually diagnosed after age 3 or 4 years
- Five times more frequent in males than in females
- Increased frequency of Asperger's disorder and autistic disorder among family members

## Signs and Symptoms

- Continuous and lifelong disorder
- Normal IQ, with many exhibiting exceptional skill or talent in a specific area
- Often obsessively preoccupied with a particular subject
- Normal language development, but with attempts at conversation often being one-sided lecturing
- Increased interest in forming social relationships during adolescence
- Impaired nonverbal social behavior such as eye contact, facial expression, body posture, and gestures to regulate social interaction, with problems in social interactions possibly leading to developing relationships with much older or younger people

- Learning to use areas of strength to compensate for areas of weakness by adolescence
- Rigid adherence to routines or rituals
- Repetitive motor mannerisms such as hand or finger flapping and complex whole-body movements

## Classroom Guidelines

- Teach social skills through discussion, modeling, and practice.
- Given that two thirds of communication is considered to be non-verbal, teach students how to observe, understand, and respond to nonverbal cues. Teach body language of active listening using the mnemonic device "OFFER":

  O = open posture
  F = face person
  F = lean forward
  E = make eye contact
  R = relax

- Teach adolescent to recognize when he or she is talking too much. A vibrating watch set at 3 minutes at the beginning of interactions can be a silent reminder to stop talking and give the other person a chance.
- Be aware that TEACCH (Treatment and Education of Autistic and Related Communication Handicapped Children) provides a lifelong continuum of services, including assessment, diagnosis, treatment, use of community resources, and supported employment and living situations.

## Attendance Guideline

- Exclusion from school is not required.

## Medication

- Mood stabilizers such as clonidine (Catapres) and guanfacine (Tenex) may reduce temper tantrums.

## Communication

- Coordinate social modeling with parental efforts.
- Ask parents/caregivers how they respond to the need for rigid routines.

## Resource

- National Alliance for Autism Research
  414 Wall Street
  Research Park
  Princeton, NJ 08540
  (888) 777-NARR
  www.naar.org

# Asthma

## Description

Asthma is a disease in which airways in the lungs are narrowed and inflamed, causing episodes of wheezing, difficulty in breathing, tightness in the chest, and coughing (asthma attack). Triggers (exercise, cold air, allergens, or other irritants) and/or viral infections (e.g., a cold) cause the airways to get narrow or blocked and make breathing difficult. If asthma attacks become severe, emergency treatment is needed.

## Primary Groups Affected

- Adolescents of any age
- Most common respiratory chronic illness among adolescents
- Most common in African Americans, urban residents, and boys
- Usually develops by age 5 years

## Signs and Symptoms

- Wheezing noises
- Difficulty in breathing—**911**
- Tightness in the chest
- Feeling of fear and confusion
- Tingling or numbness in the fingers or toes
- Unable to talk without stopping for breath—**911**

## Classroom Guidelines

- Identify and control triggers as much as possible (e.g., dust mites and mold, animal fur or feathers, pollen, smoke, air pollution, paint fumes, strong odors, cockroaches, cold air, exercise).

- Know signs and symptoms of an asthma attack.
- Have copy of asthma action plan and review with student and parent/caregiver.
- Seat adolescent's desk away from open windows if asthma attacks are brought on by pollen, grass, and the like.
- In case of an asthma attack, check adolescent and activate local emergency system if breathing difficulty does not get better quickly.
- Care for adolescent by assisting in getting to comfortable breathing position, giving medication if ordered, and staying calm and reassuring the youth—**911.**
- Understand that an adolescent with asthma may feel drowsy or tired, anxious about medications, and/or embarrassed about disrupting school activities.
- Know medication side effects such as increased heart rate after inhalers are used.
- Encourage adolescent to participate in physical activities whenever possible.
- Allow quiet activity if adolescent is recovering from an asthma attack.
- Maintain confidentiality.
- Have many copies of asthma action plan in classroom and take on field trips and other school outings.
- Develop clear procedure with adolescent and parent/caregiver for handling missed schoolwork.

## Attendance Guideline

- Exclusion from school is not required. Follow asthma action plan for specific guidelines. Written asthma action management plan should include medications, peak flows, triggers, phone numbers, and when to go to an emergency room.

## Medications

- For long-term control, anti-inflammatory medications may be used.
- "Quick relief" medications include the use of bronchodilators.

## Communication

- Ask whether adolescent has asthma. If student does, check whether a copy of the asthma action plan is on file.

- Ask for information/demonstration of medication such as an inhaler or a peak flow meter.
- Communicate often about triggers and asthma management.

## Resources

- www.aafa.org
- www.mdnet.de/asthma

# Attention Deficit/ Hyperactivity Disorder

Also known as: ADHD, ADD

## Description

Attention deficit/hyperactivity disorder is a persistent pattern of inattention and/or hyperactivity/impulsivity. Those who are affected have significant problems with family and peer relationships. Often, they experience impaired academic achievement.

## Primary Groups Affected

- Symptoms are most prominent during elementary grades.
- Males with ADHD outnumber females by three to one.
- ADHD persists into adulthood in 30% to 70% of affected individuals.

## Signs and Symptoms

- Inattention: appear to be not listening; difficulty in organizing tasks; forgetful in daily activities; not following rules of games or activities; inability to think abstractly, conceptualize, or generalize
- Hyperactivity: signs of excessive gross motor activity (less common), feelings of restlessness, difficulty in participating in quiet sedentary activities
- Impulsivity: engaging in potentially dangerous activities without consideration of possible consequences, interrupting or intruding on others inappropriately

## Classroom Guidelines

- Do not confuse ADHD with sensory integration dysfunction.
- Remember that rules and expectations should be clearly stated. Ask adolescent to repeat what was heard.
- Establish a behavioral contract that establishes clear behavioral expectations, states how these are to be achieved, and relates achievement to rewards.
- Deal with disruptive behavior immediately, decisively, and as quietly as possible.
- Encourage the use of a notebook or tape recorder to record assignments, requirements, and due dates.
- Do not exempt student from curricular requirements and outcomes.
- Acknowledge adolescent's talents and skills, and celebrate his or her achievements.
- Encourage hobbies and extracurricular interests.

## Attendance Guideline

- Exclusion from school is not required.

## Medications

- Medications provide a "window of opportunity" to allow other strategies to be more effective. Stimulant medications increase activity in the parts of the brain that are underactive, improving attention and reducing impulsiveness and hyperactivity.
- Ritalin is rapidly metabolized and might need to be given as often as five times per day.
- Adolescent may be taking Cylert.
- Dexedrine and Adderall may be too stimulating for the hyperactive adolescent.
- Side effects are minimal and transient. Symptoms may become worse (rebound effect) as the medication wears off.

## Communication

- If possible, have student be responsible for informing parents about academic responsibilities.
- Establish a team spirit with child, parents, and yourself to problem solve difficulties as they arise.

## Resource

- Children and Adults with Attention Deficit/Hyperactivity Disorder (CHADD)
  8181 Professional Place, Suite 201
  Landover, MD 20785
  (800) 233-4050
  www.chadd.org

# Autistic Disorder

Also known as: autism

## Description

Autism is a disorder of the brain characterized by social isolation, communication impairment, and strange repetitive behaviors. It is the most severe form of pervasive developmental disorders.

## Primary Groups Affected

- Onset prior to age 3 years
- Four to five times higher in males than in females
- Females with the disorder more likely to be cognitively impaired
- Siblings at increased risk for the disorder

## Signs and Symptoms

- During adolescence, there may be some developmental gains such as increased interest in social interactions.
- Behavior in some adolescents worsens, while in others it improves.
- The most striking feature is profound social isolation. Adolescent has no pleasure in sharing experiences with others and cannot anticipate thoughts and actions of others.
- Adolescent dislikes being touched or looking people in the eye.
- Student presents a bizarre picture of disturbed motor behavior such as whirling, lunging, darting, rocking, and toe walking.
- Adolescent throws tantrums for no apparent reason.

- Student shows an obsessive interest in a single object, activity, or person.
- Youth resists changes in routines.
- Adolescent displays abnormal language development. He or she may be mute, may make unintelligible sounds, may say words repeatedly, and cannot use or understand abstract language.
- Student displays odd responses to sensory stimuli such as over-sensitivity to sounds or being touched and exaggerated reactions to light or odors.
- Adolescent may exhibit self-injurious behaviors such as head banging and finger, hand, or wrist biting.
- Of these individuals, 5% to 10% will become independent as adults, 25% will require supervision as adults, and the remainder will continue to be severely impaired and in need of a high level of care.

## Classroom Guidelines

- Teach social skills through discussion, modeling, and practice.
- Given that two thirds of communication is considered to be nonverbal, teach students how to observe, understand, and respond to nonverbal cues. Teach body language of active listening using the mnemonic device "OFFER":

  O = open posture
  F = face person
  F = lean forward
  E = make eye contact
  R = relax

- Be aware that TEACCH (Treatment and Education of Autistic and Related Communication Handicapped Children) provides a lifelong continuum of services, including assessment, diagnosis, treatment, use of community resources, and supported employment and living situations.

## Attendance Guideline

- Exclusion from school is not required.

## Medications

- Mood stabilizers such as clonidine (Catapres) and guanfacine (Tenex) may reduce temper tantrums.

## Communication

- Coordinate social modeling with parental/caregiver efforts.
- Coordinate response to temper tantrums with parental/caregiver response.
- Ask parents/caregivers how they respond to the need for rigid routines.
- Discuss the best way in which to communicate with youth.

## Resource

- National Alliance for Autism Research
  414 Wall Street
  Research Park
  Princeton, NJ 08540
  (888) 777-NARR
  www.naar.org

# Autoerotic Asphyxia

Also known as: AeA, head rushing, scarfing, accidental sexual asphyxiation

## Description

Autoerotic asphyxia is caused by intentionally strangling oneself while masturbating so as to intensify the orgasm through reduced oxygen flow to the brain. The adolescent fashions a tourniquet-like device that constricts the neck, decreasing the blood and oxygen supply to the brain. The person then masturbates and, at the point of orgasm, releases the bonds to enhance the sensation or sexual high. Tragically, this practice causes many deaths. The vagal nerve complex in the carotid artery is stimulated by pressure around the neck, slowing the heart rate and decreasing oxygen flow to the brain even further. The adolescent becomes unconscious, slumps forward, and accidentally hangs himself.

## Primary Groups Affected

- AeA typically begins experimentally during adolescence. It may continue as a compulsion into adulthood.
- AeA is primarily a male affliction.
- As many as 500 to 1,000 young men die from AeA every year in the United States.

## Signs and Symptoms

- May appear to be a suicide at first
- No evidence of suicidal ideation, no suicide note, no history of depression

- No evidence of unexplained marks of violence on the body
- Often in a secluded location
- Body often found with erotic pictures or magazines
- Partially or completely nude

## Classroom Guidelines

- Understand that the taboo against discussing this practice is as dangerous as the behavior itself given that it prevents adolescents from seeking help.
- Be aware that the topic should be discussed during sex education classes or in health classes. Adolescents need to be educated on the dangers of hypoxia and strangulation.
- If a peer dies from AeA, discuss the situation with classmates.

## Medication

- No medication is required.

## Communication

- Provide family/caregiver with information on support groups.
- Be aware that parents may find it comforting that their son did not commit suicide but rather died as the result of a tragic accident.
- Also be aware that parents may choose to tell others that their son committed suicide because that is easier for others to understand.

## Resources

- Yahoo AeA Support Club
- One LIST/eGroupsAeA Support Club
- www.silentvictims.org

# Behavior Disorder: Conduct Disorder

Also known as: CD

## Description

Conduct disorder is characterized by a persistent pattern of aggressive and destructive behavior along with disregard for the rights of others and the norms of society. The problematic behavior is usually present at home, in school, and in the community.

## Primary Groups Affected

- Onset before age 10 years is more typical in boys than in girls.
- Some adolescents with CD may have had oppositional defiant disorder during early childhood.
- Many adolescents with CD also have attention deficit/hyper-activity disorder.

## Signs and Symptoms

- Mild to severe problems
- Deliberate destruction or theft of property
- Often lies to obtain goods or favors or to avoid obligations ("cons" others)
- Often stays out at night or runs away from home overnight despite parental prohibitions, beginning before age 13 years
- Often truant from school, beginning before age 13 year; often drops out of school
- Tends to have normal peer relationships but often displays conduct problems in the company of others

- May lack appropriate feelings of guilt
- Likely to disappear by adulthood if onset is during adolescence
- Becomes sexually active at a young age
- At high risk for substance use disorders

## Classroom Guidelines

- Discuss and model the resolution of interpersonal conflict—compromising, negotiating, and dealing with frustration.
- Teach the problem-solving process.
- Discuss peer likeability factors such as the following:

  - Trustworthiness—doing what they say they will do
  - Responsibility—acknowledging their contributions to situations in which they are involved
  - Sense of humor—laughing with others and not ridiculing others

- Provide frequent, immediate, and consistent feedback on behaviors.
- Establish reasonable and meaningful consequences for both compliant and noncompliant behavior.
- Use behavioral contracts to establish expectations, how they will be achieved, and the specific rewards. A token economy may be used.

## Attendance Guideline

- Exclusion from school is not required unless the student is suspended or expelled for antisocial behavior.

## Medication

- No medication is required.

## Communication

- Encourage parent/caregiver to help youth use problem-solving skills at home.
- Explain that this is considered a mental disorder and not just childhood rebellion. As such, it requires professional intervention.

## Resource

- Center for Mental Health Services
  (800) 789-2647
  www.mentalhealth.org

# Behavior Disorder: Oppositional Defiant Disorder

Also known as: ODD

## Description

Oppositional defiant disorder is a recurrent pattern of disobedient and hostile behavior toward authority figures. Disruptive behavior occurs at a more frequent rate, at greater intensity, and for longer periods of time than do the usual behavioral problems of peers.

## Primary Groups Affected

- Transient oppositional behavior is very common in adolescents and does not warrant the diagnosis of ODD.
- ODD is equally prevalent in males and females after puberty.

## Signs and Symptoms

- Frequently disruptive, argumentative, hostile, and irritable
- Deliberately defies adult rules
- Tends to blame others for one's own mistakes and difficulties
- Behavior leading to social problems with peers and adults
- Behavior leading to impaired academic functioning
- Problem behaviors that end during adolescence (for most)

## Classroom Guidelines

- Discuss and model the resolution of interpersonal conflict—compromising, negotiating, and dealing with frustration.
- Teach the problem-solving process.
- Discuss peer likeability factors such as the following:
  - Trustworthiness—doing what they say they will do
  - Responsibility—acknowledging their contributions to situations in which they are involved
  - Sense of humor—laughing with others and not ridiculing others
- Provide frequent, immediate, and consistent feedback on behaviors.
- Establish reasonable and meaningful consequences for both compliant and noncompliant behavior.
- Use behavioral contracts to establish expectations, how they will be achieved, and the specific rewards. A token economy may be used.

## Attendance Guideline

- Exclusion from school is not required.

## Medication

- No medication is required.

## Communication

- Ask parent/caregiver whether the problem behavior occurs outside of the school setting.
- Encourage parent/caregiver to help child use problem-solving skills at home.
- Explain that this is considered a mental disorder and not just adolescent rebellion. As such, it requires professional intervention.

## Resource

- Center for Mental Health Services
  (800) 789-2647
  www.mentalhealth.org

# Bipolar Disorder

Also known as: manic depressive disorder

## Description

Bipolar disorder is characterized by periods of normal mood alternating with periods of depression and periods of mania. Intense mood swings typically last only 1 to 2 hours. There is a tendency for remission and recurrence throughout the life span.

## Primary Groups Affected

- Onset may occur at any age, but incidence increases with age.
- Three quarters (75%) of adolescents with manic depressive disorder also have attention deficit/hyperactivity disorder.
- Nearly half (42%) of adolescents with manic depressive disorder also have conduct disorder.

## Signs and Symptoms

- Eating and sleeping disturbances
- Academic difficulties
- Depression:

  - Depressed mood
  - Severe self-criticism and guilt
  - Suicidal thoughts and plans
  - Very low self-esteem

- Mania:

  - Elation or irritability
  - Overtalkativeness
  - Increased physical activity

- Poor attention span/concentration
- Argumentative and/or assaultive
- Risk-taking behavior

## Classroom Guidelines

- Set firm limits on unacceptable behavior.
- If concentration is a problem, provide a quiet, nonstimulating environment and keep activities simple and short.
- Limit decision making until adolescent is able to make appropriate decisions more easily.
- Work with the adolescent to "stop and think" before acting impulsively.
- Understand that adolescent might not be able to participate in vigorous physical or mental activities due to his or her inability to stay focused or lack of energy.
- Help adolescent to engage in quiet activities with one peer.
- Make sure that adolescent eats lunch—he or she may have no appetite or be "too busy" to eat.
- Be aware that adolescent may find that drawing or painting his or her feelings is easier than verbalizing them.
- Look for any cues that adolescent may be suicidal such as giving favorite objects away, making reference to hurting himself or herself, or asking whether others will miss him or her.

## Attendance Guidelines

- Attendance is not appropriate when behavior is out of control or adolescent is unable to participate in curriculum. Education may be provided in an alternative setting.
- Readmission usually will require permission of therapist or psychiatrist.

## Medications

- Antidepressant such as Prozac, Paxil, Zoloft, Effexor, Elavil, Tofranil, Aventyl, and Welbutrin may be prescribed.
- Mood stabilizers such as lithium and Tegretol may be prescribed.

## Communication

- Ask parent/caregiver what the usual signs of impending relapse for the adolescent are.

- Discuss ways in which youth has learned to improve concentration.
- Ask whether there is a history of suicidal thoughts.

## Resource

- National Depressive and Manic Depressive Association
  730 N. Franklin, Suite 501
  Chicago, IL 60649
  www.ndmda.org

# Body Piercing Infection/Reaction

## Description

This is a reaction of the body due to a perforation of any human body part other than an ear lobe for the purpose of inserting jewelry or another decoration or for some other nonmedical purpose. Healing times for piercing are usually as follows: ear lobe, 6 to 8 weeks; ear cartilage, 4 months to 1 year; eyebrow, 6 to 8 weeks; nostril, 2 to 4 months; nasal septum, 6 to 8 months; nasal bridge, 8 to 10 weeks; tongue, 4 weeks; lip, 2 to 3 months; and navel, 4 months to 1 year.

## Primary Groups Affected

- Adolescents of any age may get their bodies pierced with parental consent.

## Signs and Symptoms

- Reaction to body piercing may include swelling, clear yellow-green drainage, rash or bumps around the piercing, increased temperature (99 degrees or above), redness, fatigue, and nausea or vomiting.
- In rare instances, hepatitis B or C can occur.

## Classroom Guidelines

- Restrict adolescent from participating in swimming or field trips at beaches or public pools until healing occurs.
- Ensure that adolescent avoids public pools and beaches until piercing is completely healed.

### Attendance Guideline

- Exclusion from school is not required unless adolescent has increased temperature.

### Medications

- Antibiotics and mild pain relievers may be ordered for adolescent.

### Communication

- Ask whether adolescent needs to clean piercing site with any special solutions.
- Notify parent/caregiver and school health provider if adolescent complains of any of signs and symptoms listed previously after having body part pierced.
- Ask parent/caregiver/adolescent about schedule of medications so as to support/monitor adolescent's compliance with treatment plan.

### Resource

- www.vh.org/navigation/vh/topics/piercing_and_tattoos.html

# Burns

## Description

A burn is an injury that results in cell/tissue death as a result of a thermal, chemical, or electrical source. The type of agent and the length of time it remained in contact with the tissue will affect the severity of the burn. Burns are classified as first, second, or third degree. If no infection occurs, minor burns generally heal without complications except for scarring. Serious burns will require the constant wearing of special pressure garments after healing has occurred (e.g., jacket, tights, arm sleeve, face mask).

## Primary Groups Effected

- Higher incidence in children under age 5 years and in lower socioeconomic families, but any age group may be susceptible

## Signs and Symptoms

- First-degree burns are red, warm, tender. and painful but usually do not blister (outer skin only).
- Second-degree burns have the same symptoms, but blistering does occur (through the outer skin and into the inner skin)—**911.**
- Third-degree burns involve the destruction of nerve endings (through the inner skin [dermis] and into the underlying subcutaneous tissue), so pain may be reduced—**911.**

## Classroom Guidelines

- Remove adolescent from the heat source immediately and apply cool water to the affected area with running water or towels.

- Seek immediate assistance from school health care provider.
- Call **911** if the burn appears to be large or deep, was an electrical burn, or involves smoke inhalation.
- Cleanse minor burns with soap and water, and cover them with a topical antibiotic and dressing.
- Be aware that serious burns (deep second- and third-degree burns) will require hospitalization and possible skin grafting.
- Evaluate the area of the burn and determine whether adolescent will have difficulty with any activities.
- Adjust the assignment/expectations of adolescent to accommodate his or her level of functioning.
- Ensure that the wound dressing does not become wet or soiled during school activities.
- Ask adolescent if he or she is experiencing pain, especially if you notice attitude or work quality changes.
- Prepare the class for the return of the adolescent if it has been a significant burn, stressing how the burn may have affected his or her outward appearance and ability to interact or to participate in physical activities.
- Request that school health care provider be involved with adolescent's burn treatment plan.

## Attendance Guideline

- Exclusion from school is not required except in the case of serious burns requiring hospitalization and rehabilitation. This may cause a significant lapse in school attendance.

## Medication

- Acetaminophen (Tylenol) is used to control pain, but adolescent may require a stronger prescription drug depending on the severity of the burn.

## Communication

- Ask parent/caregiver/adolescent whether the burn is over a joint surface or causes difficulty with motion.
- Ask how much pain adolescent is experiencing.
- Ask whether adolescent will require pain medication at school. Ask what the medication is and whether the side effects will affect concentration in classes.

- Ask what should be done if there is excessive drainage or bleeding on the wound dressing.
- Ask for instructions if adolescent is to wear a special pressure garment on the burned area.

## Resource

- American Burn Association
  625 N. Michigan Avenue, Suite 1530
  Chicago, IL 60613
  (312) 642-9260
  www.ameriburn.org/search.htm

# Cancer

Also known as: malignancy, leukemia, lymphoma

## Description

Cancer involves the abnormal growth of cells in organs and tissue. Cancer affects only 14 of every 100,000 American children every year. The most common childhood cancers are leukemia, lymphoma, and brain cancer. Leukemia is a cancer that causes abnormalities of the white blood cells in the bone marrow. This cancer leads to anemia, infection, and bleeding problems. Lymphoma affects the lymph system that travels through the whole body and fights off infection. Lymphoma results when the cancerous lymphocytes (a type of white blood cells) multiply and crowd out normal cells. In most cases, cancer in adolescents occurs as the result of mutations in the genes; therefore, there is no effective way in which to prevent cancer. Cancer treatment includes medications to kill cancer cells (chemotherapy), radiation, and surgery. Chemotherapy involves the use of anti-cancer medicines given through intravenous feedings. Radiation uses energy rays like X rays to destroy or damage abnormal cancer cells. Surgery involves an operation to remove the cancer.

## Primary Groups Affected

- Any age group

## Signs and Symptoms

- Fevers
- Frequent infections
- Weight loss
- Nausea
- Anemia

- Poor appetite
- Headaches
- Tires easily
- Bruises/Bleeds easily
- Frequent nosebleeds
- Pain in joints
- Swollen glands (lymph nodes)
- Seizures
- Poor coordination
- Weakness on one side of the body
- Headaches, particularly in the early morning, combined with nausea and vomiting
- Slurred speech
- Dizziness
- Sudden change in vision or sense of smell

## Classroom Guidelines

- Assist adolescent and classmates in understanding the side effects of cancer treatments.
- Be aware of chemotherapy side effects:

  - Nausea
  - Fatigue
  - Hair loss
  - Infection

- Be aware of radiation side effects:

  - Fatigue
  - Nausea and vomiting
  - Diarrhea

- Ensure proper hand washing to minimize the spread of infection (*see* Procedure A).
- Develop a plan to assist student in learning during periods of absence from school.
- Schedule frequent rest periods to accommodate adolescent's decreased energy levels.
- Provide opportunity for frequent small snacks to aid with nausea and vomiting.

## Attendance Guideline

- Exclusion from school is not required except when contagious illness is in the classroom.

## Medications

- Acetaminophen (Tylenol) or ibuprofen (Motrin) may be given for fever and pain relief with parent/caregiver permission.
- Medications may be used to control nausea and diarrhea. Consult with parent/caregiver regarding how and when to administer.

## Communication

- Ask parent/caregiver/adolescent which activities and sports are safe for student to participate.
- Communicate with parent/caregiver if there are contagious illnesses in the classroom, given that individuals undergoing cancer treatment can become seriously infected quite easily.

## Resource

- www.candlelighters.org

# Cellulitis

## Description

Cellulitis is a serious bacterial infection of the skin that usually spreads after some type of injury to the skin. This injury usually is an open wound that gets infected; however, it can occur in areas where the skin is not broken. Cellulitis most commonly occurs on the face or lower legs. As the infection spreads, the adolescent may complain of feeling sick and develop a fever. An adolescent who has been bitten by an animal, a saltwater fish, or a shellfish needs to be watched for signs of cellulitis. In addition, many different types of bacteria can cause cellulitis.

## Primary Groups Affected

- Any adolescents whose skin is injured from cuts, bruises, or scrapes
- Adolescents who are living with diabetes or taking medicines that affect the immune system

## Signs and Symptoms

- Swelling of skin
- Tenderness
- Warm skin
- Pain
- Bruising
- Blisters
- Fever
- Headache
- Chills
- Feeling weak

- Red streaks from original site of cellulitis
- Very large area of red inflamed skin—**911**
- Affected area causing adolescent to complain of numbness, tingling, or other changes in hand, arm, leg, or foot—**911**
- Skin appears to be black—**911**
- Area that is red and swollen is around adolescent's eye(s) or behind his or her ear(s)—**911**

## Classroom Guidelines

- Have adolescent wear protective clothing/gear during active play or sports.
- If adolescent gets a scrape, wash site well with soap and water and cover with bandage.
- Be aware that if adolescent has an extremity affected, activity restrictions may be necessary and arm or leg might need to be elevated.
- Be aware that warm wet dressings may be prescribed for the infection site and may be applied during the school day.
- Understand that adolescent may be on an antibiotic that adheres to a time schedule.

## Attendance Guidelines

- Exclusion from school is not required unless prescribed by health care provider.
- Adolescent may need rest, intravenous antibiotics, and/or surgery.

## Medication

- Oral antibiotics (which may or may not be given with food) may be prescribed.

## Communication

- Notify parent/caregiver and urge to seek medical treatment if adolescent has a large cut, deep puncture wound, or bite.
- Ask parent/caregiver/adolescent about any activity restrictions.
- Ask about schedule of medications to be given to adolescent.
- Ask about need for warm wet dressings during the school day.

## Resources

- www.kidshealth.org
- www.mayoclinic.org

# Cerebral Palsy

Also known as: CP

## Description

Cerebral palsy is a nonprogressive permanent neurological disorder that occurs during infancy/early childhood when the brain suffers trauma or is deprived of oxygen. The extent of the disorder will vary greatly from child to child. There is no known cure for this disorder. The prognosis is dependent on the severity of the brain dysfunction. A small group of children have normal IQs with only slight evidence of motor dysfunction, whereas others are profoundly cognitively disabled and incapable of any purposeful movement. Most adolescents fall between these two extremes.

## Primary Groups Affected

- Affects males and females equally

## Signs and Symptoms

- Distinctive posturing of motor movement, with the majority being spastic movements
- May appear to be having great difficulty in moving or unable to move at all
- May have other problems that include seizures, mentally and cognitively disabled (ranging from mild to profound), inability to swallow, and impairments of speech, hearing, vision, and sensory input

## Classroom Guidelines

- Be aware that the needs of each adolescent will be dependent on the severity of his or her brain lesion.

- Arrange for adolescent's safe exit from classroom in case of an unexpected event that requires students to leave classroom or school.
- Allow for adolescent's independence as much as possible.
- Dispense medications according to schedule and school policy.
- Follow seizure precautions if adolescent has a history of seizures (*see* Epilepsy and Seizure Disorders).
- Inquire as to whether adolescent can participate in physical education/recess and to what extent.
- Ensure that adolescent wears braces/splints as instructed.
- Provide for extra time allowance between classes if needed.
- Observe adolescent's ability to maneuver the hallways/stairs, especially if using an assistance device.
- Develop a system of communication to interact with adolescent if he or she cannot speak.
- For adolescent with poor motor tone/gag reflex that leads to oral dysfunction, inability to swallow properly, and inability to manage body fluids or excretions, be aware of the following:

  - No eating/drinking via the mouth, possible use of a gastrostomy tube for feedings (*see* Procedure E)
  - Oral/nasal suctioning, possible tracheostomy (*see* Procedure D)
  - May need diapering if adolescent has inability to control bowel or bladder soiling
  - May require repositioning every 2 hours
  - May require wheelchair for mobility
  - May need communication board or a system to allow adolescent to communicate needs.

## Attendance Guidelines

- Exclusion from school is not required.
- Because of the level of care required, adolescent may have an aide assigned and experience multiple absences due to medical appointments.

## Medications

- Medications vary with adolescents' symptoms. For those who are unable to swallow, medications may be administered through a gastrostomy tube (*see* Procedure E).
- Adolescents with a history of seizures may be on antiseizure medication with a side effect of drowsiness.

## Communication

- Ask parent/caregiver what adolescent can do for himself or herself and what will require assistance.
- Ask about adolescent's mental cognitive abilities.
- Ask about adolescent's system for communication.
- Ask about adolescent's method for mobility—independent, walker, or wheelchair.
- Ask whether adolescent has a gastrostomy tube, and if so, whether he or she is allowed to have anything by mouth.
- Ask whether adolescent requires medications at school and what the schedule is for regular medications.
- Ask whether adolescent has a history of seizures.
- Ask whether adolescent has splints/braces, and if so, what the wearing schedule is.

## Resources

- United Cerebral Palsy Association
  www.ucpa.org
- http://dir.yahoo.com/health/diseases_and_conditions/cerebral_palsy
- www.mayoclinic.org

# Chest Injury

Also known as: myocardial contusion, chest wall injury, "hit in the chest," "blow to the chest," chest wall trauma

## Description

This rare, but dangerous, injury results from blunt force to the chest wall that injures the heart muscle. This can be from a baseball, a baseball bat, or a kick that forcefully comes in contact with the chest wall. This injury could be life-threatening, causing irregular heartbeat and bleeding within the heart muscle.

## Primary Groups Affected

- Any age group, especially if adolescents are involved in sports

## Signs and Symptoms

- Injury may be severe without any visible signs and symptoms.
- Adolescent may complain of chest pain and/or shortness of breath—**911.**

## Classroom Guideline

- This injury usually does not occur in the classroom, but any adolescent who experiences a severe hit to the chest needs the local emergency medical system activated for more intense medical evaluation.

## Attendance Guideline

- This injury warrants immediate evaluation by the health care provider. The adolescent will need to be hospitalized for observation and treatment. After a period of rest, the adolescent may slowly resume activities.

## Medication

- The child will probably be hospitalized, treated for pain, and observed for any complications.

## Communication

- If the injury occurred at school, it is very important that the exact events are relayed to either parent/caregiver/school nurse or emergency medical personnel who come to the scene.
- Ask parent/caregiver/adolescent about any physical activity restrictions.

## Resource

- http://health.discovery.com

# Chicken Pox

Also known as: varicella

## Description

Chicken pox is caused by the varicella zoster virus. The disease is highly contagious but generally causes only a mild illness. The disease may more seriously affect infants and persons who already have an impaired immune system. Chicken pox can also cause severe health problems in pregnant woman, causing damage to their unborn infants. Adolescents with chicken pox are contagious for 1 to 2 days before the characteristic rash begins and continues until all of the lesions (pimples) have scabs. Chicken pox is spread by person-to-person contact when a susceptible person is exposed to respiratory secretions or directly to fluid from the open lesions of an infected person. The varicella virus will always remain in the body and may later take the form of shingles (herpes zoster), which is a painful skin rash. The chicken pox vaccine has been available since 1995 and is approved for healthy children over age 12 months. At least 70% of those who receive the vaccine are protected from chicken pox; the remainder will usually develop very mild symptoms with fewer lesions and lower fever and will recover more quickly. Vaccinated children who get this milder form of chicken pox can still spread the disease to others who are not protected.

## Primary Groups Affected

- Can occur at any age, with adults more likely to have more complications
- Most common at ages 2 to 8 years
- Occurs most often during late winter and spring

## Signs and Symptoms

- Itchy rash of small red lesions (pimples) that spreads to the stomach, back, and face (a few lesions to as many as 500 lesions)
- Fever
- Malaise
- Poor appetite

## Classroom Guidelines

- Ensure proper hand washing (*see* Procedure A).
- Ensure proper disposal of children's tissues.
- Urge students to avoid sharing of personal articles such as drinking glasses and eating utensils.
- Urge students to keep fingernails short and clean.
- Try to distract adolescent from scratching scabs.
- Be aware that a cooler environment may lessen itching.
- Teach adolescent to apply pressure to area that itches rather than to scratch it.
- Try to help individual understand that scars will form from scratching.

## Attendance Guideline

- Exclusion from school is required until scabs have formed over last group of lesions (pimples).

## Medication

- Topical calamine lotion may be used to reduce itching.

## Communication

- Notify all staff members and parents/caregivers that a case of chicken pox has occurred.
- Contact local health department (required in some areas).

## Resource

- CDC Hotline
  (800) 232-2522 (English) or (800) 232-0233 (Spanish)

# Cold Sores

Also known as: herpes simplex type 1, fever blisters

## Description

Cold sores are a form of the herpes simplex virus and are contagious. It is a common illness, and once adolescents are infected with herpes, they carry the virus for life. It can reappear on adolescents' lips as "cold sores" or "fever blisters." The virus is spread by direct contact with infected mucus or saliva, most frequently through kissing or through sharing towels or eating utensils. The herpes simplex type 1 virus can be spread even when blisters are not present. But the greatest risk for contacting the virus is from the initial appearance of the blister to when it has completely crusted over. Symptoms might not be apparent for as long as 20 days after exposure. Cold sores are very different from canker sores. Canker sores are not contagious and are small sores inside the soft tissue of the mouth, a place where cold sores are not found.

## Primary Groups Affected

- Adolescents of any age who have come in contact with the virus

## Signs and Symptoms

- Small, fluid-filled blisters develop on a raised red area of skin, usually the lip but sometimes the nostrils, cheeks, or fingers. Blisters will break and ooze, form a yellow crust, and finally come off to uncover pinkish skin.
- If cold sores are inside of mouth, they are found on gums or roof of mouth.

- Pain or tingling often precedes blisters by 1 to 2 days.
- A small hard spot on lip may develop but is not visible.
- Fever, menses, and exposure to sun may initiate an outbreak.
- Once symptoms appear, they usually last for 7 to 10 days.

## Classroom Guidelines

- Urge adolescents not to share eating utensils or drinking glasses.
- Urge adolescents to wash hands frequently and properly (*see* Procedure A).
- Urge students to use sunscreen on lips and face before long exposure to sun if they are prone to cold sores.
- Be aware that an adolescent with a cold sore should be kept away from others who have an immune system disorder or who have undergone an organ transplant.
- Be aware that ice may be applied to blister if it is painful.
- Urge adolescent not to squeeze, pinch, or pick at blister.

## Attendance Guidelines

- Each adolescent's situation should be evaluated on an individual basis.
- Exclusion from school is required until lesions are dry.

## Medications

- Antiviral medications may be ordered in some extreme circumstances.
- Over-the-counter creams may be used to provide comfort. Disposable gloves should be used when applying ointment or cream.

## Communication

- Ask parent/caregiver/adolescent about any medications ordered and schedule of administration.
- Notify parent/caregiver if adolescent complains of pain or feeling like something is in his or her eye, sensitivity to light, and/or drainage from eye and urge follow-up with health care provider. Eye infection with virus is a complication that can cause blindness.

## Resources

- www.mayoclinic.org
- www.vh.org/navigation/vh/topics/adult_patient_mouth_disorders.html

# Color Blindness

Also known as: color vision deficiency

## Description

Color blindness is the inability to identify various colors and shades. There are several different kinds and degrees of color deficiency. It is very rare to be totally color-blind (monochromasy). Most color vision problems are present at birth due to a hereditary color vision deficiency, and there is currently no known cure or treatment. At school, adolescents living with color vision deficiency may be especially challenged when confronted with color-enhanced instructional materials in the classroom such as colored paper and crayons, when they cannot see chalk boundaries on grass, or when they are unable to follow directions of connecting lines to colored objects. When these adolescents are asked to retrieve a specific colored ball during gym class, they might not be able to respond appropriately because the words red, orange, yellow, and green are simply different labels for the same color. The same may be true for violet, purple, lavender, and blue. Among the colors most often confused are pink/gray, orange/red, green/yellow, brown/maroon, and beige/green. Differentiating among pastel colors also presents a challenge.

## Primary Groups Affected

- Approximately 5% to 8% of males and fewer than 1% of females (1 in every 12 males and 1 in every 200 females)

## Signs and Symptoms

- Adolescent experiences difficulty in distinguishing among red, green, brown, and gray. Red and black may look the same. Pink and purple may be seen as gray or blue. Dull yellow, orange, and light green may look the same. Pastels and different shades are confusing.

- Adolescent is not accurate in identifying colors.
- Adolescent is challenged when drawing lines connecting certain colored objects.
- Adolescent may have difficulty in distinguishing writing with yellow chalk on green chalkboard.
- Adolescent may color faces, arms, legs, and the like with crayons/markers/paints that do not depict normal color, such as coloring a face green.
- Adolescent may have difficulty in distinguishing lines on a field for a sports event.
- Adolescent may be frequently observed wearing different colored socks.

## Classroom Guidelines

- Label coloring utensils with names of the colors.
- Use white chalk rather than colored chalk on blackboards. Avoid using yellow, orange, or light tan chalk on green chalkboards.
- Photocopy textbooks or instructional materials printed with colored ink. Black print on red or green paper is not helpful because it may appear as black on black to adolescent living with color blindness.
- Assign classmate to assist adolescent with assignments that require color recognition such as different countries on a world map.
- Teach adolescent the colors of common objects such as grass, flowers, and the sky so that he or she can use labeled coloring utensils.
- Try teaching adolescent all of the colors. Rarely are adolescents unable to distinguish all colors; it is usually different shades or tints that challenge them.

## Attendance Guideline

- Exclusion from school is not required.

## Medication

- No medication is required.

## Communication

- If you suspect that an adolescent has a color deficiency, request that the adolescent be tested before he or she uses color-enhanced instructional materials.
- Discuss with parent/caregiver/adolescent the best approach to working with this deficiency. Attempt to be consistent in efforts and to decrease frustration for the adolescent in performing color-related tasks.

## Resources

- www.preventblindness.org
- http://members.aolcom/nocolorvsn/color4.htm
- www.firelily.com/opinions/color.html
- www.color-vision.com

# Common Cold

Also known as: stuffy nose, runny nose, upper respiratory infection (URI), rhinovirus, nasopharyngitis

## Description

Although the common cold is usually mild and symptoms last only a week or less, it is the most frequent reason for adolescents being absent from school. Colds seem to be related to adolescents' lack of resistance to infection and to contacts with others in school. Statistics from 1996 indicate that colds caused approximately 22 million days lost from school that year. There is no known cure for the common cold, especially given that more than 200 viruses are known to cause cold symptoms. Most colds occur during the fall and winter. Increases in colds begin in late August or early September, and the number of colds remains high until March or April.

## Primary Groups Affected

- Adolescents of any age who have come in contact with cold viruses

## Signs and Symptoms

- Nasal discharge
- Difficulty in breathing through nose
- Swelling of sinus membranes (possible tenderness under and above eyes)
- Sneezing, coughing, sore throat (sometimes accompanied by hoarseness)
- Headache
- Watery eyes

- Decreased appetite
- Usually slight fever, but can go to 102 degrees
- Fatigue
- Symptoms that last 2 to 14 days, with symptoms that last longer than 2 weeks possibly being due to an allergy
- Possible infections of ear and/or sinuses (including high fever, swollen glands, severe facial pain in sinuses, and cough that produces mucus) that may require treatment by health care provider

## Classroom Guidelines

- Urge adolescents not to share eating utensils or drinking glasses.
- Urge adolescents to wash hands frequently and properly (*see* Procedure A).
- Take adolescent's oral temperature.
- Have adolescent use tissue to cover nose and mouth when sneezing or coughing and to dispose of tissue in an appropriate receptacle.
- If possible, avoid prolonged contact with others suffering from colds.
- Be aware that an adolescent with a cold should be kept away from others who have an immune system disorder or who have undergone an organ transplant.
- If possible, clean environmental surfaces with virus-killing disinfectant. Some rhinoviruses can survive up to 3 hours outside of the nasal passages and on inanimate objects.
- Urge adolescent to drink fluids.

## Attendance Guidelines

- Each youth's situation should be evaluated on an individual basis as to whether or not he or she is too ill (e.g., coughing excessively, discolored or white nasal drainage) to participate in classroom activities.
- Adolescent may return to school when there is no elevated temperature for 24 hours.

## Medications

- Adolescent may be taking over-the-counter medications, cough medicines, and antihistamines that may cause drowsiness.

## Communication

- Notify parent/caregiver if adolescent is too sick to participate in classroom activities.
- Ask parent/caregiver/adolescent about any medications adolescent is taking.

## Resources

- www.kidsource.com/health/the.common.cold.html
- www.schoolnurse.com

# Cystic Fibrosis

## Description

Cystic fibrosis is a genetic disease that causes the body to produce an abnormally thick sticky mucus. This is due to the faulty transport of sodium and chloride (salt) within the cell lining. The thick mucus obstructs the lungs and pancreas. Vitamin deficiencies may occur because enzymes are prevented from reaching the intestines to help break down and digest food. Treatment depends on the stage of disease and the organs affected.

## Primary Groups Affected

- Affects approximately 30,000 children and adults in the United States
- Affects 1 of every 2,000 white infants

## Signs and Symptoms

- May produce a variety of symptoms
- Salty-tasting skin
- Persistent coughing
- Wheezing or pneumonia
- Frequent respiratory infections
- Excessive appetite but poor weight gain
- Diarrhea and foul-smelling stools

## Classroom Guidelines

- Carefully observe adolescent for breathing difficulties or respiratory infections—**911.**

- Consult parent/caregiver/adolescent for individualized treatment routine.
- Be aware that adolescent might need to see school nurse for chest physical therapy (vigorous percussion by cupped hands on the back and chest to dislodge the thick mucus from the lungs).
- Observe adolescent's appetite and eating pattern.
- Communicate with parent/caregiver and school nurse frequently.

## Attendance Guidelines

- Athletes need individualized plans for participation but generally may participate.
- Fluids should be recommended for adolescents to keep hydrated during activities.

## Medications

- Antibiotics may be useful for lung infections.
- Enriched diets with vitamins and enzymes may be recommended.

## Communication

- Check with parent/caregiver/adolescent regarding treatment routine and antibiotic time schedule.
- Ask about activities in which adolescent can participate.

## Resource

- www.cff.org

# Dating Violence

Also known as: domestic violence, interpersonal violence, physical violence

## Description

Dating violence refers to a pattern of behavior that dominates, controls, lowers self-esteem, or takes away freedom of choice. It is systematic persecution of another individual, ranging from subtle words or actions to violent battering. Common reasons adolescents give for dating violence are betrayal and jealousy. Unfortunately, many perpetrators and victims interpret violence as a sign of love. Dating violence may include date rape (*see* Rape).

## Primary Groups Affected

- Most frequently, the first acts of partner violence occur in dating relationships.
- Physical abuse occurs in 10% to 20% of high school students and in 30% to 40% of college students who are dating.

## Signs and Symptoms

*Perpetrator*

- Chooses to be violent and gives self permission to be violent
- Control over victim established by repetitive abuse
- Often extremely jealous and possessive
- Inflexibility that hinders ability to find alternative solutions to conflict
- Blame abusive behavior on victim
- Experience of violence in family of origin suggesting that the use of physical force is appropriate

*Victim*

- May exhibit signs of depression
- Stays in the relationship because of promises to reform on the part of perpetrator
- Kept in a constant state of fear by perpetrator threats
- Isolated from friends and family by abuser
- Guilt and feelings of self-blame, further immobilizing and keeping victim from leaving relationship or seeking help from family or friends
- Belief that being in a bad relationship is better that being alone (fear of loneliness)
- Belief that the violence itself is evidence of personal worthlessness
- Often continues to be threatened and stalked after ending relationship

## Classroom Guidelines

- Create as safe a space as possible for students to honestly discuss their experiences, opinions, and feelings.
- Plan strategies for dealing with any cases of violence.
- Suggest that school programs be developed that include the following characteristics:
  - Are developmentally appropriate and culturally sensitive
  - Involve adolescent in the development and oversight of the program
  - Discuss gender stereotypes and dating myths
  - Teach that all violence is unacceptable
  - Discuss respect in friendships
- Understand that perpetrators must be held accountable for what they are doing.
- As a leader (teacher), speak out against violence.

## Attendance Guideline

- Exclusion from school is not required.

## Medication

- No medication is required.

## Communication

- Encourage family to discuss the issue of dating violence.
- Teach family members to listen to and respect each person's point of view during the discussions.
- As required by law, report incidents of abuse in minor students.

## Resource

- Domestic Violence Hotline
(800) 799-SAFE (for hearing impaired: (800) 787-3224

# Depression

Also known as: unipolar mood disorder, clinical depression

## Description

Depression is an altered mood state involving a loss of interest in usually pleasurable activities and diminished interest in daily activities of living. Depression negatively influences the normal development of adolescents who are unable to complete age-appropriate tasks. Academic progress and peer relationships are often compromised.

## Primary Groups Affected

- The incidence of depression in adolescence is often underestimated. At least 8% of adolescents are depressed at any point in time.
- Half of all adults with depression report onset before age 20 years.
- Girls are twice as likely as boys to develop depression during adolescence.
- Those who have a family history of depression are at higher risk.

## Signs and Symptoms

- Intense mood swings
- Academic difficulties
- Argumentative and/or assaultive
- Risk taking or antisocial behavior
- Excessive sleeping
- Very low self-esteem
- Suicidal ideation and plans

## Classroom Guidelines

- Help student to understand that negative thinking is part of the disorder and not necessarily fact. Ask questions such as the following: "What do you say about yourself?" "Is that true?" "Have these thoughts increased as you began to feel worse?"
- Encourage review of past achievements and present successes to counteract the negative thinking.
- Allow enough time for adolescent to comprehend expectations and instructions given that thinking processes may be slowed. Clarify adolescent's understanding through the use of questions and feedback.
- Help the depressed individual to plan short pleasurable activities that can be accomplished with one or two peers. Understand that adolescent might not have the energy to interact with peers and that this can result in social isolation.
- Encourage adolescent to help someone else. The end result is usually that the helper feels better about himself or herself.
- Give adolescent limited choices until his or her decision-making ability is improved. You might say, for example, "You can work on your assignment now in class, or you can take it home and do it this evening."

## Attendance Guideline

- Exclusion from school is not required unless adolescent is actively suicidal and in need of hospitalization.

## Medications

- Antidepressant medication is given to adolescents with severe symptoms and to those with chronic or recurrent episodes.
- Medications are often given several times throughout the day.

## Communication

- Encourage family to help adolescent participate in after-school activities.
- Ask whether school problems seem to be contributing to the depression.

## Resource

- National Foundation for Depressive Illness
  P.O. Box 2257
  New York, NY 10116
  (800) 239-1265
  www.depression.org

# Diabetes

Also known as: diabetes mellitus, sugar diabetes, type 1 diabetes (juvenile diabetes, insulin-dependent diabetes, IDDM), type 2 diabetes (adult-onset diabetes, non-insulin-dependent diabetes, NIDDM)

## Description

Diabetes mellitus is a chronic disease caused when either a person does not make enough of a hormone called insulin or the body cannot use the insulin properly. Insulin has the task of moving glucose from the blood into cells, where it is converted into energy. In diabetes, because insulin is not working properly, glucose does not get moved into the cells as it should, and this results in high blood sugar level and can lead to many other problems. The type of diabetes mellitus most commonly seen in children and adolescents is type 1 diabetes. In type 1 diabetes, the pancreas usually does not make any insulin. Because insulin is not made, those with type 1 diabetes will need to inject insulin and watch their diets very carefully. Type 2 diabetes occurs most commonly in adults and especially in overweight people. People with type 2 diabetes make some insulin and can often control their diabetes with just dietary changes. Oral medications that stimulate the pancreas to work better might be needed. Insulin may also be added to help control this condition. When blood sugars are not controlled well, serious complications can result, including kidney failure, heart disease, and blindness.

## Primary Groups Affected

- Children of any age, from infancy to adult
- Greatest incidence for type 1 diabetes in girls ages 10 to 12 years and in boys ages 12 to 14 years

## Signs and Symptoms

- Very thirsty
- Very hungry
- Needing to urinate often, bed-wetting
- Unexplained rapid weight loss
- Fatigue
- Sores that are slow to heal
- More infections than usual
- Tingling or numbness in hands or feet
- Sudden vision changes
- Loss of consciousness—**911**

## Classroom Guidelines

- Understand signs of low blood sugar (usually from taking too much insulin or eating too little), called hypoglycemia, that include dizziness, shakiness, sweating, confusion, and the need to drink or to eat sugar.
- Be aware that adolescent might need to check blood sugar levels. This may involve puncturing skin to obtain a drop of blood.
- Recognize that many adolescents have difficulty in accepting the diagnosis of diabetes. Be respectful of their need for privacy with blood testing and insulin administration.
- Encourage adolescent to make good food choices.
- Be aware that adolescents with diabetes do best when they eat three meals and two snacks per day and eat at about same time each day, avoiding or limiting foods with added sugar.

## Attendance Guideline

- Exclusion from school is not required.

## Medication

- Insulin given by injection or an insulin pump is used.

## Communication

- Ask parent/caregiver/adolescent about the signs of hypo-glycemia and what food is used to correct this (often skin milk, juice, and/or hard candy).

- Ask how to assist with insulin administration if needed.
- Ask how to assist with insulin pump use if necessary.
- Ask about acceptable and unacceptable foods for adolescent to eat.

## Resources

- www.childrenwithdiabetes.com
- www.idf.org

# Diarrhea

Also known as: intestinal flu, stomach flu, runny bowels, loose stools, the runs

## Description

Acute diarrhea, an increase in frequency and a change in consistency of bowel movements, is usually caused by bacteria, virus, or parasite infection. Foods, juices, laxatives, and antibiotics can also cause acute diarrhea. Most cases of acute diarrhea last 2 to 3 days and require no medical treatment other than supportive care to avoid dehydration. Chronic diarrhea lasts longer than 2 weeks and is usually caused by malabsorption syndrome, food allergies, lactose intolerance, or irritable bowel syndrome. Children with chronic diarrhea will need medical evaluation.

## Primary Groups Affected

- Children of any age
- More serious for infants, young children, and those with poor immune systems
- Leading cause of illness in children under age 5 years

## Signs and Symptoms

- Bowel movements that are more frequent, looser, or more watery than usual
- Nausea and vomiting
- Abdominal cramps
- Headaches
- Fever
- Blood in stools

- Loss of appetite
- Weight loss (chronic diarrhea)

## Classroom Guidelines

- Ensure that adolescents' hands are washed after use of bathroom and before and after handling food (*see* Procedure A).
- Ensure that adolescents use disposable paper towels for hand washing.
- Clean bathroom surfaces and food preparation areas daily.
- Because diarrhea can cause dehydration, ensure that child with diarrhea receives plenty of fluids.
- Because classroom pets (especially reptiles) can spread germs, wash pet cages/bowls in separate sink from where food is prepared.

## Medications

- Antidiarrhea medications may be used for chronic diarrhea.

## Communication

- Notify parents/caregivers of children who have direct contact with child with diarrhea.
- Notify local health department if two or more children in one classroom have diarrhea within a 48-hour period.
- Notify local health department if it is learned that diarrhea is due to *Shigella, Campylobacter jejuni, Salmonella, Giardia, Cryptosporidium,* or *Escherichia. coli* (*E. coli*).

## Resource

- www.kidshealth.org

# Down Syndrome

Also known as: trisomy 21, cognitive impairment, mental retardation

## Description

Down syndrome occurs when an infant is born with three, rather than two, copies of chromosome 21. It is this extra genetic material that disrupts normal physical and cognitive development.

## Primary Groups Affected

- It can happen to anyone and occurs in 1 of every 800 to 1,000 live births.
- Women over age 35 years have a significantly increased risk of giving birth to a child with Down syndrome.

## Signs and Symptoms

- Poor muscle tone
- Facial abnormalities: flat facial profile, small nose, upward slant to eyes, abnormal shape and small size of ears, small skin folds on inner corners of eyes, enlargement of tongue in relationship to size of mouth
- Single deep crease across the center of palm
- Excessive ability to extend the joints
- Congenital heart defects (affects 50% of individuals with Down syndrome)
- Increased susceptibility to infection, respiratory problems, and childhood leukemia
- Chronic ear infections associated with hearing loss (40% to 60% of individuals)
- Cognitive impairment in the mild to moderate range of disability

## Classroom Guidelines

- Understand that the Individuals with Disabilities Education Act protects the rights of adolescents in the least restrictive environment.
- Be aware that adolescent will need an individualized education program with inclusion in the regular classroom.
- Maintain consistency and predictability in the classroom setting.
- Recognize that adolescent might need repetitive directions and prompts about what his or her behavior should be.
- Use "time-outs" for inappropriate behavior.
- Use clear, concrete, and simple directions given that adolescent may have difficulty in understanding abstract thinking or nonverbal communication.
- Gear teaching to adolescent's capabilities at the current time.

## Attendance Guideline

- Exclusion from school is not required.

## Medication

- No medication is required.

## Communication

- Communication among teachers, caregivers, and therapists must be clear and frequent.
- Older adolescents should be involved in their coordinated treatment plans.

## Resource

- National Association for Down Syndrome
  (708) 325-9112

# Drug Abuse: Cocaine/ Amphetamines

Also known as: coke, crack, blow, snow, C, powder, dust, flake, nose candy (street names for cocaine); benzedrine, methedrine, dexedrine, methamphetamine, MDMA (types of amphetamines); bennies, speed, dexies, uppers, crystal, crank, meth, speed, ice, Ecstasy, and Adam for MDMA (street names for amphetamines)

## Description

Adolescent drug use is related to many factors. If parents are users, there may be a genetic influence as well as a modeling influence. Developmentally, adolescents may abuse drugs as a means of rebelling against parents, in a search for identity, and/or in an effort to separate from their families. Other risk factors include sensation-seeking tendencies, risk-taking tendencies, and the availability of drugs. Some adolescents experiencing family dysfunction, problems in school, problems with peers, and/or emotional or physical trauma may feel overwhelmed and attempt to escape through the use of substances. Some adolescents suffering from mental disorders may try to self-medicate with alcohol or drugs.

## Primary Groups Affected

- Peak initiation is between the 10th and 12th grades.

## Signs and Symptoms

- Administration: oral, smoking, intravenous

- Cocaine:
  - Initial rush of euphoria that lasts only 10 to 20 seconds, followed by a less intense feeling of euphoria lasting 15 to 20 minutes; following use, intense pleasure replaced by equally unpleasant feelings called a "crash"
  - Increased energy and mental alertness, more talkative and playful
  - Feeling of self-confidence and increased sexual arousal
  - Impaired judgment
  - May become paranoid and violent
  - Overdose: euphoria, grandiosity, anger, combativeness, increased pulse and blood pressure, sweating or chills, nausea and vomiting, seizures, respiratory failure, possible death—**911**

- Amphetamines:
  - In small amounts: sense of mental alertness, euphoria, self-confidence, increased sex drive
  - As use increases: hypervigilance, grandiosity, agitation, irritability
  - Ice (the smokeable form): more likely to become violent and unpredictable in behavior
  - MDMA: warm state of empathy and good feelings for everyone around users, a sense of connectedness to others
  - Overdose: euphoria, hyperactivity, talkativeness, anxiety, anger, fighting, impaired judgment, rapid and irregular pulse, high blood pressure, high temperature, seizures—**911**
  - MDMA combined with high levels of physical activity such as at a rave dance: Possible death resulting from greatly increased body temperature, high blood pressure, muscle breakdown, and kidney failure—**911**

## Classroom Guidelines

- If you suspect drug abuse during school hours, confront the issue rather than ignore it.
- Be aware that if a student is moderately to severely impaired, emergency treatment might be necessary—**911**.
- Understand that it is very painful for adolescents to stop denying that drugs are causing problems for themselves and others.
- Help students to identify the negative academic consequences of drug abuse.

- Help students to develop problem-solving skills given that they have avoided problems through the use of drugs.
- Help adolescents to identify their strengths and abilities and to decrease their feelings of helplessness and hopelessness.
- Encourage adolescents to improve fitness through regular exercise or by becoming involved in a sport.
- Check with administration about providing drug education classes for students.

## Attendance Guideline

- Students should not attend school while under the influence of drugs.

## Medication

- Gabapentin (Neurontin) may reduce craving.

## Communication

- Ask family whether student engages in high-risk behaviors outside of school.
- Determine whether there are multiple family problems.
- Have family and adolescent plan structured daily activities to replace drug-using activities.

## Resource

- 800 Cocaine Information
  (800) 262-6284
  www.drughelp.org

# Drug Abuse: Hallucinogens

Also known as: LSD, mescaline, PCP, psilocybin, ketamine, GHB; acid, cid, microdots, windowpane, blotter (street names for LSD); angel dust, crystal, hog, tranks, tea (street names for PCP); magic mushrooms, shrooms (street names for psilocybin), green mauve, LA, special coke, Special K, bumps (street names for ketamine); G, Liquid G (street names for GHB)

## Description

Adolescent drug use is related to many factors. If parents are users, there may be a genetic influence as well as a modeling influence. Developmentally, adolescents may abuse drugs as a means of rebelling against parents, in a search for identity, and/or in an effort to separate from their families. Other risk factors include sensation-seeking tendencies, risk-taking tendencies, and the availability of drugs. Some adolescents experiencing family dysfunction, problems in school, problems with peers, and/or emotional or physical trauma may feel overwhelmed and attempt to escape through the use of substances. Some adolescents suffering from mental disorders may try to self-medicate with alcohol or drugs.

## Primary Groups Affected

- Peak initiation is between the 10th and 12th grades.

## Signs and Symptoms

- Administration: oral, smoking, inhalation, intravenous
- Vivid visual images
- Altered perceptions and sensation of slowed time
- Euphoria

- Anxiety
- Mood swings
- Hostility
- Depression
- Impulsivity
- Inability to perform simple tasks
- Overdose: severe anxiety, delusions, fears of losing one's mind, paranoia, impaired judgment, hallucinations, dilated pupils, rapid pulse, sweating, tremors, lack of coordination, possible death (due to accident or suicide)—**911**

## Classroom Guidelines

- If you suspect drug abuse during school hours, confront the issue rather than ignore it.
- Be aware that if a student is moderately to severely impaired, emergency treatment might be necessary—**911**.
- Understand that it is very painful for adolescents to stop denying that drugs are causing problems for themselves and others.
- Help students to identify the negative academic consequences of drug abuse.
- Help students to develop problem-solving skills given that they have avoided problems through the use of drugs.
- Help adolescents to identify their strengths and abilities and to decrease their feelings of helplessness and hopelessness.
- Encourage teens to improve fitness through regular exercise or by becoming involved in a sport.
- Check with administration about providing drug education classes for students.

## Attendance Guideline

- Students should not attend school while under the influence of drugs.

## Medication

- No medication is required.

## Communication

- Ask family whether student engages in high-risk behaviors outside of school.

- Determine whether there are multiple family problems.
- Have family and adolescent plan structured daily activities to replace drug-using activities.

## Resource

- Narcotics Anonymous
  (800) 992-0401
  www.wsoinc.com

# Drug Abuse: Inhalants

Also known as: sniffing, snorting, bagging, huffing

## Description

Inhalants are used to produce a quick form of intoxication. Most commonly used are volatile solvents such as butane gas fumes, gasoline, paint thinner, spray paint, cleaning fluids, hair spray, and air fresheners. Another popular type of inhalant is nitrous oxide or "laughing gas," which is often sold in large balloons from which the gas is released. Effects occur within minutes and last up to 45 minutes. Problems associated with inhalant abuse include cardiac arrest, depletion of oxygen in the body, and accidents while intoxicated. Inhalant abuse has reached epidemic proportions in the United States.

## Primary Groups Affected

- Inhalant abuse can start in grade school and continue through adolescence.

## Signs and Symptoms

- Initial intoxicating effects: giddiness, euphoria, unsteady gait, hallucinations (followed by confusion and poor impulse control)
- Continued use: anemia, hepatitis, possible liver or kidney failure
- Toxicity: abnormal heartbeat and respiratory depression that are potentially fatal—**911**

## Classroom Guidelines

- If you suspect inhalant use during school hours, confront the issue rather than ignore it.
- Be aware that student should be referred for emergency treatment given that cardiac arrest is a fatal complication—**911**.
- Look for ways in which to build adolescent's self-esteem in the classroom.
- Check with administration about providing drug information classes.

## Attendance Guideline

- Adolescents should not attend classes while under the influence of inhalants.

## Medication

- No medication is required.

## Communication

- Ask family whether there has been a sudden change in behavior in adolescent.
- Ask whether family sees signs that inhalants are being used such as clothing with strong chemical odors, strong-smelling rags and empty containers hidden in closets or drawers, unusual-smelling breath, and signs of intoxication.

## Resources

- www.inhalants.org
- National Clearing House for Alcohol and Drug Information (800) 729-6686
- www.health.org
- National Council on Alcoholism and Drug Dependence (800) NCA-CALL
  www.ncadd.org

# Drug Abuse: Marijuana

Also known as: cannabis, hashish; grass, joint, pot, ganja, blang, reefer, weed, Mary Jane, Acapulco gold, Colombian, roach (street names)

## Description

Adolescent drug use is related to many factors. If parents are users, there may be a genetic influence as well as a modeling influence. Developmentally, adolescents may abuse drugs as a means of rebelling against parents, in a search for identity, and/or in an effort to separate from their families. Other risk factors include sensation-seeking tendencies, risk-taking tendencies, and the availability of drugs. Some adolescents experiencing family dysfunction, problems in school, problems with peers, and/or emotional or physical trauma may feel overwhelmed and attempt to escape through the use of substances. Some adolescents suffering from mental disorders may try to self-medicate with alcohol or drugs. Medical marijuana is useful in treating nausea and vomiting, glaucoma, epilepsy, multiple sclerosis, hypertension, anorexia, and pain.

## Primary Groups Affected

- Peak initiation is between the 9th and 11th grades.
- Marijuana is the most widely used illegal drug in the United States, with 60 million people having tried marijuana and some 20 million using it regularly.

## Signs and Symptoms

- Administration usually by smoking; may be taken orally when mixed with food
- Pleasure that may progress to euphoria
- Apathy and detachment
- Passivity
- Enhanced appetite
- Slowed sense of time
- Altered perceptions
- Sexual arousal

## Classroom Guidelines

- If you suspect drug abuse during school hours, confront the issue rather than ignore it.
- Be aware that if a student is moderately to severely impaired, emergency treatment might be necessary—**911**.
- Understand that it is very painful for adolescents to stop denying that drugs are causing problems for themselves and others.
- Help students to identify the negative academic consequences of drug abuse.
- Help students to develop problem-solving skills given that they have avoided problems through the use of drugs.
- Help adolescents to identify their strengths and abilities and to decrease their feelings of helplessness and hopelessness.
- Encourage adolescents to improve fitness through regular exercise or by becoming involved in a sport.
- Check with administration to provide drug education classes for students

## Attendance Guideline

- Students should not attend school while under the influence of drugs.

## Medication

- No medication is required.

## Communication

- Ask family whether student engages in high-risk behaviors outside of school.

- Determine whether there are multiple family problems.
- Have family and adolescent plan structured daily activities to replace drug-using activities.

## Resource

- KidsPeace
  National Center for Kids Overcoming Crisis
  5300 KidsPeace Drive
  Orefield, PA 18069
  (800) 8KID-123
  www.kidspeace.org

# Drug Abuse: Opioids

Also known as: heroin, morphine, codeine, Dilaudid, Percodan, Demerol, methadone, Vicodin; smack, dope, H, horse, Miss Emma, lords, D, dollies, china white (street names)

## Description

Adolescent drug use is related to many factors. If parents are users, there may be a genetic influence as well as a modeling influence. Developmentally, adolescents may abuse drugs as a means of rebelling against parents, in a search for identity, and/or in an effort to separate from their families. Other risk factors include sensation-seeking tendencies, risk-taking tendencies, and the availability of drugs. Some adolescents experiencing family dysfunction, problems in school, problems with peers, and/or emotional or physical trauma may feel overwhelmed and attempt to escape through the use of substances. Some adolescents suffering from mental disorders may try to self-medicate with alcohol or drugs.

## Primary Groups Affected

- Peak initiation is between the 10th and 12th grades.

## Signs and Symptoms

- Administration: oral, smoking, inhalation, injection, intravenous
- Initial brief intense sensation (called a rush or thrill), followed by a longer-lasting period (called a high) that includes a sense of calmness

- Sedated appearance
- Slowed body movements
- Slurred speech
- Impaired attention and memory
- Decreased awareness
- Euphoria, pleasure, relaxation
- Overdose: clammy skin, shallow respirations, pinpoint pupils (may be dilated if there is severe lack of oxygen), coma, possible death (from respiratory failure)—**911**
- Possible poisoning problem given that heroin is often "cut" with substances that may contain impurities

## Classroom Guidelines

- If you suspect drug abuse during school hours, confront the issue rather than ignore it.
- Be aware that if a student is moderately to severely impaired, emergency treatment might be necessary—**911**.
- Understand that it is very painful for adolescents to stop denying that drugs are causing problems for themselves and others.
- Help students to identify the negative academic consequences of drug abuse.
- Help students to develop problem-solving skills given that they have avoided problems through the use of drugs.
- Help adolescents to identify their strengths and abilities and to decrease their feelings of helplessness and hopelessness.
- Encourage adolescents to improve fitness through regular exercise or by becoming involved in a sport.
- Check with administration about providing drug education classes for students.

## Attendance Guideline

- Students should not attend school while under the influence of drugs.

## Medications

- Naltrexone (ReVia, Trexan) and acamprosate (Campral) may be given to decrease the craving.
- Methadone may be given to decrease the symptoms of withdrawal and in maintenance programs.

## Communication

- Ask family whether student engages in high-risk behaviors outside of school.
- Determine whether there are multiple family problems.
- Have family and adolescent plan structured daily activities to replace drug-using activities.

## Resource

- Narcotics Anonymous
  (800) 992-0401
  www.wsoinc.com

# Drug Abuse: Sedatives/Sleepers/ Antianxiety Drugs/ Date Rape Drugs

Also known as: barbiturates, Valium, Librium, Xanax, Halcion, Ativan; downers, ludes, red devils, reds, blue angels, blues, yellow jackets, trenks, barbs (street names); two new designer drugs, Rohypnol (roofies, forget pills, R2) and GHB (G-riffic, Grievous Bodily Harm, Liquid G), called "date rape" drugs

## Description

Adolescent drug use is related to many factors. If parents are users, there may be a genetic influence as well as a modeling influence. Developmentally, adolescents may abuse drugs as a means of rebelling against parents, in a search for identity, and/or in an effort to separate from their families. Other risk factors include sensation-seeking tendencies, risk-taking tendencies, and the availability of drugs. Some adolescents experiencing family dysfunction, problems in school, problems with peers, and/or emotional or physical trauma may feel overwhelmed and attempt to escape through the use of substances. Some adolescents suffering from mental disorders may try to self-medicate with alcohol or drugs.

## Primary Groups Affected

- Peak initiation is between the 10th and 12th grades.

## Signs and Symptoms

- Taken orally but can be used intravenously
- Drowsiness
- Sedated appearance
- Lack of coordination
- Euphoria
- Rapid mood swings
- Irritability
- Anxiety
- Impaired attention and memory loss
- Date rape drugs: short-term memory loss, initial feeling of euphoria that, when combined with alcohol, can lead to unconsciousness, coma, or even death—**911**

## Classroom Guidelines

- If drug abuse is suspected during school hours, confront the issue rather than ignore it.
- Be aware that if a student is moderately to severely impaired, emergency treatment might be necessary—**911**.
- Understand that it is very painful for adolescents to stop denying that drugs are causing problems for themselves and others.
- Help students to identify the negative academic consequences of drug abuse.
- Help students to develop problem-solving skills given that they have avoided problems through the use of drugs.
- Help adolescents to identify their strengths and abilities and to decrease their feelings of helplessness and hopelessness.
- Encourage adolescents to improve fitness through regular exercise or by becoming involved in a sport.
- Check with administration about providing drug education classes for students.

## Attendance Guideline

- Students should not attend school while under the influence of drugs.

## Medication

- No medication is required.

## Communication

- Ask family whether student engages in high-risk behaviors outside of school.
- Determine whether there are multiple family problems.
- Have family and adolescent plan structured daily activities to replace drug-using activities.

## Resource

- Narcotics Anonymous
  (800) 992-0401
  www.wsoinc.com

# Drug Abuse: Steroids

Also known as: Anadrol, Anavar, Dianobol, Durabolin, Equipose, Finajet, Halotestin, Maxibolin, Winstrol, Durabolin, Depo-testosterone; roids, andro, gym candy, pumpers, stackers, juice, weight trainers (street names)

## Description

Athletes and bodybuilders use anabolic steroids to build body muscle mass and strength and to improve physical appearance. There is little evidence that athletic skill is enhanced by steroids, although the ability to train longer and harder is enhanced. Some people report an increase in energy and might even experience a "high." Users often "pyramid"—set up a 6- or 12-week cycle beginning with low doses, slowly increase the doses, start decreasing the doses about midway, and end with zero use. This may be a continuous cycle, or the user may take a break from steroid use between cycles.

## Primary Groups Affected

- Athletes and bodybuilders between ages 10 and 17 years
- Adolescents usually introduced to steroids at gyms, by coaches, or by family members
- Males at higher risk than females

## Signs and Symptoms

- Administration is oral or intramuscular injection.
- Females may increase muscle mass, develop a deeper voice, have absent menses and be infertile, and develop a larger clitoral size.

- Males may experience a decreased sex drive, shrinking of the testicles, enlargement of the prostate gland, and infertility.
- Roid rage includes dramatic mood swings, manic-like episodes, and a tendency toward aggressive behavior and violence.
- Toxicity may involve abnormal liver function.

## Classroom Guidelines

- Ask administration to implement ATLAS (Athletes Training and Learning to Avoid Steroids) program.
- Discuss the side effects of steroid use with students.
- Discuss toxic effects of steroid use such as liver tumors, high blood pressure, wild mood swings, cancer, depression, and violent behavior.

## Attendance Guideline

- Exclusion from school is not required.

## Medication

- No medication is required.

## Communication

- Inform parents that steroid use is banned at the high school, college, and professional levels of athletics.
- Ask whether adolescent has experienced changes in mood, relationships, and/or physical appearance.

## Resources

- ATLAS (Athletes Training and Learning to Avoid Steroids)
  U.S. Department of Education
  Safe and Drug Free Schools
  www.ohsu.edu/som-hpsm/atlas

- Illinois Masonic Foundation
  *Student Assistance Program: What It's All About*
  www.ilmason.org/pubrel/prdrugab.htm

# Dystonia

## Description

Dystonia is a chronic neurological (brain) movement disorder that has to do with the way in which adolescents move and develop. It is rare to be born with signs of dystonia. It is characterized by involuntary skeletal muscle contractions, causing certain parts of the body into abnormal, and sometimes painful, movements or posturing that can affect any part of the body. Adolescents living with dystonia may have affected legs, arms, trunks, necks, faces, and/or eyelids. Dystonia does not affect adolescents' intelligence, strength, vision, or hearing. Dystonia has no known cause or cure and is not considered fatal, but its prognosis is difficult to predict.

## Primary Groups Affected

- Children of any race, age, or ethnicity
- Usually begins during early childhood after a period of normal development
- Often begins in leg and foot

## Signs and Symptoms

- Muscle contractions can cause twisting and repeated movements or abnormal posture.
- Adolescent's neck may jerk in a backward position, and he or she may complain of neck stiffness or pain.
- Adolescent might not be able to properly grasp a pencil, resulting in poor handwriting.
- Adolescent may frequently complain about cramps or fatigue in hands and legs.
- Adolescent may have difficulty in sitting and walking.

- Dystonia can spread to other muscles in adolescent's body.
- Adolescent may have targets (things he or she can do to make spasms disappear) such as sitting or walking or touching the back of the head while walking.
- Adolescent with neck dystonia may experience shortness of breath.
- Adolescent may experience eye irritation, sensitivity to bright lights, and increased blinking.
- Adolescent may experience face or jaw spasms, difficulty in chewing, and changes in speech.

## Classroom Guidelines

- Arrange for adolescent's safe exit from classroom in case of an unexpected event that requires students to leave classroom or school.
- Plan suitable activities designed to meet the needs of adolescent.
- Treat adolescent like a normal student.
- Allow for handwriting difficulties.
- Be aware that dystonia that affects breathing or involvement of vocal cords may cause activity or speaking to be restricted according to medical guidelines.

## Attendance Guideline

- Exclusion from school is not required unless adolescent is recovering from surgery to lengthen tendons.

## Medications

- Anticholinergics may be used.
- A combination of medications may be prescribed.

## Communication

- Ask parent/caregiver/adolescent about activity restrictions.
- Ask about schedule of medications.
- Ask about known targets to assist in controlling spasms.
- Ask whether adolescent desires to inform classmates of disorder.

## Resource

- www.dystonia-foundation.org

# Eating Disorder: Anorexia

Also known as: self-starvation, anorexia nervosa

## Description

People with anorexia lose weight by dramatically decreasing their food intake and sharply increasing their amount of physical exercise.

## Primary Groups Affected

- Although more girls are identified as having anorexia, significant numbers of boys suffer from this disorder as well.
- The disorder typically begins at about ages 13 to 17 years, but early onset begins between ages 7 and 12 years.

## Signs and Symptoms

- Nausea, abdominal pain, feeling full, or being unable to swallow; rapid and dramatic weight loss; irregular heartbeat; dry cracked skin
- Muscle wasting, loss of menses, arrested sexual development, anemia, kidney failure
- May suffer from delayed growth and osteoporosis (thin bones)
- A desperate need to please others, resulting in overcompliant behavior; may overachieve in academic and extracurricular activities
- Excessive and compulsive exercise routines
- Terrified of weight gain and fat
- Have no insight into disorder; believe that not eating is the solution, not the problem

- Severely distorted body image; even when emaciated, perceive self as fat

## Classroom Guidelines

- Discourage excessive physical activity during recess and lunch break.
- Allow for snack breaks if this is part of the behavioral treatment plan.
- Avoid discussing food or physical complaints.
- Design classroom activities that will foster positive self-esteem.
- Encourage problem-solving activities and appropriate decision making.
- Avoid making statements that reinforce the culture's high value placed on thinness.

## Attendance Guidelines

- Exclusion from school is not required.
- If under 75% of ideal body weight, adolescent is likely to be placed in an inpatient eating disorder program.

## Medication

- No medication is required.

## Communication

- Ask parent/caregiver about the treatment program: specific goals and rewards and how it should be carried through during the school hours.
- Ask about extracurricular activities that might be a factor in the eating disorder.

## Resources

- National Association of Anorexia and Associated Disorders
  P.O. Box 7
  Highland Park, IL 60055
  Hotline: (847) 831-3438
  www.anad.org

- Anorexia and Bulimia Hotline
  (800) 772-3390

# Eating Disorder: Bulimia

Also known as: binge and purge syndrome, bulimia nervosa

## Description

Adolescents with bulimia develop cycles of binge eating followed by purging. The severity of the disorder is determined by the frequency of the binge–purge cycles.

## Primary Groups Affected

- Although more girls are identified as having bulimia, significant numbers of boys suffer from this disorder as well.
- Female athletes are at risk in sports that emphasize a thin body such as gymnastics, ballet, figure skating, and distance running.
- Males are at higher risk in sports such as bodybuilding and wrestling.
- Female and male dancers and models are also at higher risk.
- The disorder typically begins at about ages 17 to 23 years.

## Signs and Symptoms

- The cycle consists of the following:
  - Skipping meals sporadically or overly strict dieting
  - Binge eating—ingestion of huge amounts of food within a short time (usually occurs when person is alone and at home and is most frequent during the evening)

- Purging—forced vomiting, excessive use of laxatives (50 to 100 per day) and diuretics
- Feels compelled to binge, purge, and fast; is helpless to stop the behavior; and is full of self-disgust for continuing the pattern
- Disrupted activities and relationships
- May resort to stealing food or to stealing money to buy food
- Sporadic exercise
- May experience multiple fears
- Not pleased with body shape and size
- Irritability, depression
- Irregular menses, fertility problems
- Abdominal pain, bowel irregularities
- Dental decay, chronic sore throat, swollen salivary glands

## Classroom Guidelines

- Allow for snack breaks if this is part of the behavioral treatment plan.
- Avoid discussing food or physical complaints.
- Design classroom activities that will foster positive self-esteem.
- Encourage problem-solving activities and appropriate decision making.
- Avoid making statements that reinforce the culture's high value placed on thinness.

## Attendance Guideline

- Exclusion from school is not required.

## Medication

- Adolescent may be on antidepressant medications.

## Communication

- Ask parent/caregiver about the treatment program: specific goals and rewards and how it should be carried through during the school hours.
- Ask about extracurricular activities that might be a factor in the eating disorder.

## Resources

- National Association of Anorexia and Associated Disorders
  P.O. Box 7
  Highland Park, IL 60055
  Hotline: (847) 831-3438
  www.anad.org

- Anorexia and Bulimia Hotline
  (800) 772-3390

# Eczema

Also known as: atopic dermatitis (AD), chronic dermatitis, infantile eczema, contact dermatitis

## Description

Eczema is a very common skin irritation, and the term actually refers to a number of different skin conditions. A red, irritated skin rash that becomes moist, oozing, and crusted characterizes this condition. The cause of eczema is unknown; however, it often appears in children who have or will later acquire allergies, hay fever, and/or asthma or who have family members with these conditions.

## Primary Groups Affected

- Most common in infants, but can affect any age group
- Affects about 10% of all infants and children
- Becomes worse during winter months

## Signs and Symptoms

### First Phase

- Usually ages 2 to 6 months, always by age 5 years
- Itchy, dry red bumps beginning on the face and scalp and spreading to remainder of body
- Eventually becomes oozy and then crusted lesions
- Symptoms that flare up and then diminish periodically

### Second Phase

- Usually between ages 4 and 10 years
- Round, raised, itchy scaly area on elbows and wrist and behind knees and ankles
- Extremely dry

*Third Phase*

- Usually subsides by early adulthood
- Itching, dry scaly areas

## Classroom Guidelines

- Dispense medication according to school regulations.
- Remind adolescent not to scratch or itch areas. Try distraction strategies.
- Be sensitive to emotional concerns of adolescent.
- Urge adolescent to avoid long hot showers/baths that dry the skin and to use warm water and mild soaps.
- Urge adolescent to apply ointments (e.g., petroleum jelly) within a few minutes of showering.
- Try cold compresses on irritated areas.
- Urge adolescent to avoid overheating and overstress, because both cause the condition to worsen.
- Get rid of allergens that may increase flare-up such as certain foods (eggs, milk, peanuts, soy, wheat, and seafood are common problem foods), dust, and pet dander.

## Attendance Guideline

- Exclusion from school is not required. Condition is not contagious.

## Medications

- Topical corticosteroid creams or ointments are commonly used.
- Antihistamines may be used to help control itching.
- Oral or topical antibiotics may be used to treat secondary infections caused by itching.
- Ultraviolet light treatments may be prescribed.

## Communication

- Ask parent/caregiver about schedule of medications so as to support/monitor adolescent compliance with it.

## Resources

- www.eczema-assn.org
- www.eczema.com

# Epilepsy and Seizure Disorders

## Description

Epilepsy and seizure disorders are the most common serious neurological problems affecting children. Seizures occur when there are excessive electrical discharges in some nerve cells of the brain. When this happens, the brain loses control over certain muscles of the body. This loss of muscular control is temporary, and the brain functions normally between seizures. When seizures occur frequently, the disease is called epilepsy. The most familiar types of seizures are partial, complex partial, absence (petit mal), general tonic/clonic (grand mal), and febrile. There is no known cure for epilepsy, and seizures are not contagious.

## Primary Groups Affected

- Half (50%) of all cases develop before age 10 years.
- 1 of every 50 children has epilepsy.
- Epilepsy can affect both females and males.

## Signs and Symptoms

- Aura: a warning sign; varies from person to person; may be a change in body temperature, a feeling of tension or anxiety, a musical sound, a strange taste, a curious odor, or some other individual sign
- Absence (petit mal): 5- to 15-second lapses in consciousness; appears to be staring into space, and eyes roll upward;

not preceded by an aura, and activity resumes immediately afterward
- Partial: strange or unusual sensations, including sudden jerky movements of one body part, distortions in hearing or seeing, stomach discomfort, and/or sudden sense of fear; consciousness not impaired
- Complex partial: appears dazed and confused, with purposeless behaviors such as random walking, mumbling, head turning, and pulling at clothing; stares and smacks lips (in children)
- General tonic/clonic: loses consciousness and falls, and body becomes rigid (beginning of seizure); body jerks and twitches (next phase); consciousness slowly resumes (after seizure); may be preceded by an aura
- Febrile: often occurs with a fever (high temperature) at the time of an attack; generally lasts less than 15 minutes and does not recur within a 24-hour period; little confusion afterward

## Classroom Guidelines

- Understand that safety of the adolescent must be a key consideration. Uncontrolled seizures can present safety hazards to the unsupervised adolescent. Be informed and prepared.
- Be aware that once seizure has begun, there is nothing anyone can do to stop it.
- Keep calm. If possible, hold blanket up to screen adolescent from other students and to give adolescent privacy.
- Be aware that tonic/clinic seizures are most often dramatic and frightening. Other students might need to be reassured and calmed.
- Loosen adolescent's collar and put something soft under his or her head.
- Do not try to restrain adolescent.
- Remove hard, sharp, or hot objects from the area.
- Do not force anything between the adolescent's teeth.
- After the seizure, turn adolescent to one side and allow him or her to rest.
- If adolescent has loss of bowel and/or bladder control during seizure, maintain adolescent's privacy and allow him or her to change clothes without embarrassment.
- If seizure lasts longer than 2 to 3 minutes, or if adolescent seems to pass from one seizure to another without regaining consciousness, call—**911**.

- Contact parent/caregiver.
- Reassure adolescent and remain calm.
- Dispense medications according to school policy.

## Attendance Guideline

- Exclusion from school is not required.

## Medications

- Anticonvulsant therapy is preferred when possible and is effective with most persons.
- Medications include barbiturates, phenytoin, valproic acid, and Ethosuximide.
- About 50% of adolescents who take medications will see their seizures eliminated, 30% will see their seizures reduced in intensity and frequency, and 20% are resistant to medications or require larger doses to control.
- Side effects vary and may include drowsiness, dizziness, nausea, irritability, and hyperactivity.

## Communication

- Ask parent/caregiver/adolescent about seizures, what they look like, and how long they last.
- Ask about treatment, medication schedule, and compliance with routine.

## Resources

- Epilepsy Foundation of America
  www.efa.org

- U.S. National Institutes of Health
  (800) 352-9424

# Eye Injury

Also known as: corneal abrasion, corneal laceration, eye scratch, eye trauma

## Description

The cornea may be scratched or cut by contact with toys, dust, dirt, sand, wood shavings, metal particles, or paper. Most often, the scratch is superficial. If the scratch becomes infected, there is a risk for developing a corneal ulcer, which is a more serious injury.

## Primary Groups Affected

- Adolescents of any age, especially during outdoor activity time and in windy weather conditions
- Adolescents engaged in doing projects such as sanding and carving wood

## Signs and Symptoms

- Pain in eye (may complain of excessive pain due to many sensory nerve endings in eye)
- Tears
- Blurred vision
- Sensitivity or redness around eyes

## Classroom Guidelines

- Do not touch, or attempt to remove, any foreign body sticking to or embedded in eye.
- Seek medical attention immediately for any foreign body sticking to or embedded in eye—**911**.

- If object is large and makes closing eye difficult, cover eye and object with a paper cup—**911.**
- Wash hands (*see* Procedure A).
- Try to locate object in eye visually. Have adolescent sit down, and examine eye by gently pulling lower lid downward and instructing adolescent to look at the ceiling. Reverse procedure for upper lid; hold upper lid and examine eye while student looks at the floor. If there is no penetrating object, tilt adolescent's head and run lukewarm tap water over eye or splash eye with clean water, aiming for inner corner so that water washes over eye.
- If pain, vision problems, or redness persists, or if flushing proves to be unsuccessful in removing the foreign body, apply loose clean cloth over eye or both eyes (if the adolescent can tolerate this) and seek medical attention—**911.**
- Have adolescent blink several times unless foreign body is penetrating, large, or obvious.
- Pull upper eyelid over lower eyelid if an object is under eyelid unless foreign body is penetrating, large, or obvious.
- Caution adolescent not to rub eye because doing so can make the situation worse.
- Do not apply patches or ice packs to eye.
- Do not press on the eyeball.
- Be aware that adolescent may experience anxiety due to vision limitations. Keep adolescent safe and calm.
- Provide any special accommodations necessary to respond to adolescent's vision limitations such as distance considerations from blackboard and visual supplements used in classroom.
- Be aware that adolescent may have difficulty in reading and that vision may be blurred or limited while eye injury is healing.

## Attendance Guideline

- Exclusion from school is not required.

## Medication

- Only medication as ordered by health care provider as follow-up should be used.

## Communication

- Notify parent/caregiver of injury.
- Ask parent/caregiver/adolescent about any restrictions or special accommodations to be implemented while eye injury heals.

## Resource

- www.mayoclinic.org

# Eye Splash

Also known as: chemical splash in eye, chemical burn

## Description

Eye splash is characterized by the eye coming in contact with a chemical (alkali or acid) or radiation burns. Acid and alkali burns of the eye are often severe. Alkali burns to both eyes are more serious in the cornea (the clear transparent covering of the eye).

## Primary Groups Affected

- Adolescents of any age, especially during science experiments or when using cleaning products

## Signs and Symptoms

- Pain, burning in eye (may complain of excessive pain due to many sensory nerve endings in eye)
- Difficulty in opening eye
- Tears
- Blurred vision or loss of vision
- Swelling or redness around eyes

## Classroom Guidelines

- Immediately flush eye for at least 20 minutes (using jug if easier), tilting adolescent's head with good eye uppermost, and run cool tap water over other eye or splash eye with clean water. Aim for inner corner so that water will wash over eye.
- Do not let water splash in adolescent's face. Dry adolescent's face.

- Close eyelid and apply loose, clean moist cloth over eye or both eyes and seek emergency medical attention.
- Be aware that adolescent may experience anxiety due to vision limitations. Keep adolescent safe and calm.
- Provide any special accommodations necessary to respond to adolescent's vision limitations such as distance considerations from blackboard and visual supplements used in classroom.
- Be aware that the adolescent may have difficulty in reading and that vision may be blurred or limited while eye is healing.

## Attendance Guideline

- Exclusion from school is not required.

## Medication

- Only medication as ordered by health care provider as follow-up should be used.

## Communication

- Notify parent/caregiver of splash.
- Ask parent/caregiver/adolescent about any restrictions or special accommodations to be implemented while eye heals.

## Resource

- www.mayoclinic.org

# Eye Stye

## Description

A stye is common bacterial infection of the oil glands at the edge of the upper or lower eyelid. It can also be an infection of the hair follicle (the small pit from which the eyelash grows) of an eyelash that usually goes away on its own. A stye resembles a pimple and is usually caused by bacteria that infect the gland or root of the eyelash. Contaminated mascara brushes and eye makeup have been linked with styes. A chalazion, or a small eyelid lump resulting from a blocked mucus gland under the eyelid, is frequently mistaken for a stye. A chalazion is a painless swelling, whereas a stye is fairly painful.

## Primary Groups Affected

- Adolescents of any age group

## Signs and Symptoms

- Small, red, pimple-like bump at base of an eyelash
- Gritty feeling as if something is in eye
- Painful

## Classroom Guidelines

- Urge adolescent to wash hands frequently and properly, given that styes spread easily (*see* Procedure A).
- Ensure that adolescent uses warm, moist clean compresses for 10 minutes three or four times per day.
- Remind adolescent not to rub eye or squeeze stye, given that doing so can cause stye to spread.
- After the stye bursts, wash it thoroughly with warm water.

- Teach adolescent not to share washcloths or towels with someone who has a stye.
- If adolescent has vision difficulties, the stye enlarges after 3 days and fails to drain, or there are frequent occurrences of styes, notify parent/caregiver and urge to see health care provider.

## Attendance Guidelines

- Exclusion from school may be required, depending on personal habits, pain, and level of functioning in understanding treatment of stye.
- Adolescent may return to classroom after treatment is verified.

## Medication

- Antibiotic drops or ointments are usually prescribed. Do not let tip of bottle or tube touch eye.

## Communication

- Ask parent/caregiver/adolescent about any medications ordered.
- Notify parent/caregiver if adolescent complains of vision disturbances, the stye enlarges after 3 days, adolescent has more than one stye, or eye becomes red and painful. Urge to seek treatment from health care provider.

## Resources

- http://momo.essortment.com/eyestyes_rakx.htm

# Fever

Also known as: pyrexia

## Description

Fever is a body temperature that is higher than normal and usually indicates that something abnormal is going on in the body. The normal oral temperature for children is 98.0 to 98.6 degrees. An increase in body temperature may also be the effect of exercise, hot weather, drinking hot fluids, and/or common childhood immunizations. Fever in itself is not an illness but rather a symptom that something is not right with the body.

## Primary Groups Affected

- Adolescents of any age

## Signs and Symptoms

- Oral temperature above 99.8 degrees
- Flushed face
- Hot dry skin
- Not interested in eating
- Headache
- Aching body
- Nausea or vomiting
- Symptoms that, if accompanying a fever, should prompt you to call parent/caregiver and urge health care treatment immediately or to activate local emergency medical system:

  - Seizures/convulsions—**911**
  - Irregular breathing—**911**
  - Stiff neck—**911**
  - Confusion—**911**

## Classroom Guidelines

- Take adolescent's temperature if oral thermometer is available.
- Notify parent/caregiver if adolescent has elevated temperature.
- Allow adolescent to lie down if possible.
- Keep adolescent from chilling.
- Have adolescent remove coat and/or sweater if he or she is not experiencing chilling.
- Reduce room temperature unless adolescent is shivering.
- Apply cool moist compress to adolescent's forehead.
- Give cool fluids unless fever is accompanied by nausea or vomiting.

## Attendance Guideline

- Exclusion from school is required while adolescent has elevated temperature. Adolescent should not attend school for 24 hours after a fever.

## Medication

- Acetaminophen (Tylenol) may be administered according to school policy and with parent/caregiver permission.

## Communication

- Notify parent/caregiver immediately and urge to see health care provider.

## Resource

- www.vh.org/navigation/vch/topics/pediatric_patient_fever.html

# Fifth Disease

Also known as: human parvovirus B19, erythema infectious, "slapped cheek disease"

## Description

Fifth disease is an infection caused by parvovirus B19 and is spread through direct contact or respiratory secretions. The period of infectiousness is before the onset of the characteristic face rash. Most persons who get fifth disease appear to have a cold and recover without serious consequences. However, because it can affect the red blood cells, children with sickle cell anemia, chronic anemia, or an impaired immune system may become seriously ill when infected with parvovirus B19. If a pregnant woman becomes infected, the fetus may be damaged; therefore, she should contact a health care provider for advice. The virus infects only humans and should not be confused with the parvovirus that infects cats and dogs.

## Primary Groups Affected

- Any age, but most common in elementary school-age children
- Most infections during winter and spring

## Signs and Symptoms

- Low-grade fever, joint pain, and malaise (1 to 2 weeks after exposure)
- Red rash on the face, chiefly on the cheeks, giving a "slapped cheek" appearance (3 weeks after exposure); lasts 1 to 4 days
- Pimple-like lacy rash on upper and lower extremities (appears about 1 day after face rash appears); lasts up to 1 week and will reappear if skin is irritated or traumatized (by sun, heat, cold, or friction)

- Possibly itchy rash
- Possible to have no symptoms at all

## Classroom Guidelines

- Ensure proper hand washing (*see* Part III, Procedure A).
- Ensure proper disposal of tissues.
- Urge adolescents to avoid sharing of personal articles such as drinking glasses and eating utensils.

## Attendance Guideline

- Exclusion from school is not required, given that adolescent is no longer contagious once rash appears.

## Medications

- Topical calamine lotion may be used to reduce itching.
- Acetaminophen (Tylenol) may be used for fever and joint pain.

## Communication

- Notify all staff members and parent/caregiver of fifth disease outbreak.
- Be aware that pregnant women and parents/caregivers of adolescents who have an impaired immune system, sickle cell anemia, or other blood disorders might want to consult their health care providers.
- Ask parent/caregiver about schedule for acetaminophen and how to apply calamine lotion.

## Resource

- www.cdc.gov

# Fracture

Also known as: broken bone

## Description

A fracture is a break in the bone. A fracture happens when a bone is subjected to more stress than it can handle, possibly from a direct blow, sudden twisting motion, or crushing force. Surrounding tissues or organs may also be injured by the force that caused the break or by the force of the bone moving out of position. Fractures are described by type and extent and may be complete (total break through cross section of bone) or incomplete (partial break through cross section). Incomplete or "greenstick" fractures are more common in children. If the bone protrudes through the skin or mucus membrane, it is called an open fracture; if not, it is called a closed fracture.

## Primary Groups Affected

- Any adolescent is subject to a fracture in a given set of circumstances.
- Adolescents participating in athletic or strenuous activities may be more at risk.
- Adolescents not normally physically active participating in strenuous activities may be at increased risk given that their muscles might not be well enough developed to protect their bones.

## Signs and Symptoms

- Pain usually continuous, becoming more severe until bone is immobilized—**911**
- Loss of use of injured part, for example, loss of ability to bear weight—**911**

- Abnormal movement (too much, loss of, or unusual mobility)—**911**
- Possible deformity—**911**
- Grating sensation when adolescent moves limb—**911**
- Noticeable shortening of limb (if long bone such as arm or leg)
- Swelling or discoloration of soft tissue surrounding fracture—**911**
- Bone protruding through the skin—**911**

## Classroom Guidelines

- Be aware that further damage may result from movement before immobilization.
- Be certain that adolescent is out of further danger.
- If adolescent must be moved for safety reasons before splint placement, firmly but gently support extremity above and below fracture, keeping the long axis of bone stable and moving slowly and cautiously.
- Immobilize joints above and below injury before moving adolescent.
- Be aware that, if necessary (in absence of air or solid splint), long bone may be splinted with anything solid such as rolled newspaper or by securing injured part to adjacent part.
- If bone protrudes through skin (open fracture), keep wound clean; cover with clean (preferably sterile), dry, lint-free cloth; and call—**911.**
- Inform parent/caregiver and, for obvious injury, call—**911.**
- Arrange for adolescent's safe exit from classroom in case of an unexpected event that requires students to leave classroom or school.
- If cast is present, keep cast dry and promptly report symptoms of impaired circulation.
- Keep cast out of water or from becoming wet (*see* Procedure C).
- Allow for adolescent to have extra time if going to a different classroom.
- Understand that adolescent might need to elevate limb to prevent swelling.

## Attendance Guidelines

- Exclusion from school is not required.
- Participation in activities might be limited. Follow health care provider guidelines.

## Medications

- Pain medications may be ordered initially.

## Communication

- Ask parent/caregiver/adolescent for health care provider recommendations for activity limitations and signs/symptoms to report.

## Resources

- American Academy of Orthopaedic Surgeons
  www.ortho.aaos.org

- American Academy of Pediatrics
  www.aap.org/pubserv/fracture.htm

# Frostbite

## Description

Frostbite is an injury to body parts resulting from exposure to prolonged freezing temperatures. Usual sites of injury are hands, fingers, feet, toes, nose, cheeks, and ears.

## Primary Groups Affected

- Adolescents who do not wear adequate protective clothing in severe cold weather

## Signs and Symptoms

- Early signs: shivering, numbness, tingling, burning in affected area
- Cold, white, shiny, and soft or firm skin
- Increased risk if previous history of frostbite to that same area
- May complain of itching in frostbite area
- May be mild-superficial or deep frostbite
- After thawing, may be bluish in color (deep or severe frostbite) and may develop blisters (1 to 7 days) and noticeable swelling

## Classroom Guidelines

- Do not rub affected area.
- Remove adolescent's wet clothing.
- Take adolescent's temperature to check for hypothermia (low temperature—less than 95 degrees)—**911**.
- Protect affected area from further injury.

- Keep other areas of adolescent's body warm with blankets.
- If possible, raise affected area to decrease swelling.
- Understand that the degree of frostbite cannot be known until the affected area is rewarmed.
- Be aware that areas around the head should be covered with warm moist towels, keeping a constant temperature.
- Use warm immersion towels for arms and legs until normal color returns to affected site.
- Be aware that normal color might not return for 20 to 30 minutes.
- If blisters appear, notify local emergency medical system for physician evaluation.
- Give adolescent warm fluids to drink.

## Attendance Guideline

- Exclusion from school is not required.

## Medications

- Pain medications may be prescribed.
- Antibiotics may be ordered.

## Communication

- Ask parent/caregiver/adolescent about antibiotic and analgesic time schedule.
- Ask whether adolescent has any activity restrictions.

## Resource

- www.cdc.gov

# Grief

Also known as: mourning, bereavement

## Description

Bereavement is the feelings, thoughts, and responses that loved ones experience following the death of a person with whom they have shared a significant relationship. Mourning or grieving is the active process of learning to adapt to the loved one's death. It is the progression through a series of phases that include recognition and acceptance of the death, the experience of emotional and physical pain, and the rebuilding of a life without the loved person. The process of grieving is influenced by family, religious beliefs, and cultural customs.

## Primary Groups Affected

- Grieving occurs at any age and with any significant loss experience.

## Signs and Symptoms

- Cognitively, adolescents can understand death in adult terms. They might show few signs of grieving in the beginning, when numbness and denial protect them from overwhelming pain.
- Bereaved adolescents struggle with many complex feelings and responses, yet they are often pressured to act as though they are doing better than they really are. Confusion, lack of concentration, somatic (physical) symptoms, mood changes, guilt, anger, and sadness are to be expected.
- Adolescents may be tempted to "strike out" as a way in which to manage their anger. This may be directed at others or at themselves (possibly through suicide).

- Adolescents may associate the tragedy with their age-appropriate search for independence. If a parent dies while the adolescent is individuating, there is often a sense of guilt and unfinished business.
- Some adolescents may become closer to their families and might even feel responsible for their families' survival. Others may begin acting out as their attempts to become their own persons are complicated with grief.
- Signs of complicated grieving include symptoms of chronic depression, academic failure, less participation in school-related activities, withdrawal from family and friends, and risk-taking behaviors such as substance abuse.

## Classroom Guidelines

- Understand that adolescents benefit if their usual school activities are maintained as much as possible after a significant loss. The classroom can offer structure and consistency during this crisis period.
- Do not assume that peers will be able to comfort grieving adolescents. Unless friends have experienced grief themselves, they tend to manage their discomfort by ignoring the subject of loss completely.
- Let adolescents know that you are willing to be a "listening ear" when they need to talk about their grief.
- Recognize that adolescents need caring adults to confirm that it is normal to be sad, angry, guilty, worried, and even relieved when someone they love dies.
- Acknowledge that the process and length of grieving is a very individual phenomenon. Feelings do not necessarily stop after a certain period of time.
- Help adolescent to find an appropriate outlet for angry feelings such as screaming into a pillow, punching a pillow, writing in a journal, drawing a picture, or working out in a gym.
- Understand that adolescents need help in understanding that the grieving process will not last forever.
- Suggest a peer support group where adolescent can tell his or her story as much as is needed.

## Attendance Guideline

- Exclusion from school is not required.

## Medication

- No medication is required.

## Communication

- Ask parent/caregiver which symptoms of grieving the adolescent is expressing at home.
- If there are signs of complicated grieving, suggest professional assessment and intervention.

## Resources

- Teen Age Grief
  P.O. Box 220034
  Newhall, CA 91322-0034
  (661) 253-1932
  www.smartlink.net/~tag

- Klicker, R. L. (2000). *A student dies, a school mourns*. Philadelphia: Accelerated Development.

# Headache

Also known as: head pain

## Description

"My head hurts" is the most common complaint of all adolescents. Headaches are one of the most common health care problems that result in absenteeism. The majority of headaches have no underlying disease but may be related to stress, anxiety, odors, bright lights, food ingredients, and/or head injuries. Not every headache warrants going home from school. Some headaches are related to specific events such as staying up too late and being out in the sun for an extended period of time. Adolescents whose headaches necessitate limiting their activities for a long period of time might need to be seen by a health care provider. Migraines are a type of severe and disabling headache and may be experienced by adolescents.

## Primary Groups Affected

- Adolescents of any age

## Signs and Symptoms

- Complaints of "head hurting," holding head, crying
- Migraine headaches: severe and disabling pain, complaints of nausea, sensitivity to light, tingling on one side of face or body

## Classroom Guidelines

- Offer adolescent cold cloth to hold on head.
- If possible, allow adolescent to lie down in a dark quiet room.

- Consider referral to school counselor if, along with headaches, adolescent appears to be withdrawn or anxious.
- If adolescent complains of a headache and has a fever, stiff neck, rash, mental confusion, loss of balance, numbness, difficulty in speaking, and/or weakness, notify parent/caregiver immediately and urge medical treatment—**911.**
- If adolescent has headaches for long periods of time that restrict activity or limit participation with other students, notify parent/ caregiver and urge to seek medical treatment.
- Be aware that adolescent with diagnosed migraine headaches may be on medications that adhere to strict time guidelines.

## Attendance Guidelines

- Exclusion from school is not required unless prescribed by health care provider.
- Adolescent might need rest and decreased stimuli.

## Medications

- Pain medications, both over-the-counter and prescribed, may be used.

## Communication

- Notify parent/caregiver and urge to seek medical treatment if adolescent has frequent complaints of headaches.
- Ask about the amount of sleep adolescent is getting if, along with headaches, adolescent appears to be tired.
- Ask parent/caregiver/adolescent about schedule of medications.

## Resources

- www.mayoclinic.org
- www.schoolnurse.com

# Head Injury

## Description

Head injuries in adolescents are frequently due to falls, sporting accidents, or abuse. Head injuries occur at the moment of impact and following the impact. Head injuries are either open or closed. An open injury involves a skull fracture in which there is a break in the barrier between the brain contents and the outside environment. A closed injury is a blunt injury in which the skull and skin remain intact. Most injuries in adolescents are mild to moderate.

## Primary Groups Affected

- Two to three times more common in males

## Signs and Symptoms

- Depending on severity of head injury, adolescent may experience dizziness, headache, blurred or double vision, restlessness, changes in breathing, changed eye pupils, slurred speech or loss of speech, unsteady walking, noncoordination of arms or legs, decreased feeling in arms or legs, loss of consciousness, and nausea or vomiting—**911**.
- Adolescent with skull fracture may have wound or bruise on head as well as clear pinkish blood draining from the nose and/or ears—**911**.
- Adolescent may have blood showing in whites of eyes—**911**.

## Classroom Guidelines

- Keep adolescent quiet and lying down. Keep adolescent immobile, with slightly raised head and shoulders. If you think that adolescent could have a neck and/or spine injury, lay him or her flat and keep neck and spine immobile.

- Never lay adolescent down so that head is lower than the rest of the body.
- If adolescent's head is bleeding, apply ice and only gentle pressure. Activate local emergency medical system—**911.**
- Make sure that adolescent is breathing. If breathing stops, start CPR—**911.**
- Do not give adolescent anything to drink. If a scalp wound is present, do not clean. Do not bend neck given that a fracture may be present. If possible, place sterile dressing on wound and apply only gentle pressure on wound given that bone may be broken in skull—**911.**
- Be alert for any evidence of memory impairment, unusual impulse behavior, or aggressive behavior—**911.**
- Be alert for increasing drowsiness in adolescent and notify parent/caregiver and school health care provider.

## Attendance Guideline

- Exclusion from school is not required once adolescent has been seen by health care provider.

## Medication

- No medication is required.

## Communication

- Notify parent/caregiver of any head injury because problems can occur hours later as result of head injury.
- Report to school nurse or parent/caregiver if adolescent had seizure associated with head injury.

## Resource

- www.cdc.gov

# Head Lice

Also known as: pediculosis humanus capitis, cooties

## Description

Head lice continues to be one of the most common communicable childhood diseases, and outbreaks are possible wherever there are groups of children. Head lice are small wingless insects that live on the human scalp. They are about one-eighth inch in length and dark gray in color. Head lice can sometimes be seen crawling around in the hair or anchored to the skin. Nits are usually seen at the shaft of the hair. Nits are the head lice eggs. These eggs are sometimes mistaken for dandruff or hair spray droplets. These oval-shaped nits are found firmly attached to the hair shaft. The nits take about 1 week to hatch and are yellow to white in color. Head lice are most frequently found on the scalp behind the ears and near the neckline at the back of the neck. Head lice are rarely found on the body, eyelashes, or eyebrows (*see* Sexually Transmitted Disease: Crab Louse).

## Primary Groups Affected

- Preschool and elementary school-age children, ages 3 to 10 years; occasionally found in adolescents
- More frequent in girls than in boys
- Caucasian children with straight hair most apt to become infected; very rare in African American children

## Signs and Symptoms

- Tickly feeling of something moving in the hair
- Itching (usually an allergic reaction to the bites of the insect), which is the most common symptom and frequently the only symptom

- Irritability
- Sores on the head from scratching (may become infected)
- Swollen lymph glands in the back of the neck (severe cases)

## Classroom Guidelines

- Emphasize that anyone can get head lice. It does not mean that the infected adolescent is not clean.
- Isolate adolescent from the other students without embarrassing him or her. Adolescents with head lice are very sensitive to the reactions of the teacher and peers.
- Ensure that adolescents use proper hand-washing technique (*see* Part III, Procedure A).
- Be aware that all students in the classroom will have to be examined for head lice. Contact is common during school, in contact sports, and in sharing of lockers.
- Advise adolescents not to share hats, scarves, coats, sports uniforms, or hair ornaments. Vacuum inside of sports helmets.
- Advise adolescents not to share combs, brushes, or towels.
- If adolescent with head lice has come in contact with objects that cannot be cleaned or heat-dried, store objects in sealed plastic bag for 10 to 14 days. Head lice rarely survive off the scalp for more than a week.
- Understand that lice survive only on humans and cannot infect any classroom pets.
- Recognize that head lice provide an opportunity for teachers to instruct students on responsible personal health behaviors. Adolescents can learn communicable disease prevention concepts and be responsible for their health.

## Attendance Guidelines

- Some schools have a "nit-free policy" requiring that students have all nits removed before returning to the classroom.
- Adolescents with head lice may return to school the morning after their treatment and should be checked. Students with multiple infestations should be rechecked every 2 weeks until clear for two consecutive checks.

## Medication

- Over-the-counter or prescription shampoos may be used at home.

## Communication

- Make sure that parent/caregiver understands the "no nit" standard if mandated by school policy. This policy should be explained prior to an outbreak and allows for early intervention and minimization of inappropriate responses.
- Encourage blame-free communication to enhance parent/caregiver involvement.
- Inform parent/caregiver and/or school administration about student with head lice as soon as possible so that any classmates with lice can be identified and treated.
- Instruct parent/caregiver that there are shampoos and rinses, both over-the-counter and prescription, for the treatment of head lice. Stress the importance of following directions. Advise *not* to cut hair or shave adolescent's head.
- Suggest that parent/caregiver contact health care provider for specific instructions, especially for any student living with certain preexisting medical conditions and/or on certain prescribed medications. Repeated exposures to pesticidal products with each infestation may put certain adolescents, as well as families with pregnant or nursing mothers, at risk.

## Resources

- www.cdc.gov
- National Pediculosis Association
  www.headlice.org

- www.mayoclinic.org
- www.schoolnurse.com

# Hearing Loss

Also known as: hard of hearing, deaf, hearing impaired

## Description

Hearing loss occurs in many different degrees, ranging from slight to profound. Approximately 1 of every 1,000 children in the United States is profoundly hearing impaired (hears very little or no sound). Many young people have moderate to severe hearing loss, which usually involves speech impairment, the need for speech therapy, and difficulty with normal conversation. It is estimated that 50% of hearing deficit is inherited. Exposure to rubella accounts for another large percentage of hearing loss. Untreated or repeated otitis media (ear infection) can also lead to hearing impairment.

## Primary Groups Affected

- Any age group; often detected during school mandatory hearing screenings

## Signs and Symptoms

- Inattentiveness
- Lack of response to voice
- Confusion with instructions
- Frustration
- Need for repetition
- Speaks loudly or quietly
- Daydreams
- Articulation errors
- Favors one ear over the other
- Prefers solitary activities

## Classroom Guidelines

- Position hearing-impaired adolescent in classroom to promote hearing (with "good" ear closest to you).
- Face class when speaking. Move to side of room with hearing-impaired adolescent or stand in front of him or her.
- Eliminate distracting noises in classroom such as those from machinery, fans, and music.
- Use multimodalities for presenting material (visual, auditory, and interactive).
- Avoid walking while talking.
- Use round tables for group work so that adolescent can see other speakers.
- Allow adolescent to turn and face classmates when others behind are talking.
- Use a "buddy system" with another classmate for note taking.

## Attendance Guideline

- Exclusion from school is not required.

## Medications

- Medications to reduce wax buildup or to clear infection may be used.

## Communication

- Ask parent/caregiver about schedule of medications.
- Determine whether tubes have been placed in ears and whether there are any restrictions.
- Determine whether any hearing loss has occurred and how to best meet adolescent's needs.
- If hearing aids or amplifiers are used, determine any assistance adolescent might need.

## Resource

- kidshealth.com

# Heat Exhaustion

Also known as: heat prostration

## Description

   Heat exhaustion occurs in adolescents when they are outside in hot weather for a long period of time without taking in fluids. It can also occur if adolescents are dehydrated from diarrhea and/or vomiting and are outdoors.

## Primary Groups Affected

- Adolescents of any age

## Signs and Symptoms

- Thirsty
- Lack of energy
- Complain of muscle cramping
- Head hurting
- Nauseated and vomiting
- Body temperature normal or only slightly elevated
- Pale and damp skin
- May be sweating excessively
- May feel light-headed or dizzy when going from sitting to standing position and may faint—**911**

## Classroom Guidelines

- Activate local emergency system.
- Take adolescent to a cool, shaded, and well-ventilated room. Have adolescent rest and remove excessive clothing.

- Have adolescent lie down with feet elevated.
- Apply cool wet cloths and fan adolescent.

## Attendance Guideline

- Exclusion from school is not required.

## Medication

- If adolescent is not vomiting or nauseated, give sips of salt water (1 teaspoon salt per glass, one-half glass every 15 minutes, over a 1-hour period).

## Communication

- Notify parent/caregiver if adolescent experiences heat exhaustion.

## Resource

- www.cdc.gov

# Heatstroke

## Description

Heatstroke is serious and may be life-threatening to adolescents. It can cause an increased temperature of 104 degrees or higher.

### Primary Groups Affected

- Adolescents outside in hot weather for a long period of time

### Signs and Symptoms

- Temperature of 104 degrees or higher—**911**
- Dry skin
- Rapid pulse—**911**
- Increased breathing
- No sweating
- Decreased level of consciousness—**911**

### Classroom Guidelines

- Activate local emergency system.
- Report occurrence of heatstroke to school health care provider and parent/caregiver.
- If possible, put adolescent in a cool, well-ventilated room. Put adolescent in cool water (do not add ice) and apply cool wet cloths to head and neck until temperature is decreased.
- Do not give stimulants such as soda/soft drinks with caffeine or iced tea.
- Do not over-chill adolescent once body temperature falls below 102 degrees.
- Restrict time and strenuous activities when adolescents are outside on extremely hot days.

- Allow adolescents to drink water more frequently on extremely hot days.
- Assess that adolescents are dressed appropriately on extremely hot days. Urge students to avoid sweaters, long sleeves, and the like.

## Attendance Guideline

- Exclusion from school is not required.

## Medication

- No medication is required.

## Communication

- Notify parent/caretaker if adolescent experiences heatstroke symptoms.

## Resource

- www.cdc.gov

# Hemophilia

Also known as: a "royal" disease because it showed up in the English, Spanish, and Russian royal families; hemophilia A (factor VIII deficiency), 80% of all cases; hemophilia B (factor IX deficiency), also called Christmas disease, about 20% of all cases; hemophilia C (factor XI deficiency), 1% to 2% of all cases.

## Description

Hemophilia refers to a rare bleeding disorder that prevents the blood from clotting properly. Affected persons have problems with factor VIII, and their bleeding tendency varies from mild to severe. Bleeding can occur in any area of the body, including joints, bladder, bowel, and even brain or spinal cord. Approximately 1 of every 10,000 boys are born with hemophilia in the United States. Girls are carriers of hemophilia but are rarely affected by this sex-linked genetic condition. Newborns are not usually diagnosed because it is unlikely that they would sustain an injury that would lead to bleeding; even during circumcision, only about 30% of males with hemophilia will bleed excessively. Hemophilia may be suspected once a child begins walking and a pattern of bruising and bleeding is noticed, especially if this includes bleeding in the joint. Sometimes, bruises occur in unusual places, and child abuse often is suspected before the diagnosis is finally made. Hemophilia is diagnosed with several blood tests. There is no cure for hemophilia, but the condition can be managed successfully with periodic intravenous infusions of clotting factor replacement therapy.

## Primary Groups Affected

- Boys
- Girls very rarely affected
- Jewish children: hemophilia C, both sexes, less severe symptoms

## Signs and Symptoms

- Prolonged nosebleeds
- Excessive bleeding following an apparent minor fall or accident
- Excessive bleeding following a tooth extraction
- Excessive bleeding following surgery
- Blood in urine (hematuria)
- Pain and swelling in joints
- Heavy menstrual periods

## Classroom Guidelines

- Prevent injuries in classroom.
- Call **911** for any injury resulting in bleeding.
- While waiting for emergency medical system responders, elevate affected joint or limb, apply pressure to affected area to decrease bleeding, apply ice to affected area, and apply topical antifibrinolytic agent (if available) to nose and mouth injuries. An older youth (age 8 years or over) might be able to self-administer antihemophilic factor (ANF).

## Attendance Guideline

- Exclusion from school is not required.

## Medications

- Clotting factor replacement therapy may be used.
- Corticosteroids may be used.
- Nonsteroidal anti-inflammatory drugs (NSAIDS), such as ibuprofen and acetaminophen (Tylenol), may be used for pain relief.
- Adolescents with severe hemophilia may have a permanent intravenous catheter (called a portacath) in place for rapid administration of emergency medications.

## Communication

- Ask parent/caregiver which activities and sports are not safe for adolescent (usually these include football, boxing, and hockey).
- Ask how emergency situations should be handled, including administration of medications.

## Resource

- www.hemophilia.org

# Hepatitis A

Also known as: infectious hepatitis

## Description

Hepatitis A is an acute liver disease that generally causes mild illness. It is considered to be the least harmful of the hepatitis viruses because it rarely causes permanent liver damage. The virus enters the body through the mouth, multiplies in the body, and is excreted in the feces (bowel movements). The virus is carried on the infected person's hands and is spread by touching the food or drink of another person, contaminated water, shellfish, contaminated diapers, or changing tables. The greatest period of communicability is the 2 weeks before symptoms become apparent. Many people show no symptoms at all, and most recover in a few weeks without any complications. Once people recover from the disease, they are immune for life and do not continue to carry the virus. Immune globulin, which protects others, can be given within 10 to 14 days of exposure for those in close contact such as household members, day care centers for children not yet toilet trained, and institutionalized persons. The hepatitis A vaccine (HAV) is available and recommended for day care workers.

## Primary Groups Affected

- Preschool children and those age 15 years or under
- Common in day care settings with children in diapers

## Signs and Symptoms

- Fatigue
- Poor appetite
- Fever

- Vomiting
- Darker colored urine (tea colored)
- Jaundice (yellow) coloring of skin and whites of eyes

## Classroom Guidelines

- Ensure proper hand washing after use of bathroom and before and after handling food (*see* Procedure A).
- Ensure use of disposable paper towels for hand washing.
- Clean bathroom surfaces and food preparation areas daily.
- Wash all fruits and vegetables well.
- Avoid shellfish, especially raw oysters.

## Attendance Guidelines

- Exclusion from school is required until fever and jaundice have resolved and appetite has returned.
- Some health care providers may recommend 4 to 6 weeks of bed rest, although this is rarely necessary.

## Medication

- None is required unless for symptomatic relief of fever.

## Communication

- Notify parents/caregivers of adolescents who have direct contact with someone with hepatitis A.

## Resource

- www.cdc.gov

# Hepatitis B

Also known as: serum hepatitis

## Description

Hepatitis B is a liver disease caused by a virus that may be found in blood, saliva, semen, and other body fluids. Hepatitis B is spread by direct contact with the body fluids of an infected person, usually by a needle stick or by sexual contact. An infected pregnant woman can pass the infection on to her unborn child. Hepatitis B is diagnosed by a blood test. The usual treatment is rest; occasionally, some people need to be hospitalized if they are too ill to eat or drink. Most infected people recover completely within 6 months. However, in some instances, hepatitis B can be very harmful to a person's health, causing liver damage, cirrhosis, and an increased chance of liver cancer. Newborns are now routinely receiving the hepatitis B vaccine series. People in high-risk categories should be vaccinated.

## Primary Groups Affected

- Infants born to mothers who are hepatitis B carriers
- Drug abusers who share needles
- Health care workers who have direct contact with infected blood
- People who have unprotected sexual activity
- Hemodialysis patients

## Signs and Symptoms

- Fatigue
- Poor appetite
- Fever

- Vomiting
- Abdominal pain
- Dark-colored urine (tea colored)
- Jaundice (yellow) skin color and whites of the eyes
- Joint pain
- Hives
- Rash

## Classroom Guidelines

- Review all immunization records of adolescents.
- Ensure proper hand washing (*see* Part III, Procedure A).
- Ensure proper disposal of tissues.
- Ensure that adolescents avoid sharing of personal articles such as drinking glasses, toothbrushes, and eating utensils.
- Clean up blood spills immediately while wearing gloves.
- Disinfect area of blood spill with freshly prepared bleach solution.

## Attendance Guideline

- Exclusion from school is required until fever and jaundice have resolved and appetite has returned.

## Medication

- None is required unless for symptomatic relief of fever. Acetaminophen (Tylenol) may be used for this purpose.

## Communication

- Notify parents/caregivers of adolescents who have direct contact with someone with hepatitis B.
- Ask parent/caregiver of adolescent with hepatitis B about schedule of medications for fever relief.

## Resource

- www.hepb.org

# Hepatitis C

Also known as: formerly called non A non B hepatitis

## Description

Hepatitis C is a liver disease caused by a virus that is usually spread by direct blood-to-blood contact between two people. The most common means of transmission is through sharing needles or liquid drug preparation that has been exposed to hepatitis C. Another means of exposure to hepatitis C is through blood transfusions, although this risk has been greatly decreased with blood screening programs. Other methods of exposure to hepatitis C include a mother passing the disease to her fetus, tattooing, body piercing, acupuncture, and sharing razors. Unlike hepatitis B, hepatitis C is not present in other body fluids such as saliva, semen, and urine. The majority of persons with hepatitis C will have no symptoms for a decade or longer, some will never have symptoms, and others will have serious or even fatal liver damage.

## Primary Groups Affected

- Drug abusers who share needles or drug containers
- Persons who have received infected blood donations
- Infants born to mothers who are hepatitis C carriers
- Health care workers who have direct contact with infected blood
- Persons who have unprotected sexual activity if blood exchange is involved
- Hemodialysis patients

## Signs and Symptoms

- No signs or symptoms in 80% of persons
- Fatigue

- Poor appetite
- Fever
- Vomiting
- Abdominal pain
- Dark-colored urine (tea colored)
- Jaundice (yellow) skin color and whites of the eyes

## Classroom Guidelines

- Review all immunization records of adolescents.
- Ensure proper hand washing (*see* Part III, Procedure A).
- Ensure proper disposal of tissues.
- Ensure that adolescents avoid sharing of personal articles such as drinking glasses, toothbrushes, and eating utensils.
- Clean up blood spills immediately while wearing gloves.
- Disinfect area of blood spill with freshly prepared bleach solution.

## Attendance Guideline

- Exclusion from school is required until fever and jaundice have resolved and appetite has returned.

## Medication

- None is required unless for symptomatic relief of fever. Acetaminophen (Tylenol) may be used for this purpose.

## Communication

- Notify parents/caregivers of adolescents who have direct contact with someone with hepatitis C.
- Ask parent/caregiver of adolescent with hepatitis C about schedule of medications to reduce fever.

## Resources

- www.hepatitiscaware.org
- www.hepatitisinfo.com

# High Blood Pressure

Also known as: hypertension, high blood

## Description

Hypertension is defined as an elevation of the systolic (top) number or diastolic (bottom) number of a blood pressure reading. Most cases have an unknown cause and are labeled "essential hypertension." Elevated blood pressure reading with a specific cause, such as kidney or heart disease, is called "secondary hypertension." Children with hypertension may also have hyperlipidemia and/or obesity. These conditions are significant risk factors for heart disease.

## Primary Groups Affected

- Only about 1% to 3% of the pediatric population, with hypertension usually being identified after age 6 years
- African American adolescent males

## Signs and Symptoms

- Adolescents with hypertension may not show any symptoms
- Headache
- Shortness of breath
- Heart palpitations

## Classroom Guidelines

- Understand that a child with hypertension should be sent to the school nurse for a blood pressure check if there are complaints of chest pain, shortness of breath, heart palpitations, dizziness, or headache.

- Notify parent/caregiver if adolescent complains of any of the preceding symptoms.
- Teach African American adolescents about their greater risk for hypertension and developing complications when they reach adulthood.
- Recognize that adolescents on antihypertensive medications might need to use the restroom more frequently as a side effect of the medication.

## Attendance Guideline

- Exclusion from school is not required.
- Adolescents may miss school for scheduled office visits to monitor condition or for diagnostic tests.

## Medications

- Adolescents are usually placed on a diet low in fat and salt and high in fiber, fruits, and vegetables. After a period of lifestyle changes regarding diet and exercise, adolescents might need to be started on antihypertensive medications.

## Communication

- Document the condition of hypertension on the school health/ physical form.
- Ask parent/caregiver/adolescent about any activity restrictions or release to participate in competitive sports.
- Ask about medications and side effects.

## Resource

- www.mayoclinic.org

# High Cholesterol Level

Also known as: hyperlipidemia

## Description

High cholesterol (hyperlipidemia) is a condition of excess fat in the blood that may eventually lead to atherosclerosis (buildup of fatty plaque in the arteries) and cardiovascular disease. Usually, adolescents do not die from atherosclerosis. Hyperlipidemia, however, begins during childhood and progresses through adulthood and can lead to heart disease, which is currently the leading cause of death in the United States. This condition is diagnosed by a blood test.

## Primary Groups Affected

- Some adolescents may have a genetic predisposition to a high cholesterol level due to a defect in lipid (fat) metabolism.

## Signs and Symptoms

- Children with hyperlipidemia usually do not have any symptoms.

## Classroom Guidelines

- Recognize that there are no specific guidelines other than ongoing education regarding diet, exercise, and weight control.
- Encourage parents/caregivers/adolescents to provide "healthy treats" for student celebrations and events that require food to be brought into the classroom.

- Encourage school administration to provide healthy snacks in vending machines and at school-sponsored events.
- Encourage participation in aerobic exercises in gym class and school-related activities.

## Attendance Guideline

- Exclusion from school is not required. Adolescents might need to miss school in the morning for a fasting (nothing to eat or drink for 12 hours) blood test.

## Medication

- Most children with hyperlipidemia can be managed with modifications in diet and exercise. If these interventions are not successful, medication that lowers the fat levels in the blood may be prescribed for children over age 10 years.

## Communication

- Note that parent/caregiver should document the condition on adolescent's school physical form.
- Ask parent/caregiver/adolescent about any dietary restrictions.

## Resource

- www.mayoclinic.org

# HIV/AIDS

Also known as: human immunodeficiency virus (HIV), acquired immunodeficiency syndrome (AIDS)

## Description

AIDS is a chronic, life-threatening illness caused by the human immunodeficiency virus, for which there is no cure. The virus damages the cells of the immune system (referred to as immunocompromised) and stops the body from being able to fight off infections caused by bacteria, fungi, and viruses. HIV is the virus, and AIDS denotes the later stages of the HIV infection. Sexual contact, receiving blood, or sharing the needles or syringes of an infected person spreads the HIV virus. HIV can also be passed from an untreated mother to her infant during pregnancy, birth, or breast-feeding. Symptoms will vary depending on the phase of the disease. Some people will remain symptom free for 8 to 10 years; however, the immune system is slowly deteriorating. Sweat or tears, or sharing food or clothing, does not transmit HIV. Nor does kissing someone with HIV, being bitten by a mosquito, or donating blood. Behaviors that place people at greatest risk for being infected with HIV, in addition to being newborns of HIV-positive mothers, include having sex with multiple partners and not using a latex or polyurethane condom, sharing needles with someone who is HIV positive, and having received a blood product before 1985 when testing began.

## Primary Groups Affected

- Any age group

## Signs and Symptoms

### HIV (early signs)

- Swollen lymph glands
- Weight loss
- Poor growth
- Diarrhea
- Fever
- Persistent cough
- Shortness of breath
- Delayed mental development
- Development of cerebral palsy

### AIDS (later signs)

- Night sweats
- Fever higher than 100 degrees for several weeks, chills
- Chronic diarrhea
- Headaches
- Blurred vision
- Recurrent infections (more severe forms of otitis media, pneumonia, meningitis, and tonsillitis)
- Cancer (Kaposi's sarcoma, cervical cancer, and lymphoma)

## Classroom Guidelines

- Follow guidelines to prevent blood-borne infections: Ensure proper hand washing (see Procedure A), do not allow sharing of toothbrushes, clean up blood spills immediately using protocol set by the facility, disinfect surfaces with freshly prepared bleach solutions, and cover open wounds.
- Understand that many of the medications are on an extremely strict schedule and that not administering them on time can have very grave effects for adolescent.
- Understand that many of the medications must be given with food, whereas some are to be taken on an empty stomach.
- Understand that the adolescent living with HIV/AIDS may be sensitive to other student's reaction. Teacher needs to role model acceptance of student.
- Maintain privacy and confidentiality of student's health status.

## Attendance Guideline

- Exclusion from school is required during outbreaks of infectious diseases such as fifth disease and chicken pox (due to compromised immune system).

## Medications

- A variety of medications may be used to inhibit replication of HIV virus.

## Communication

- Ask parent/caregiver about schedule of medications so as to support/monitor compliance with treatment plan.
- Ask for written schedule of medications.

## Resource

- STD and HIV Hotline
  (800) 342-AIDS (English) or (800) 344-7432 (Spanish)
- www.hivatis.org
- www.aidsinfo.nih.gov

# Impetigo

Also known as: impetigo contagiosa

## Description

Impetigo is a skin infection caused by one of two bacteria: *group A streptococcus* or *Staphylococcus aureus*. The bacteria are contagious and likely to enter through broken skin and be transmitted through direct contact with the infected skin or by touching clothing or bed linens that have been in contact with infected skin. Impetigo often occurs on skin that has been previously affected by poison ivy, eczema, or allergies.

## Primary Groups Affected

- Most common in preschool and school-age children, with majority under age 2 years
- More common during summer months

## Signs and Symptoms

- Most common on face around mouth and nose or at site of trauma
- *Group A streptococcus* impetigo: begins with tiny blisters that in time break open; next, small wet patches of red skin; eventually, honey-colored crust over affected area; itching
- *S. aureus* impetigo: larger blisters containing clear and then cloudy fluid, blisters remaining intact longer, itching
- Less common symptoms: fever, diarrhea, weakness

## Classroom Guidelines

- Ensure proper hand washing (*see* Procedure A).
- Keep wound area as clean as possible.

- Dispense medications according to school regulations.
- Remind adolescent not to scratch or itch areas. Try distraction strategies.
- Be sensitive to emotional concerns.
- Eliminate any shared articles such as towels, hats, and personal articles.
- Minimize close contact with infected persons until they are treated.

## Attendance Guidelines

- Exclude from school until at least 48 hours after antibiotic treatment has started.
- Understand that wound usually heals by 7 to 10 days with antibiotic treatment.

## Medications

- Oral and topical (on the skin) antibiotics are commonly ordered.

## Communication

- Ask parent/caregiver about schedule of medications so as to support/monitor compliance.

## Resource

- www.emedicine.com

# Inflammatory Bowel Disease

Also known as: ulcerative colitis (UC), Crohn's disease (CD), IBD

## Description

Inflammatory bowel disease refers to two chronic disorders that cause inflammation in the intestines: ulcerative colitis and Crohn's disease. UC and CD have similar symptoms but two distinct differences. Both conditions can have mild to very severe symptoms, with periods of flare-ups and remissions. CD is often more disabling and has more complications. Medical and surgical treatment for CD is often not as effective as it is with UC. Both diseases cause inflammation of the digestive tract. CD can occur anywhere in the system, from the mouth to the anus (most often the small intestines), and often spreads deep into the layers of tissue. UC causes inflammation and ulcerations in only the inner lining of the large intestines (colon). It is believed that environment (living in cities), diet (high-fat and refined foods), and possibly genetics play a role in both of these diseases. Smoking may also play a role in CD. Researchers no longer believe that stress is the main causative factor, although stress can often aggravate symptoms.

## Primary Groups Affected

- Usually diagnosed between ages 15 and 30 years
- Nearly one third (30%) between ages 10 and 19 years
- More common in Euro-Americans; five times more common in Jewish persons and in those of European descent
- Parent or sibling with disease in 20% of cases

## Signs and Symptoms

- Diarrhea (sometimes bloody) requiring as many as 20 or more trips to the bathroom per day
- Abdominal pain and cramping
- Fatigue
- Poor appetite
- Weight loss
- Fever
- Constipation (less common)
- Poor growth due to malnutrition
- Delay in onset of puberty

## Classroom Guidelines

- Understand adolescent's fatigue, irritability, and anxiousness.
- Provide easy access to bathroom.
- Encourage a well-balanced diet. Eating small frequent meals throughout the day will lessen symptoms.
- Be aware that foods that tend to cause increased symptoms include seeds, popcorn, and corn as well as foods high in fat and sodium-laden fast-foods. The adolescent will eventually figure out which foods trigger attacks.
- Dispense medications according to school regulations.

## Attendance Guideline

- Exclusion from school is not required.

## Medications

- Anti-inflammatory medications and medications to suppress the immune system may be used.
- Vitamin, iron, and folic acid supplements may be prescribed.
- Sometimes surgery is necessary.

## Communication

- Ask parent/caregiver about schedule of medications so as to support/monitor compliance with treatment plan.
- Ask about foods that initiate attacks.

## Resource

- www.living-better.com

# Influenza

Also known as: flu, influenza A, influenza B, influenza C

## Description

Influenza is a highly contagious viral infection that can make persons of any age ill. There are basically three types of influenza viruses, identified as A, B, and C. Influenza types A and B usually cause the outbreak of respiratory illness that occur nearly every winter. Influenza C usually causes either a very mild respiratory illness or no symptoms at all. The flu tends to pass from person to person through sneezing and coughing. The virus can also live for a short time on objects such as doorknobs, pens, pencils, telephone receivers, eating utensils, and drinking glasses. This permits it to be spread to another person by handling an object that was touched by an infected person. At high risk for flu are persons who have asthma or other chronic lung conditions, who have cardiac problems, who are on medications to suppress their immune system, and who have sickle cell anemia, HIV, diabetes, or chronic kidney disease. "Stomach flu" is an incorrect term sometimes used to describe gastrointestinal (stomach and intestines) illnesses caused by other germs.

## Primary Groups Affected

- School-age children/adolescents, especially those who are malnourished, are sleep deprived, and get little exercise

## Signs and Symptoms

- High fever (usually lasts 3 to 5 days)
- Headache
- Sneezing and coughing (may last several weeks)

- Fatigue (may last several weeks)
- Severe aches and pain
- Sore throat (in some cases)
- Nausea or vomiting (rarely seen)

## Classroom Guidelines

- Notify parent/caregiver if any signs or symptoms are apparent in adolescent.
- Encourage all adolescents to wash hands to reduce (but not eliminate) risk of infection (*see* Procedure A).
- Encourage adolescent who is coughing or sneezing to cover nose and mouth with a tissue to limit spread of disease.
- Provide a receptacle for used tissues.

## Attendance Guideline

- Exclusion from school is required for period of time when adolescent is showing respiratory symptoms.

## Medication

- Acetaminophen (Tylenol) may be given for fever with parent/caregiver permission.

## Communication

- Notify parent/caregiver if adolescent is exhibiting flu-like symptoms.

## Resource

- http://2g.isg.syssrc.com

# Insect Stings/Bites

## Description

Many children may suffer from insect venom allergies. There is an increased incidence related to the spread of the fire ant throughout the United States. Adolescents stung by bees, wasps, yellow jackets, hornets, spiders, or ants can be thrust into life-and-death situations (*see* Anaphylaxis). A normal response to an insect bite is redness and swelling, but it is necessary to recognize signs of anaphylaxis. If an adolescent has a known allergy to insect venom, an emergency kit should be at the school and taken on all field events. Responsible persons should be trained in administering first aid for insect bites.

## Primary Groups Affected

- Adolescents of any age, especially during outdoor activity times

## Signs and Symptoms

- Redness
- Swelling around site of sting or bite
- Itching and hives over much of body
- Pain
- Nausea or vomiting, stomach cramps—**911**
- Confusion—**911**
- Difficulty in breathing—**911**
- Swelling in throat and tongue—**911**
- Rapid fall in blood pressure—**911**
- Shock, loss of consciousness—**911**

## Classroom Guidelines

- Talk calmly to adolescent who has been stung/bitten by insect.
- Remove stinger as soon as possible if stinger is still in skin. Scrape area with swinging motion using edge of credit card or stiff cardboard. Do not use forceps or tweezers, and do not pinch or grasp stinger at top (doing so may squeeze the poison sac and allow it to enter the wound).
- For a sting in the mouth, give adolescent ice cube or Popsicle to suck on or cold water to drink so as to decrease swelling.
- Wash sting site with soap and water, apply ice (for at least 10 minutes), and raise affected part if possible.
- For a bee sting, apply a paste of baking soda and water and leave it on for 15 to 20 minutes.
- Watch for more severe reactions. Activate local emergency medical system and be prepared to resuscitate.
- Any adolescent who has a history of severe reaction to stinging insect bites should carry an Epi-pen for emergency use.
- Fire ant bites should be treated with ice and call the local poison control center or emergency room for further treatment guidelines.
- Notify parent/caregiver.
- Teach adolescents methods to minimize contact with stinging insets, including refraining from wearing brightly colored clothing with flowery patterns, avoiding sweet-smelling cosmetics and hair sprays, wearing enclosed shoes to guard against getting stung by stepping on insects, keeping arms and legs covered during hiking and other activities that may expose them to insects, not swatting or crushing insects, staying clear of insect nests, and keeping food and garbage covered. Teach adolescents that insect repellents do not work against stinging insects and that they should not drink from open soda/soft drink cans because insects can crawl inside and end up biting the inside of the mouth.

## Medications

- Acetaminophen (Tylenol) may be used if parent/caregiver permission is obtained.
- Antihistamines may be used.
- Corticosteroids may be used to decrease inflammation.

## Attendance Guideline

- Exclusion from school is not required.

## Communication

- Ask parent/caregiver/adolescent to describe reaction.
- Ask parent/caregiver to give adolescent with severe reaction Medic-Alert bracelet to wear.
- Ask whether adolescent with severe reaction is getting venom immunotherapy.
- Ask whether adolescent with known allergic response to insect bites has an EpiPen or bee sting kit (*see* Procedure K).

## Resources

- www.allergic-reactions.com
- www.allergy.meg.edu

# Juvenile Rheumatoid Arthritis

Also known as: juvenile arthritis, children's arthritis, JRA

## Description

Juvenile rheumatoid arthritis is common rheumatic inflammatory disease that results in swelling, pain, redness, and heat in the joints. It may affect one joint or include nearly all joints in the body. The majority of adolescents with JRA have mild disease and do quite well. In approximately 85% of adolescents, the disease goes into remission by adulthood. There may, however, be permanent residual joint deformities. If the mobility impairment is severe, there may be a need for total joint replacement during either childhood or adulthood.

## Primary Groups Affected

- Approximately 200,000 children in the United States
- Affects individuals under age 18 years
- Often a family history of some rheumatological condition (any variety of disorders that cause inflammation and/or degeneration of joints and related structures)

## Signs and Symptoms

- Arthritis (pain, swelling, redness, heat) present in the joints
- Affected joints that vary from adolescent to adolescent
- Stiffness, especially during the morning or after being immobile for a period of time

- Fatigue, irritability
- Anemia
- May include spiking fevers and rash
- Poor growth pattern when the disease is active

## Classroom Guidelines

- If the adolescent consistently complains of pain or exhibits difficulty in performing school activities, report these findings to parent/caregiver and school health care provider.
- Be aware that adolescents often complain of pain for other reasons and that arthritis might not be the cause.
- Understand that because adolescent is very stiff in the morning, early classes may often be missed.
- Understand that during a flare-up of the disease, adolescent may have multiple absences due to pain.
- Allow adolescent to get up and stretch as needed, for example, by passing out papers and erasing the blackboard.
- Expect adolescent to have good and bad days and for performance to fluctuate accordingly.
- Determine whether adolescent can tolerate a full day of classes when the disease is flaring up.
- Understand that adolescent's face and body may become more rounded due to effects of medications.
- Upper extremities:

  - Provide extra time for writing assignments if needed, or reduce the amount of writing required.
  - Understand that penmanship may suffer.
  - Ensure that adolescent wears splints as instructed.
  - Provide assistance for adolescent with lockers, lunch tray, milk cartons, dressing, and toileting as needed.
  - Determine whether adolescent can carry books.

- Back/neck:

  - Investigate the need for a book stand for adolescent's desk to decrease neck strain.

- Lower extremities:

  - Provide indoor activities when the weather is cold or damp.
  - Ensure that adolescent wears brace/splints as instructed or uses crutches/walker appropriately.
  - Be sure that adolescent has enough time to change classes.

    – Arrange for adolescent's safe exit from classroom in case of an unexpected event that requires students to leave classroom or school.

## Attendance Guideline

- Exclusion from school is not required because this is not a contagious disease.

## Medications

- Anti-inflammatory medication may be used as per parent/caregiver instructions.
- Acetaminophen (Tylenol) may be used with parent/caregiver permission.
- Low-dose chemotherapeutic (anti-cancer) drugs and/or steroids, via oral or intravenous route, possibly may be prescribed.

## Communication

- Ask parent/caregiver/adolescent about treatment plan, especially regarding restriction of activities.
- Ask about schedule of medications.
- Ask what should be done for extremely painful episodes.
- Ask about use of splints and the wearing schedule.

## Resources

- American Juvenile Arthritis Organization
  1314 Spring Street, N.W.
  Atlanta, GA 30309
  (404) 872-7100

- www.arthritis.org

# Lupus

Also known as: systemic lupus erythematosus (SLE)

## Description

Lupus is characterized by inflammation that can affect many parts of the body (skin, joints, kidneys, blood cells, heart, and lungs). It can be mild to life-threatening. Flare-ups may come and go.

## Primary Groups Affected

- Rare in very young children
- Occurs most often between ages 9 and 15 years
- Higher incidence noted in African American, Asian, and Hispanic children

## Signs and Symptoms

- Complaints of weakness or feeling tired
- Rashes (butterfly-shaped rash across bridge of nose and cheeks or scaly, disk-shaped rash on face, neck, or chest); may look like severe sunburn or hives
- Fever
- Shortness of breath
- Joints swelling and achy; pain in hip joint that may cause difficulty in walking and running
- Seizures, headaches, excitability, forgetfulness, dizziness, difficulty in concentrating, mood swings—**911**
- Nausea, vomiting, loose stools, stomach pain
- Thinning hair or loss of hair
- Sensitivity to light (photosensitivity)

## Classroom Guidelines

- Take adolescent's complaints seriously and notify parent/ caregiver.
- Urge adolescent to minimize exposure to sun and ultraviolet light and to use sunscreen or a wide-brimmed hat (*see* Procedure I).
- Arrange for adolescent's desk to be away from windows with a lot of direct sunlight.
- Keep adolescent indoors and arrange for participation in alternative activities during extremely cold weather.
- Adhere to any dietary modifications as indicated by parent/ caregiver/adolescent; request list of written restrictions and allowed foods.
- Provide psychological support and show patience when adolescent has difficulty in concentrating. Adolescent may easily cry and become frustrated with himself or herself and need to develop effective coping skills.
- Observe adolescent for fatigue during strenuous activities and plan for involvement that decreases exertion.
- Provide for adolescent's safety and privacy if seizures occur.
- Be aware that adolescent should wear Medic-Alert bracelet regarding the disease and if he or she is on steroids (anti-inflammatory drugs).

## Attendance Guideline

- Adolescent may experience excessive absences depending on which symptoms are being experienced and the response to medications.

## Medications

- As ordered by health care provider, these usually include numerous medications for symptoms and pain.

## Communication

- Notify parent/caregiver if adolescent complains of any symptoms at school.
- Ask parent/caregiver/adolescent about any restrictions or special accommodations to be implemented to decrease stress and fatigue.

- Ask parent/caregiver/adolescent to provide sunscreen when adolescent is participating in outdoor activities.
- Ask whether adolescent has experienced seizure activity associated with lupus.
- Notify parent/caregiver if adolescent seems depressed or withdraws from other children or activities.

## Resource

- www.mayoclinic.org

# Lyme Disease

Also known as: *Borrelia burgdorferi* infection

## Description

Lyme disease is an illness affecting many parts of the body. It occurs from being bitten by an infected tick commonly carried by deer, dogs, and cats. The tick must feed on the person for 36 hours to transmit the disease. Development of the disease occurs in three stages. Stage 1 occurs shortly after the bite and is characterized by a red rash and flu-like symptoms. Stage 2 occurs 1 to 4 months after the bite and is characterized by Lyme arthritis. Stage 3 occurs several month later and is characterized by central nervous system changes and continuing Lyme arthritis.

## Primary Groups Affected

- May occur at any age; immunity to future exposures not acquired
- Risk highest from May through July but can occur at any time of year
- Risk highest in areas that are heavily wooded, brushy, or grassy; higher incidence in northeastern coastal states, Wisconsin, Minnesota, and the coast of Oregon and northern California; also reported in Europe and Asia

## Signs and Symptoms

- The disease develops with a slowly expanding red rash starting as a flat or raised red area, at the site of the tick bite, spreading to form an intense red-ringed border with some clearing toward the center. Blisters or scabs may develop at the center, or a bluish discoloration may occur.

- Flu-like symptoms include complaints of fatigue, headache, stiff neck, mild fever, and muscle and joint aches.
- Left untreated, adolescent develops Lyme arthritis, with pain and swelling of joints, most commonly the knees.
- Central nervous system changes that occur during stage 3 include arm and leg weakness, Bell's palsy, encephalitis, meningitis, and sometimes depression.

## Classroom Guidelines

- When engaging in outdoor activities in high-risk areas, ensure that adolescents wear protective clothing to prevent exposure of skin and that they tuck pant legs into socks.
- Check for ticks, especially ticks hidden in the hair, after outings in high-risk areas.
- Using tweezers or finger and wearing gloves, remove the tick by gripping it gently but firmly at the point where mouthparts are attached. Pull straight outward with gentle steady pressure until tick releases. Wash hands afterward.
- Do not use folklore remedies such as petroleum jelly and hot matches.
- Cleanse area with soap and water. If any tick parts are left under the skin, adolescent needs to see health care provider for removal.
- Save the tick for identification in case adolescent becomes ill.
- Adolescent with Lyme disease might not be able to participate in vigorous activities. Allow for periods of rest.

## Attendance Guideline

- Exclusion from school is not required.

## Medications

- Adolescents with early Lyme disease are usually treated with antibiotics and non-aspirin analgesics, such as acetaminophen (Tylenol), for aches and mild fevers.

## Communication

- Inform parent/caregiver if tick bite occurs at school or on a school outing.

- Encourage to seek medical attention promptly if parts of tick remain after removal or symptoms develop.
- Ask whether adolescent is being treated with medications.

## Resource

- www.cdc.gov/ncidod/diseases

# Measles
# (German Measles)

Also known as: three-day measles, rubella

## Description

Rubella, a virus that is spread through the air or by close contact, usually causes a mild self-limiting illness. However, the disease can also be transmitted from a mother to her fetus during early pregnancy (congenital rubella syndrome), and this can lead to serious consequences (deafness, blindness, heart defects, neurological damage, miscarriage, or stillbirth) for the fetus. A person can spread the virus from 1 week before the rash begins until 1 week after the rash disappears. Immunity can be achieved by receiving the MMR (measles, mumps, rubella) vaccination. This vaccine series begins at ages 12 to 15 months and again at ages 4 to 6 years or 11 to 12 years. The vaccine should not be given to pregnant women, and pregnancy should be avoided for 3 months after receiving the vaccine.

## Primary Groups Affected

- Any age group

## Signs and Symptoms

- Symptoms often mild, with 30% to 50% of cases having no obvious symptoms
- Young children:
  - Rash that usually begins on face and spreads down to feet; lasts about 3 days; sometimes itches

- Older children and adults:

  - 1 to 5 days of early symptoms before rash
  - Low-grade fever
  - Fatigue
  - Headache
  - Swollen glands (neck or behind ears)
  - Upper respiratory infection
  - Inflammation of eyes (conjunctivitis)
  - Joint pain (lasts for up to 1 month)
  - Rash (pink or light red spots) that occurs after 1 to 5 days of early symptoms

## Classroom Guidelines

- Review all immunization records.
- Ensure proper hand washing with hot soapy water (*see* Procedure A).
- Ensure proper disposal of tissues.
- Urge adolescents to avoid sharing of personal articles such as drinking glasses and eating utensils.

## Attendance Guideline

- Exclusion from school is required until 1 week after rash first appears.

## Medication

- Acetaminophen (Tylenol) may be used to reduce fever and discomfort.

## Communication

- Notify staff, parent/caregiver, and school nurse.
- Notify local health department.
- If adolescent is pregnant, refer to health care provider.
- Ask parent/caregiver about schedule of medications.

## Resource

- www.cdc.gov

# Measles
# (Rubeola)

Also known as: rubeola, red measles, seven-day measles, hard measles

## Description

Measles is a respiratory infection caused by a virus and known for its characteristic skin rash. Rubeola is very contagious and is spread through respiratory secretions (coughing, sneezing, or kissing) to persons who are not immune. Most people with measles become very ill but usually recover with no long-lasting effects. Young infants and adults tend to become more ill and have more complications than do children and adolescents. Measles can lead to complications such as otitis media (ear infection), pneumonia, croup, and encephalitis. Measles usually lasts 10 to 14 days from the first symptoms until the rash disappears. People are contagious from 5 days after exposure to 5 days after the rash appears. Immunity can be achieved by receiving the MMR (measles, mumps, rubella) vaccination. This vaccine series begins at ages 12 to 15 months and again at ages 4 to 6 years or 11 to 12 years. Adults born before 1957 are considered immune because they most likely have had the disease. Adults born after 1956 should receive two doses of the MMR vaccine (one dose given after 1967 at age 12 months or over). Pregnant woman should inform their health care providers of exposure given that the disease can trigger miscarriage and premature delivery. This disease is seen very infrequently since the MMR vaccine started being used.

## Primary Groups Affected

- Any age group

## Signs and Symptoms

### Early Symptoms

- 1 to 8 days, usually 3 or 4 days
- Irritability
- Runny nose
- Sore throat
- Red, watery, light-sensitive eyes (photophobia)
- Hacking cough
- Fever as high as 105 degrees
- Koplik's spots
- Small (size of grain of sand) red spots with bluish white centers seen inside cheeks

### Later Symptoms

- Continued cough
- Rash
- Begins on forehead and spreads down face, neck, and body
- Rash that is large, flat, red to brown blotches

## Classroom Guidelines

- Review all immunization records.
- Ensure proper hand washing (*see* Part III, Procedure A).
- Ensure proper disposal of tissues.
- Urge adolescents to avoid sharing of personal articles such as drinking glasses and eating utensils.

## Attendance Guideline

- Exclusion from school is required until the fifth day after rash first appeares.

## Medications

- Acetaminophen (Tylenol) may be used for fever.
- Antibiotics might be prescribed to prevent secondary bacterial infections for those with poor immune systems.

## Communication

- Ask parent/caregiver about schedule of medications.
- Notify staff, parent/caregiver, and school nurse.
- Notify local health department.

## Resource

- www.cdc.gov

# Meningitis

Also known as: viral meningitis, bacterial meningitis, spinal meningitis

## Description

Meningitis is an infection of the fluid that covers the brain and spinal cord. A virus or bacterial infection usually causes meningitis. Viral meningitis is the most common type. It is a serious infection but is rarely fatal in children with a normal immune system. Fewer than 1 of every 1,000 persons infected with the virus actually develops meningitis. Meningococcal meningitis (bacterial) can be quite severe. It occurs in epidemics and spreads easily from adolescent to adolescent by droplet infection of salvia, sputum, or nasal secretions. Pneumococcal meningitis is a form of bacterial meningitis and is the most serious type and may even be life-threatening. Pneumococcal meningitis can be spread through contact with droplets from the nose, eyes, or mouth of an infected person. The prognosis is dependent on early diagnosis and antibiotic therapy.

## Primary Groups Affected

- Fully 90% of reported cases of bacterial meningitis occur in children between ages 1 month and 5 years.
- Meningococcal meningitis occurs predominately in school-age children and adolescents. There is a higher incidence in children in boarding schools and in child care.
- Pneumococcal meningitis occurs frequently in very young children and in children with depressed immune systems, cancer, or AIDS.
- There is a greater incidence of bacterial meningitis in low-income children.

- Children who have had a recent case of pneumonia or ear infection are at higher risk; however, there is a relatively low incidence.

## Signs and Symptoms

- Varies from adolescent to adolescent; can develop over several hours or take 1 to 3 days after being in contact with the infecting organism
- High fever that inhibits adolescents from eating or drinking
- Severe headaches, stiff neck, drowsiness, confusion, irritability, agitation, seizures—**911**
- Skin rash (especially near armpits or on hands or feet)
- Joint pain with meningococcal infection
- Nausea or vomiting, chills
- Ear draining fluid—**911**
- Sensitive to bright lights, noise, and other stimuli
- Confusion, decreased level of consciousness, coma—**911**

## Classroom Guidelines

- Take adolescent's complaints seriously and notify school health care provider and parent/caregiver immediately.
- Be aware that how well an adolescent recovers may depend on how quickly he or she receives treatment.
- Isolate adolescent from other students but keep under supervision until parent/caregiver arrives or local emergency system is activated.
- Teach adolescents to wash their hands often, especially before they eat and after using the bathroom (*see* Procedure A). Also teach them the proper disposal of soiled tissues and urge them to avoid sharing drinking glasses and eating utensils so as to reduce the chances of becoming infected.
- Wash objects and surfaces with a dilute bleach solution (made by mixing 1 capful of chlorine-containing household bleach with 1 gallon of water) to inactivate the virus if exposed to viral meningitis.
- Allow adolescents to ask questions of someone knowledgeable about meningitis so as to decrease anxiety.
- Recognize that classmates may be placed on antibiotics or vaccinated if adolescent with disease has meningococcal meningitis (*Neisseria meningitis*).

## Attendance Guidelines

- Adolescent may return to school with permission of health care provider, usually 24 hours after fever is gone and adolescent is on antibiotic therapy.
- Adolescent may experience excessive absences depending on symptoms, complications from meningitis, and response to medications.

## Medications

- Antibiotics as ordered by health care provider may be used.

## Communication

- Notify parent/caregiver if adolescent complains of any symptoms.
- Ask about information regarding whether meningitis is viral or bacterial in origin. Notify school nurse and administration for purposes of notifying parents/caregivers of other students in contact with infected person as per school policy.
- Ask parent/caregiver/adolescent about any restrictions of activity and administration of medications when student returns to school.

## Resources

- www.cdc.gov
- www.choa.org/infectious/viralmenin.shtml
- U.S. National Center for Infectious Diseases
  Respiratory and Enteric Virus Branch
  (404) 639-3607

# Menstrual Cramps

Also known as: dysmenorrhea, painful periods

## Description

Menstrual cramps occur in about 60% of women at some time in their lives. In addition to painful uterine cramping with menses, women with dysmenorrhea may experience nausea, vomiting, diarrhea, headaches, weakness, and/or fainting. Symptoms may vary in severity from cycle to cycle but generally continue throughout the reproductive years. Dysmenorrhea can be an incapacitating problem, causing significant disruption in a woman's life each month. Severe cramps need to be evaluated by a health care provider to determine whether the cause is related to pelvic disease or endometriosis.

## Primary Groups Affected

- Any menstruating women

## Signs and Symptoms

- Low abdominal cramping that correlates with the menstrual cycle
- May occur several days before the period begins
- May occur just during the actual menstrual bleeding

## Classroom Guidelines

- Encourage adolescents who are experiencing painful periods to seek the advice of a health care provider to learn methods to assist with pain.

- Common pharmacological remedies include the following:

  – Over-the-counter, nonsteroidal, anti-inflammatory drugs
    (NSAIDs) such as aspirin, ibuprofen, and naproxen sodium
  – Acetaminophen usually not as helpful with this type of pain
  – Prescription anti-inflammatory medications
  – Prescription birth control pills

- Nonpharmacological methods include the following:

  – Maintaining healthy weight
  – Avoiding smoking
  – Avoiding tampons
  – Exercise and stress reduction
  – Vitamin B3 (niacin), vitamin E, calcium, omega-3, and
    omega-6
  – Evening primrose oil, flax oil
  – Decreasing dairy products, saturated fats, and animal foods
  – Increasing fish, nuts, seeds, whole grains, legumes, fruits, and
    vegetables

## Attendance Guideline

- Exclusion from school is not required unless adolescent is experiencing too much pain.

## Medications

- Over-the-counter and prescription medications may be used.

## Communication

- Ask parent/caregiver about schedule of medications/dietary changes so as to support/monitor compliance with treatment plan.

## Resource

- www.mckinley.uiuc.edu/health-info

# Mononucleosis

Also known as: mono, infectious mononucleosis, kissing disease, Epstein-Barr virus (EBV)

## Description

Mononucleosis is an acute, self-limiting, viral respiratory infection. The course of the disease is usually mild but can cause serious complications in rare instances. Mononucleosis is spread by person-to-person contact with infected saliva such as sharing eating utensils, drinking glasses, or intimate kissing. Persons between ages 4 and 15 years often have a mild form of the disease that appears to be a respiratory infection. Older persons frequently have more severe symptoms that last longer. The virus has an incubation period of 4 to 7 weeks; therefore, this amount of time will lapse from exposure until symptoms first appear. There are many different symptoms, and the disease may initially be mistaken for flu or strep throat. A blood test is used to diagnose mononucleosis. However, even after diagnosis, there is no cure for the disease; the adolescent simply requires plenty of rest and symptomatic relief for aches and fever. Most symptoms will go away in about 10 days; however, it will be 2 or 3 weeks before the adolescent can return to normal activities and often 2 or 4 months before he or she feels completely normal. If symptoms continue for longer than 6 months, it is possible that chronic fatigue syndrome is the cause.

## Primary Groups Affected

- Ages 4 to 35 years, with the highest incidence between ages 15 and 24 years

## Signs and Symptoms

- Fatigue
- Headache
- Weakness
- Sore throat
- Sore muscles
- Fever
- Swollen lymph nodes in neck and armpits
- Swollen tonsils
- Loss of appetite

## Classroom Guidelines

- Urge students to avoid sharing of personal articles such as drinking glasses and eating utensils.
- Dispense medications according to school regulations.
- Reinforce the need for a well-balanced diet.
- Urge adolescent to avoid strenuous activities. Provide opportunities for rest.

## Attendance Guideline

- Exclusion from school is required until fever resolves.

## Medications

- Acetaminophen (Tylenol) or ibuprofen (Motrin) may be used for fever.
- Adolescent should be encouraged to drink plenty of water.

## Communication

- Inquire about schedule of medications.
- Notify staff, school nurse, and parents/caregivers of all students who come in contact with adolescent.

## Resource

- Centers for Disease Control and Prevention (888) 232-3228

# Mumps

Also known as: infectious parotitis

## Description

Mumps, caused by a virus similar to the influenza virus, is known for the parotid and salivary gland swelling noticeable in the cheeks, jaw, and neck area. One third of persons affected have minimal or no obvious symptoms. However, mumps can cause serious complications such as encephalitis (brain swelling) and hearing loss. Mumps can also lead to spontaneous miscarriage when acquired during early pregnancy. One quarter of adolescent and adult males with mumps also experience swelling of one or both testicles, although this does not usually lead to sterility. Mumps is contagious and is spread via direct contact with respiratory secretions. Symptoms begin to show 2 to 3 weeks after exposure; however, those affected are contagious from 12 to 24 days after exposure. Immunity to the mumps can be achieved by receiving the MMR (measles, mumps, rubella) vaccination. This vaccine series begins at ages 12 to 15 months and again at ages 4 to 6 years or 11 to 12 years.

## Primary Groups Affected

- Any age group may be affected, although mumps is uncommon under age 1 year.
- Adolescents and adults will usually become more ill than children who are affected.

## Signs and Symptoms

- Swelling of the cheeks, neck, and jaw (below and in front of ear), often with one side swelling and then, as it begins to subside, the second side swelling

- Neck and ear pain (can be severe)
- Low-grade fever
- Headache
- Fatigue
- Loss of appetite

## Classroom Guidelines

- Review all immunization records.
- Ensure that adolescents wash hands frequently (*see* Procedure A).
- Ensure proper disposal of tissues.
- Urge adolescents to avoid sharing of personal articles such as drinking glasses and eating utensils.

## Attendance Guideline

- Exclusion from school is required until 9 days after swelling begins or until swelling subsides.

## Medication

- Acetaminophen (Tylenol) may be used to reduce fever and discomfort.

## Communication

- Notify staff, school nurse, and parents/caregivers of all students who come in contact with affected adolescent.
- Notify local health department.

## Resource

- www.cdc.gov

# Muscular Dystrophy

Also known as: MD

## Description

Muscular dystrophy is a group of hereditary muscle-destroying disorders. The muscles, usually the voluntary muscles, become progressively weaker. Duchenne's and Becker's muscular dystrophies are the most common form of the disease. Duchenne's is the most severe form. Becker's is a milder and slower progressing form. Remaining physically active for as long as possible keeps the adolescent from having to be wheelchair dependent. Sole use of the wheelchair promotes the development of contractures (abnormal shortening of muscle tissue that makes the muscle resistant to stretching) and deconditioning.

## Primary Groups Affected

- Duchenne's: found in young boys between ages 3 and 7 years
- Becker's: found in older boys and young men usually diagnosed by about age 10 years
- Landouzy-Dejerine: found during early adolescence
- Limb-girdle: found during later childhood or early adolescence
- Children living with diabetes mellitus, Down syndrome, or Turner syndrome

## Signs and Symptoms

*Duchenne's*

- Usually weakness in the pelvic area first, progressing to the shoulders

- Frequent falls and great difficulty in rising from a sitting position
- Waddling gait; most unable to walk by late childhood
- Calves and upper arm muscles enlarged
- Heart muscle enlarged
- Development of scoliosis (*see* Scoliosis)
- Mental deficiency
- Often death by late teens or early 20s due to pneumonia, respiratory muscle weakness, or cardiac complications

### Becker's

- Nearly identical symptoms to Duchenne's but often much less severe
- Heart problems sometimes more significant
- Survival well into mid- to late adulthood

### Landouzy-Dejerine

- Difficulty in raising arms over head
- Lack of facial mobility
- Forward slope of shoulders
- Slow progression that rarely affects life span

### Limb-Girdle

- Weakness of certain muscles of pelvic and shoulder areas
- Progression usually slow

## Classroom Guidelines

- Foster an atmosphere that allows adolescent living with muscular dystrophy to be as independent as possible.
- Foster an atmosphere of sensitivity concerning adolescent's knowledge of disease outcome. Because there may be other children in extended family with this disorder, adolescent may be aware of prognosis depending on type of muscular dystrophy.
- Address safety concerns associated with adolescent using assistive devices such as walker and wheelchair.
- Arrange for adolescent's safe exit from classroom in case of an unexpected event that requires students to leave classroom or school.

- Plan suitable activities devised to meet needs of adolescent, but limit activity according to directions of health care provider. Plan activities in which adolescent can be successful by using unaffected muscles.

## Attendance Guideline

- Exclusion from school is not required.

## Medications

- Medications to treat symptoms may be prescribed by health care provider.

## Communication

- Ask parent/caregiver about adolescent's knowledge of disease and progression.
- Ask parent/caregiver/adolescent about schedule of medications to be given and any treatments.

## Resources

- www.mayoclinic.org
- www.mdausa.org

# Nosebleed

Also known as: epistaxis

## Description

Bleeding from the nose usually occurs as a result of increased pressure from secretions in the nose due to respiratory tract infection, allergies, or inflammation of the sinuses. Bleeding also can occur from nose picking and blowing, being hit on the nose, or putting something in the nose. In addition, overly dry air or a broken nose can cause bleeding.

## Primary Groups Affected

- Adolescents of any age, especially during outdoor activity time and when involved in contact sports or games

## Signs and Symptoms

- Bleeding from the nose; may be light or heavy
- Heavy prolonged bleeding that can cause symptoms of shock

## Classroom Guidelines

- Have adolescent sit down while keeping head in an upright position, leaning slightly forward if possible.
- Using universal precautions on when to wear gloves (*see* Procedure A), apply firm (but not painful) pressure with fingers over bleeding nostril for at least 5 minutes. Do not apply pressure to bridge of nose given that this is too high up and does not stop bleeding.
- Apply ice wrapped in gauze or cold cloth and place on bridge of nose for soothing effect.

- If bleeding does not stop in a reasonable amount of time, activate local emergency medical system and contact parent/caregiver.
- Keep adolescent from blowing or picking at nose.
- Reassure adolescent that bleeding from nose is usually not serious.
- Be calm and approach adolescent in a positive manner.
- Discourage adolescent from swallowing.
- Explain what you are doing to stop bleeding.

## Attendance Guidelines

- Exclusion from school is not required.
- Restrict adolescent from strenuous activities for remainder of day.

## Medication

- No medication is required.

## Communication

- Notify parent/caregiver of nosebleed episode.

## Resources

- www.entnet.org/healthinfo/nose/nosebleeds.cfm
- www.mayoclinic.org

# Obesity

Also known as: extreme overweight

## Description

Obesity is the most common nutritional disorder in the United States. Genetics appears to play a major role in obesity. Studies show that if one parent is obese, there is a 50% chance that the couple's children will be as well; the chance increases to 66% when both parents are obese. Other research has found that when identical twins are reared apart, they end up with similar weights, regardless of the weights of their adoptive families. Prevention is more effective than treatment.

## Primary Groups Affected

- Affects all age groups
- Nearly one quarter (22%) of all children overweight, up from 15% a decade ago
- Minority populations, especially African American females, disproportionately affected

## Signs and Symptoms

- Body mass index (BMI, calculated by dividing weight [in kilograms] by height [in meters] squared) of 25 to 29 considered overweight; BMI of 30 or higher considered obese
- Orthopedic abnormalities such as hip problems
- Low self-esteem
- Poor peer interactions
- Discrimination in school and from the general public

- As adults, at risk for developing a number of medical conditions: diabetes, hypertension, heart disease, gallbladder disease, arthritis, and complications during pregnancy

## Classroom Guidelines

- Discuss with the entire class the concepts of stigma and discrimination. State clearly that those behaviors are not allowed in the school setting.
- Avoid sending negative messages about the way in which the obese adolescent looks.
- Limit adolescent's access to buying junk food.
- Encourage physical activity. Model healthy lifestyle activities such as taking the stairs, walking, and eating healthy foods.

## Attendance Guideline

- Exclusion from school is not required.

## Medication

- No medication is required.

## Communication

- Given that many medications for other disorders cause weight gain, ask parent/caregiver whether this is a factor for adolescent.
- Ask parent/caregiver what actions have been attempted to reduce adolescent's weight and whether they were effective.

## Resources

- Weight Watchers
  www.weightwatchers.com

- Take Off Pounds Sensibly (TOPS)
  www.tops.org

# Obesity: Prader-Willi Syndrome

## Description

Prader-Willi syndrome is a congenital disorder evidenced by morbid obesity as well as mental and behavioral problems.

## Primary Groups Affected

- Estimated prevalence of 1 of every 12,000 to 15,000 children
- Both genders affected
- All ethnic groups affected
- Congenital defect of the 15th chromosome

## Signs and Symptoms

- History of excessive and rapid weight gain between ages 1 and 6 years
- Mild to moderate cognitive impairment; adolescents with average IQs typically having learning disabilities
- Obsession with food, food foraging, and excessive appetite that is physiological and overwhelming, as adolescent cannot decide "not to eat"
- Hoarding food and stealing money to buy food
- Behavioral problems such as temper tantrums, oppositional behavior and stubbornness, and labile emotions as well as compulsive behaviors such as skin picking
- Difficulties with transitions and unanticipated changes

- Sleep disturbances or sleep apnea
- Short stature for genetic background by age 15 years
- Hypogonadism—delayed puberty, small penis, and undescended testes in males; lack of menses in females
- Nighttime enuresis (bed-wetting) common at all ages

## Classroom Guidelines

- Rigidly enforce access to food.
- Be aware that restricting food intake demands close supervision.
- Encourage exercise and sports activities, and make adaptations as needed.
- Build on areas of strength:

  - Verbal ability
  - Visual-perceptual skills
  - Long-term memory
  - Reading ability
  - Receptive language

- Understand that adolescent may have problems with short-term auditory memory.
- Recognize that adolescent may experience the stigma of obesity and become a victim of teasing. Enlist other students to offer acceptance and protection.

## Attendance Guideline

- Exclusion from school is not required.

## Medication

- No medication is required.

## Communication

- Ask parent/caregiver which exercise and sport activities adolescent prefers.
- If adolescent brings lunch to school, make provisions to prevent access to food until lunch break.

## Resources

- International Prader-Willi Syndrome Organization
  Adalbert Stiffer Strasse

8D-68259 Mannheim, Germany
+49 621-799-2193
www.ipwso.org

- Prader-Willi Syndrome Association
  5700 Midnight Pass Road
  Sarasota, FL 34242
  (800) 926-4797
  www.pwsausa.org
  E-mail: pwsausa@aol.com

# Obsessive-Compulsive Disorder

Also known as: OCD

## Description

Obsessions are unwanted repetitive thoughts such as fear of dirt or germs, fear of something dreadful happening, constant doubting, and bodily concerns. Compulsions are behaviors or thoughts used to decrease the fear or guilt associated with obsessions. Examples include repetitive hand washing or bathing, repeating movements such as touching objects and getting in and out of chairs, counting silently or out loud, needing to have objects in fixed positions, and checking doors, locks, or written work. The effects of the symptoms can range from mild (less than 1 hour per day) to incapacitating (nearly constant).

## Primary Groups Affected

- There are two peak onset ages for OCD: one at about age 10 years and another during young adulthood.
- Juvenile-onset OCD has a stronger family genetic transmission, affects boys more often than it affects girls, has a higher incidence of tics and neurological symptoms, and is less responsive to treatment.

## Signs and Symptoms

- May appear to have learning disabilities when the compelling need to count or recheck interferes with homework and testing

- Might not recognize that obsessions and/or compulsions are excessive or unreasonable
- Displays consuming, and at times bizarre, behavior
- May experience "magical" thinking such as preventing an imagined future disaster by compulsive checking
- Anxiety ranging from mild to nearly constant worry
- Constant doubts leading to difficulty with concentration and mental exhaustion, that is, doubting everything related to their compulsion and not being reassured by what they see, feel, smell, touch, or taste
- Very slow in solving problems, but symptoms do not interfere with accuracy in problem solving
- Involving parents (and sometimes siblings) in the rituals, possibly altering the lives of all family members

## Classroom Guidelines

- Avoid forcing adolescent to abandon compulsive behavior because this will only serve to increase the level of anxiety.
- Observe adolescent for behaviors that interfere with learning, for example, doing schoolwork repeatedly until it is perfect and taking too much time on exams while looking for the perfect answers.
- Recognize that until the disorder is treated effectively, adolescent will have no control over obsessive-compulsive behavior.
- Protect adolescent from teasing or bullying in relation to bizarre behavior.

## Attendance Guideline

- Exclusion from school is not required.

## Medication

- Adolescent may be on antidepressant medication, which often decreases the intensity of OCD.

## Communication

- Ask parent/caregiver how family life has been affected by the presence of this disorder.

- Find out what accommodations need to be made in the classroom so that adolescent can complete rituals.
- If adolescent is in the process of behavioral therapy, ask what can be done to support that program.

## Resources

- O-C Information Center
  2711 Allen Boulevard
  Middletown, WI 53562
  (608) 827-2390

- American Academy of Child and Adolescent Psychiatry
  3615 Wisconsin Avenue, N.W.
  Washington, DC 20016-3007
  (202) 966-7300
  www.aacap.org

# Organ Transplant

## Description

An organ transplant is a complex surgical procedure performed in a person with a life-threatening condition as a result of failure of a particular body organ. The three most prevalent organ transplant procedures available for children and adolescents are heart, liver, and kidney.

### Primary Groups Affected

- Adolescents of any age who, without organ transplants, would be considered terminal or dying

### Signs and Symptoms

- Complaints of fatigue
- Changes in emotional responses, from euphoria to depression
- Complaints of pain and discomfort
- Experiences an increase in body temperature
- Nausea or vomiting
- Diarrhea
- Weight loss or gain
- Increased or decreased appetite
- Facial changes that may occur as a result of medications
- If kidney transplant was had, possible pain over kidney and swelling of arms and legs

### Classroom Guidelines

- Ensure proper handwashing (*see* Part III, Procedure A).
- Avoid exposure of adolescent to others with colds, sore throats, and the like.

- Allow adolescent to use bathroom when needed.
- Restrict physical activity if adolescent complains of fatigue.
- Be aware that you might need to verify with veterinarian which pets would be appropriate in the classroom and which pets could potentially be harmful to the adolescent.

## Attendance Guidelines

- Exclusion from school is not required.
- Health care provider will give permission as to when adolescent may return to school.

## Medications

- Adolescent may be on numerous medications that follow a very strict timetable.

## Communication

- Ask parent/caregiver/adolescent about type of transplant.
- Ask about medication schedule.
- Ask about any physical restrictions.
- Notify parent/caregiver immediately if an outbreak of infectious/contagious disease is prevalent in the school.

## Resource

- Transplant Recipients International Organization
  (412) 687-2210

# Osgood-Schlatter Disease

Also known as: OSD

## Description

Osgood-Schlatter disease (sometimes confused with "growing pains") is the most common cause of knee pain in adolescents. OSD is not really a disease but rather an inflammation of the area just below the knee where the thigh muscles (quadriceps) attach to the lower leg. Basically, the bones are growing longer and the tendons are not able to stretch along with the bones, and this causes damage to the tendons. This condition usually goes away with time, but it may take as long as 6 to 24 months. The pain and swelling should go away when the adolescent stops growing because the tendons become much stronger. The majority of adolescents experience the inflammation on one side of the body, with a predominance of left-sided involvement. The presence of OSD has been associated with jumping activities, running downhill, and excessive knee drops as a trampoline activity.

## Primary Groups Affected

- More frequent in males, usually between ages 10 and 18 years (average age at diagnosis 12 years), especially during growth spurts
- Females between ages 10 and 16 years (average age at diagnosis 11 years)
- Adolescents who are involved in football, soccer, basketball, volleyball, gymnastics, or ballet

## Signs and Symptoms

- Aching pain in knee associated with activity (running, jumping, or climbing stairs) that occurs suddenly and sometimes at night
- Swollen, warm, tender, bony bump 2 inches below the kneecap that hurts when it is pressed or the adolescent attempts to kneel
- Tightness of surrounding muscles, especially the thigh (quadriceps) muscles

## Classroom Guidelines

- Stress the importance of performing warm-up (stretching) exercises prior to physical activity and caution adolescent to avoid overuse of knee in sporting or physical activity events. Adolescent might need to run at a slower speed or for a shorter time. Running in pool might be a better alternative.
- Encourage adolescent to report nagging knee pain to parent/caregiver, school health personnel, and/or health care provider.
- Encourage adolescent participating in school physical activity events to wear good shock-absorbing shoes, use good posture, and wear a pad over the affected knee at the point where the knee hurts or a strap across the knee tendon during high-impact activities to decrease stress on the area.
- Encourage adolescents to cross train in different sports to decrease overuse of knee.
- Be aware that adolescent with diagnosed OSD may obtain relief from RICE (rest, ice, compression, elevation). Activity may be restricted for about 6 weeks to allow the injury to heal properly (rest), ice may be applied for 15 to 20 minutes before and after working out (ice), a bandage may be used to relieve swelling but not so tight as to impair circulation (compression), and the leg may be kept up during classes to decrease swelling (elevation).
- If adolescent is using knee brace or crutches, arrange for safe exit from classroom in case of an unexpected event that requires students to leave classroom or school.
- Understand that adolescent may have activity restrictions and might need alternate activities when classmates are on field trips requiring excessive running, climbing, or jumping.
- Recognize that adolescent might need to be encouraged to use knee brace/crutches if ordered and provide for safety during rainy and icy conditions.
- Understand that adolescent might need additional time and assistance to get to classes on time.

## Attendance Guideline

- Exclusion from school is not required; however, adolescent may be excluded from physical education or sporting events for a limited time.

## Medications

- Anti-inflammatory medications may be ordered to help relieve pain and swelling.

## Communication

- Ask parent/caregiver/adolescent about any activity restrictions.
- Ask about medications and treatment schedule.

## Resource

- American Academy of Family Physicians
  http://familydoctor.org/handouts/135.html

# Panic Disorder

Also known as: panic attacks

## Description

Panic disorder is recurrent panic attacks that are usually unexpected and begin with a sudden sensation of apprehension, fear, and terror.

## Primary Groups Affected

- Far more common in adolescents than in young children

## Signs and Symptoms

- Four or more of the following symptoms must develop abruptly and peak within 10 minutes:
  - Pounding heart
  - Sweating, chills, or hot flashes
  - Chest pain or discomfort, shortness of breath
  - Nausea, stomachache, or choking feeling
  - Dizziness or light-headedness
  - Numbness or tingling
  - Feelings of unreality or detachment from self
  - Fear of losing control or going crazy
  - Fear of dying
- These symptoms are often accompanied by a variety of specific phobias, such as heights and open or closed-in spaces, that trigger panic.

## Classroom Guidelines

- Remain with adolescent. Never leave adolescent alone during a panic attack.
- Provide support and reassurance during times of panic. Speak slowly in a gentle voice and use short simple sentences such as "You're okay," "I'm here with you," and "Sit next to me."
- If adolescent has shortness of breath, instruct him or her to breathe slowly, in and out, in time with your breathing. Instruct adolescent to take a deep breath through the nose, hold his or her breath for a count of three, and then exhale slowly while silently saying the word "relax."
- Reassure adolescent that you will stay and that the attack will go away.
- At a time when adolescent is not anxious, help identify who in adolescent's support group helps him or her to feel safer.

## Attendance Guideline

- Exclusion from school is not required.

## Medications

- Adolescent may be on antidepressant medications or may be prescribed nonaddictive antianxiety medication (Buspar).

## Communication

- Ask parent/caregiver about the usual symptoms adolescent experiences during a panic attack and how long the attack usually lasts.
- Find out what measures the adolescent has developed to manage the panic episodes.

## Resources

- KidsPeace
  National Center for Kids Overcoming Crisis
  (800) 8KID-123
  www.kidspeace.org

- Anxiety Disorders Association of America
  11900 Parklawn Drive, Suite 100
  Rockville, MD 20852

(301) 231-9350
www.adaa.org

- National Mental Health Association
1021 Prince Street
Alexandria, VA 22314-2971
(800) 969-NMHA
www.nmha.org

# Pediatric Autoimmune Neuropsychiatric Disorder

Also known as: PANDAS

## Description

Pediatric autoimmune neuropsychiatric disorder is a neurological complication of streptococcal infections in some children and adolescents. The antibodies produced to fight the streptococci bacteria can trigger an autoimmune reaction. This reaction is most frequently directed against cells in the heart and joints and is referred to as rheumatic fever. In 20% to 30% of the cases, the autoimmune reaction occurs in the brain.

## Primary Groups Affected

- There is some correlation between PANDAS and obsessive-compulsive disorder (OCD), Tourette's syndrome, and attention deficit/hyperactivity disorder (ADHD).
- Some adolescents develop these disorders simultaneously with, or subsequent to, the autoimmune reaction; however, a number of them have ADHD, tic disorders, and OCD before the occurrence of the streptococcal infection.
- It is thought that these other disorders may reflect a vulnerability to PANDAS.

## Signs and Symptoms

- Sudden and dramatic onset of OCD, ADHD, and/or Tourette's syndrome, with the adolescent being described as having changed overnight
- Classic OCD symptoms that include excessive hand washing, rigid nighttime rituals, checking behavior, and obsessions about death
- Classic ADHD symptoms that include a peculiar "squirminess" in which the adolescent tries very hard to sit still but constantly wiggles and fidgets
- Classic Tourette's symptoms that include sudden uncontrollable movements, grunts, and facial grimaces
- Emotional swings with unprecipitated bouts of crying or hysterical laughter and increased irritability
- Nighttime difficulties, including severe nightmares and new bedtime fears or rituals
- Resolves completely in some adolescents, symptoms continue with less severity in others, and periods of acute symptom relapse are experienced by a few

## Classroom Guidelines

- Avoid forcing adolescent to abandon compulsive behavior because this will only serve to increase the level of anxiety.
- Observe for behaviors that will interfere with learning such as doing schoolwork repeatedly until it is perfect.
- Ask adolescent to repeat what he or she heard of instructions before beginning a task.
- Allow adolescent to carry out one instruction before being given another, and provide positive feedback for the completion of each step.
- Create a classroom climate of acceptance, belonging, and security. Do not allow teasing or bullying of adolescent in the face of seemingly "strange" behavior.

## Attendance Guideline

- Adolescent might need to be on bed rest until signs of active infection have disappeared.

## Medications

- Adolescent may be on antibiotics.

## Communication

- Because the symptoms have a sudden onset, call parent/caregiver immediately and urge to make an appointment with family health care provider.
- Ask about necessary accommodations in the classroom so that adolescent can complete rituals.
- Communicate any significant social problems with adolescent's peers.

## Resource

- American Academy of Child and Adolescent Psychiatry
  3615 Wisconsin Avenue, N.W.
  Washington, DC 20016-3007
  (202) 966-7300
  www.aacap.org

# Pelvic Inflammatory Disease

Also known as: PID

## Description

Pelvic inflammatory disease refers to an infection in the internal female organs. The infection is generally caused by untreated sexually transmitted diseases (STDs) that ascend from the vagina and cervix into the uterus, fallopian tubes, and ovaries. PID is especially associated with the STDs gonorrhea and chlamydia. This infection can cause some serious problems such as chronic pain in the pelvic area. The untreated infection can cause scar tissue to form in the fallopian tubes, and this can lead to long-term problems with fertility, causing some women to be unable to either get pregnant or maintain their pregnancies due to ectopic pregnancies (pregnancies outside the uterus, usually in the fallopian tube). It is estimated that about 150 women die from PID each year. PID can be difficult to diagnose because symptoms can be vague and/or minimal, even though damage is being done. PID can be cured with antibiotics, and early diagnosis and treatment will prevent damage to reproductive organs. Approximately 25% of women with PID will need to be hospitalized for administration of intravenous antibiotics, and some women will need surgery if there are abscesses that do not respond to antibiotics.

## Primary Groups Affected

- Sexually active women who have unprotected intercourse

## Signs and Symptoms

- Only mild symptoms in some women
- Fever
- Abnormal vaginal discharge
- Foul odor to discharge
- Painful urination
- Irregular menstrual bleeding
- Abdominal pain

## Classroom Guidelines

- Teach the following guidelines for sexual activity:
    - Practice sexual abstinence.
    - Use a latex condom with every sexual encounter.
    - Limit the number of sexual partners.
    - If possibly infected, avoid sex and see health care provider immediately.
    - Be truthful with sexual partners about their risk of exposure.
- Dispense medications according to school regulations.

## Attendance Guideline

- Exclusion from school is not required.

## Medications

- Usually an antibiotic medication will be prescribed by health care provider.
- Acetaminophen (Tylenol) may be given for fever and pain relief with parent/caregiver permission.

## Communication

- Ask parent/caregiver about schedule of antibiotics so as to support/monitor compliance with treatment plan.
- Encourage adolescents and parents/caregivers to discuss sexual issues and practices.

## Resource

- www.cdc.gov

# Phobia: Social

Also known as: extreme shyness

## Description

Fearfulness is experienced with both other teens and adults. The adolescent fears that he or she will act in a way that will be humiliating or embarrassing. Avoidance of others may become so extreme that it interferes with the development of normal social relations, and this can lead to a sense of isolation and/or depression. This disability interferes with education and social relationships.

## Primary Groups Affected

- Affects more than one of every eight adolescents

## Signs and Symptoms

- Most (60%) distressing events occurring at school
- Reluctant to speak in class; unable to write on the blackboard
- Difficulty in meeting new people
- Refuses to attend pleasant events such as parties
- Refuses to use public bathrooms
- Suffers from test anxiety
- Refuses to eat in front of others
- Physical symptoms such as choking, flushes, palpitations, and headaches

## Classroom Guidelines

- Do not force adolescent to behave in a way that will intensify fears. Protect adolescent from escalating anxiety.

- Have class discussions on how people establish friendships and how they maintain friendships.
- Discuss assertiveness skills and encourage adolescent to practice these skills in the classroom.
- Discuss conflict resolution skills and help adolescent to practice negotiating with peers.

## Attendance Guideline

- Exclusion from school is not required.

## Medication

- No medication is required.

## Communication

- Ask parent/caregiver and adolescent whether there is more than one fear situation.
- Ask adolescent how he or she has managed the phobia so far.
- If adolescent is in treatment, ask how you can support the skills on which they are working.

## Resources

- Anxiety Disorders Association of America
  11900 Parklawn Drive, Suite 100
  Rockville, MD 20852
  (301) 231-9350
  www.adaa.org

- Social Phobia/Social Anxiety Association
  www.socialphobia.org

# Phobia: Specific

Also known as: fear of [situation or object]

## Description

This type of phobia is an intense persistent fear of a specific situation or object that poses no real danger. Fears may involve animals or insects, storms, heights, water, closed places, blood, or injury as well as extreme fear of injections or other invasive medical procedures. These phobias are usually not disabling in adolescents, and they tend to disappear with age.

## Primary Groups Affected

- Common during childhood and adolescence

## Signs and Symptoms

- Exposure to the feared situation or object results in an immediate anxiety response such as restlessness, muscle tension, stomach complaints, shortness of breath, headaches, and/or dizziness.
- If phobia is of some object in the classroom or of closed places, adolescent may have difficulty in concentrating in school.
- If phobia is of dogs, adolescent may have difficulty in walking to school.

## Classroom Guidelines

- Avoid reinforcing adolescent's fear by agreeing with the perceived danger.
- Do not minimize or discount adolescent's fear. Speak slowly and calmly.

- Prepare adolescent in advance for any stressors related to the phobia.
- Model appropriate responses to the phobic situation or object.

## Attendance Guideline

- Exclusion from school is not required.

## Medication

- No medication is required.

## Communication

- Ask adolescent what measures he or she has developed to manage the associated anxiety.
- If adolescent is in a behavioral treatment program, ask parent/ caregiver what must be done in the classroom to support this intervention.

## Resources

- Anxiety Disorders Association of America
  11900 Parklawn Drive, Suite 100
  Rockville, MD 20852
  (301) 231-9350
  www.adaa.org

- National Mental Health Association
  1021 Prince Street
  Alexandria, VA 22314-2971
  (800) 969-NMHA
  www.nmha.org

# Pink Eye

Also known as: conjunctivitis

## Description

Pink eye, an inflammation (redness) of the conjunctiva (the white part of the eye), can be caused by bacterial or viral infections, allergic reactions, or a foreign object or chemical in the eye. Most cases do not cause any serious damage, but in rare situations infectious conjunctivitis can cause permanent damage or even blindness. Pink eye that is caused by a virus or bacteria is easily spread from one person to another.

## Primary Groups Affected

- Adolescents of any age

## Signs and Symptoms

- Pus-like drainage
- Crusting on eyelids
- Reddened conjunctiva
- Swollen eyelids
- Usually affects both eyes
- If foreign object pink eye, usually affects only one eye and causes tearing and pain
- Bacterial: white drainage from eyes, crusting of eyelids (especially on awakening), swollen eyelids, reddened lining of eye, sensitivity to light, moderate tearing, blurred vision that clears with blinking, minimal itching, usually both eyes affected
- Viral: usually occurs with a cold, watery drainage from eyes, reddened lining of eye, swollen eyelids, minimal itching, constant

tearing of eyes, usually one eye affected and then both eyes, sensitivity to light
- Allergic: itching and burning of eyes, watery to thick drainage, reddened lining of eye, swollen eyelids, constant tearing of eyes, lining of nose swollen and pale in color
- Foreign body: tearing of eye, pain, reddened lining of eye, usually only one eye affected

## Classroom Guidelines

- Ensure proper hand washing (*see* Procedure A).
- Ensure proper disposal of adolescent's tissues.
- Urge adolescent to avoid touching or rubbing eyes.
- Monitor other students for signs of pink eye.
- Disinfect any articles that have been contaminated.
- Eliminate any shared articles such as towels.
- Isolate adolescent from others, especially any students/faculty members with immune system disorders or who have undergone organ transplants.
- Be aware that adolescent's eye should be kept clean. Warm moist compresses are helpful for removing crusts but should not be kept on eye due to the chance of promoting bacterial growth. Wipe drainage from inner aspect of eye and outward, away from opposite eye.
- If adolescent complains of sensitivity to light and there is drainage from the eye or redness, notify parent/caregiver and urge follow-up with health care provider.

## Attendance Guidelines

- Exclusion from school is required when adolescent has white or yellow discharge until he or she has been treated with an antibiotic for at least 24 hours.
- Exclusion from school is not necessary when adolescent has watery eye discharge.
- Exclusion from school is not required when adolescent has allergic reactions or conjunctivitis caused by a foreign body.

## Medications

- Eye drops may be used about four times per day for 1 week.
- Eye ointments may be used but can cause blurring of vision; therefore, they are usually reserved for nighttime.

## Communication

- Ask parent/caregiver/adolescent/school nurse which type of infection the adolescent has experienced.
- Ask about schedule for and procedure of instilling eye drops or ointment.

## Resource

- www.cdc.gov

# Pneumonia

## Description

Pneumonia is a general term that refers to an infection of the lungs that can be caused by bacteria, viruses, chemical irritants, dusts, or allergies. A cold, a sore throat, or influenza may often precede pneumonia. The term "double pneumonia" means that both lungs are affected. The term "walking pneumonia" means that the symptoms are mild enough that the infected person might not even know he or she has it and can continue to "walk" around. Most pneumonia will be cured in 2 weeks if treated properly; however, some people will need to be hospitalized to receive intravenous medications and breathing treatments. There are vaccines to prevent various viral or bacterial types of pneumonia. Vaccines are especially recommended for those with chronic illness or with compromised immune systems due to, for example, cancer or HIV.

## Primary Groups Affected

- Any age, but most common during infancy and early childhood
- Most common during late winter and early spring
- People with weakened immune systems

## Signs and Symptoms

- Cough
- Difficulty in breathing—**911**
- Fever
- Wheezing—**911**
- Breathing faster than usual
- Chest pain—**911**
- Poor appetite

- Very fatigued
- Vomiting
- Irritable
- Restless
- Bluish or gray color lips in very ill persons—**911**

## Classroom Guidelines

- Ensure proper hand washing (*see* Procedure A).
- Dispense medications according to school regulations.
- Encourage adolescent to drink plenty of water.
- Encourage adolescent to spit up mucus (phlegm).
- Urge students to avoid sharing of personal articles such as drinking glasses, toothbrushes, and eating utensils.

## Attendance Guideline

- Exclusion from school is required until fever is resolved and energy level returns.

## Medications

- Usually an antibiotic is prescribed by health care provider for bacterial pneumonia.
- The antibiotic should be given until it is all gone.
- Acetaminophen (Tylenol) or ibuprofen (Motrin) may be given for fever and pain relief with parent/caregiver permission.
- Cough medicine may be prescribed.

## Communication

- Ask parent/caregiver about schedule of antibiotics so as to support/monitor compliance with treatment plan.

## Resource

- www.allkids.org

# Poisoning

## Description

Adolescents can be exposed to a variety of poisoning agents. It is imperative that you find out what the adolescent may have ingested, inhaled, or touched so as to take appropriate steps in responding to this emergency situation. The local poison control center number should be readily available. The poison control center is the best resource for this type of information.

### Primary Groups Affected

- Children, especially younger school-age children

### Signs and Symptoms

- Pain in the stomach
- Nausea or vomiting
- Loss of consciousness—**911**

### Classroom Guidelines

- Remain calm and contact local poison control center immediately. (Insert local poison control center telephone number here: _____.)
- Remove poison from contact with adolescent.
- Be prepared to initiate CPR if adolescent loses consciousness and stops breathing—**911**.
- Eye:
  - Turn adolescent's head to the side and gently wash with lukewarm water for at least 15 minutes from inner to outer aspect of eye.

- Have adolescent blink as much as possible while running water over eye.
- Do not allow adolescent to rub eye.

- Skin:

  - Remove contaminated clothing from adolescent.
  - Wash poison from skin with large amounts of water for at least 15 minutes.

- Mouth:

  - Remove poison from adolescent's mouth by hooking out with gloved finger anything you can see.
  - Examine mouth for any burns, cuts, irritations, or unusual coloring.

- Inhaled:

  - Get adolescent to fresh air immediately.
  - If adolescent is not breathing, begin CPR—**911**.
  - Avoid breathing the fumes.
  - Open all doors and windows.

- Swallowed:

  - Do not give anything by mouth until you call for advice from local poison control center. Ask whether you should make adolescent vomit.
  - Know availability of poison control kit in your school and telephone number of local poison control center. Send another student to obtain the kit.
  - If chemical or household products were swallowed, give water or milk immediately on receiving such advice from local poison control center.
  - Provide poison control center with following information: your name and name of adolescent who came in contact with poison, your telephone number in case you are accidentally disconnected, and age and approximate weight of adolescent. Also, if possible, read label of poison container and estimate how much poison was taken, signs of ingestion (e.g., pills found in mouth), and any unusual behavior on part of adolescent.
  - *Instructions to induce vomiting:* Use syrup of Ipecac (usually 1 tablespoon for children age 1 year or over). Give with glass of water. If adolescent does not vomit within 15 minutes, you might need to give another dose with water. Do not use salt

water to induce vomiting; this may be potentially dangerous. Never induce vomiting if adolescent is unconscious or having convulsions, if a caustic substance was swallowed, or if a petroleum-based product was swallowed.

- If instructed to take adolescent to hospital, take plant, drug container, or poison and its container with you.
- Avoid potential poisonings in classroom.: Keep all dangerous supplies locked up with "Mr. Yuk" stickers on containers. Never put a dangerous chemical in a beverage container or a recycled food container. Know names of plants in your classroom. Verify with local poison control center whether plants in classroom are dangerous. Do not rely on childproof caps. Do not store drugs/ vitamins in purses, drawers, or cabinets. Never refer to medicine as "candy."

## Attendance Guideline

- Exclusion from school is not required.

## Medication

- Medication should be taken only as directed by health care provider.

## Communication

- Notify parent/caregiver of incident.

## Resources

- www.vh.org/patients/ihb/emergency/poison/ifpoisoned. html
- Poison Control Center (contact local center)

# Poison Oak, Ivy, and Sumac

Also known as: poison oak dermatitis

## Description

Adolescents who come in contact with any of these three poisonous plants (ivy, oak, or sumac) may experience localized, streaked, or spotty oozing and painful sores. Poison oak grows as a shrub or vine, especially near lakes, rivers, and streams. All parts of the plant have oil that contains the irritant. The fur or saliva of an animal that is contaminated with the oil may transfer the poison to a person. Shoes, tools, and toys can be a source of contamination in children. As soon as an adolescent touches the oil, it penetrates the skin and initiates a reaction. Even the smoke from a burning shrub or vine can cause a skin reaction and may be dangerous to the lungs if inhaled. It is important, however, to remember that poison ivy sores are not contagious and that adolescents who are exposed to the oil do not need to be isolated from others.

## Primary Groups Affected

- Adolescents of any age who are in contact with an offending shrub or plant

## Signs and Symptoms

- Rash; not contagious (only contact with sap may cause rash)
- Itching or burning sensation (itching stops by 10 to 14 days)
- Multiple blister-like sores oozing fluids
- Sores that last 2 to 4 weeks (full-blown reaction usually seen after about 2 days)
- Swelling

## Classroom Guidelines

- Remain calm and flush irritant site with cold running water immediately (cold water neutralizes oil not yet attached to the skin), preferably within 15 minutes. Do not use harsh soaps or scrub skin. Wear gloves when washing or bathing skin of exposed adolescent.
- If there is a stream, allow adolescent to enter water (with clothes on) and let water rinse oil from both skin and clothes.
- Have adolescent change clothes completely if possible. Clothing should be laundered in hot water and detergent. Sap may be present on unwashed clothes for 12 to 24 hours after contact with leaves.
- Try to prevent adolescent from scratching contact site. Calamine lotions or vinegar compresses may serve to decrease itching.
- Avoid warm or heated compresses because they serve to increase itching.
- Prior to outdoor field events, instruct all students on how to recognize poison ivy, oak, and sumac shrubs or vines.

## Attendance Guideline

- Exclusion from school is not required unless itching interferes with classroom activities.

## Medications

- Apply calamine-drying lotion, washing off old lotion prior to new application. Do not use products containing the "caine" anesthetic.
- Adolescent may be taking prescribed oral corticosteroids for prevention or relief of inflammation.
- Adolescent may be applying prescribed topical corticosteroid gel for prevention or relief of inflammation.

## Communication

- Notify parent/caregiver of adolescent's contact with poison ivy, oak, or sumac.

## Resource

- www.cdc.gov

# Posttraumatic Stress Disorder

Also known as: PTSD

## Description

Posttraumatic stress disorder may occur after a traumatic event usually involving a serious threat to the adolescent's life or a family member's life. The types of disasters that may lead to PTSD are natural disasters (earthquakes, tornadoes, floods), accidental disasters (car or airplane crashes, large fires, collapsed structures), and human-made disasters (acts of terrorism, shootings, assaults, kidnappings, torture, war, bombings). Human-made disasters result in a more severe and longer lasting traumatic stress disorder.

## Primary Groups Affected

- Can occur at any age
- Adolescents with weak social support systems, a history of physical or sexual abuse, and family instability more vulnerable

## Signs and Symptoms

- Symptoms usually appearing within the first 3 months after the trauma (but sometimes not surfacing until months or years after the stressful event)
- Somatic complaints such as headaches and stomachaches
- Constantly searching the environment for danger; may develop a phobic avoidance of triggers that remind adolescent of the original trauma

- Chronic tension, mood instability, guilt, numbing of other emotions
- Uncontrollable flashbacks and recurring nightmares
- Low self-esteem
- Outbursts of anger and aggression that alienate family and friends

## Classroom Guidelines

- Suggest ways in which to modify environment to limit adolescent's exposure to triggers.
- Recognize that the goal of interactions with the traumatized person is to regain some degree of control over his or her life.
- Answer questions about the disaster honestly, but do not dwell on frightening details or allow adolescent to dominate classroom time indefinitely.
- Encourage adolescent to express feelings through talking, drawing, or painting.
- If adolescent becomes preoccupied with death, has unusual accident proneness, or makes suicidal threats, inform school administration and refer to primary care provider.

## Attendance Guideline

- Exclusion from school is not required.

## Medications

- Adolescent may be on antidepressants, especially Zoloft.

## Communication

- Discuss with adolescent and parent/caregiver the number of major stressors adolescent has experienced before this current crisis.
- Ask whether living arrangements have been altered as the result of the current crisis.

## Resources

- KidsPeace
  National Center for Kids Overcoming Crisis
  5300 KidsPeace Drive

Orefield, PA 18069
(800) 8KID-123
www.kidspeace.org

- American Academy of Child and Adolescent Psychiatry
  3615 Wisconsin Avenue, N.W.
  Washington, DC 20016-3007
  (202) 966-7300
  www.aacap.org

- National Youth Crisis Line
  (800) 999-9999

# Psoriasis

## Description

Psoriasis is a skin disease that is the result of a faster than normal life cycle of the skin. Normal skin takes about 1 month for new cells to move from the lowest layer to the outer layer. In psoriasis, this process speeds up to a cycle of 3 or 4 days, leaving a buildup of dead cells on the outer layer. The buildup of dead skin cells causes a scaly appearance to patches of skin over the scalp, elbows, knees, and lower back. Approximately 20,000 children under age 10 years are diagnosed with psoriasis each year. Some cases of psoriasis are hardly noticeable, whereas others cover large patches on the individuals' bodies. Psoriasis affects people both physically and emotionally. The condition will have cycles of exacerbation and then go into remission for weeks or months. Factors that cause exacerbations include systemic infections, injury to skin, stress, alcohol, exposure to some chemicals, and reaction to medications and vaccines. Self-help methods that will improve psoriasis include eating a balanced diet, getting adequate rest, avoiding scratching, having a daily bath (avoiding hot water), using specially formulated soaps and shampoos, and being exposed to only moderate sunlight (avoiding sunburn).

## Primary Groups Affected

- Approximately 10% to 15% of people with psoriasis under age 10 years
- Slightly more prevalent in females than in males
- Average age of onset 28 years, although psoriasis has been seen in newborns and as late as age 90 years

## Signs and Symptoms

- Pink or red raised patches of skin covered with flaky white or silver scales
- Small scaling dots (most common in children)
- Occurs most commonly on scalp, elbows, and knees
- Pitted fingernails
- Stiff swollen finger and toe joints (arthritis psoriasis seen in 10% of cases)

## Classroom Guidelines

- Dispense medications according to school regulations.
- Remind child not to scratch psoriasis areas. Try distraction strategies.
- Be sensitive to emotional concerns of adolescent.

## Attendance Guideline

- Exclusion from school is not required.

## Medications

- Creams and ointments may be applied.
- Some oral medications that help to block skin growth may be used.
- Ultraviolet light treatments may be used.

## Communication

- Ask parent/caregiver about schedule of medications so as to support/monitor compliance.

## Resources

- National Psoriasis Foundation
  (800) 723-9166
  www.psoriasis.org
- www.aad.org

# Rape

Also known as: date rape

## Description

Rape is a crime of violence second only to homicide in its violation of a person. The issue is not one of sex but rather one of force, domination, and humiliation. Date or acquaintance rape is forced unwanted sex with a person the victim knows. The force can come from deceit, threats, restraint, verbal intimidation, or physical violence.

## Primary Groups Affected

- Can happen to anyone, even males
- Females between ages 15 and 25 years most vulnerable

## Signs and Symptoms

- Women rarely report rapes when they know their attackers, especially if they are or were in a dating relationship with their attackers.
- Victims are often blamed by themselves and others for being naïve or provocative.
- Long-term consequences include difficulty with personal relationships, problems at school, nightmares, difficulty in sleeping, phobic reactions, sexual dysfunctions, and depression.

## Classroom Guidelines

- In the classroom setting, discuss ways in which adolescents can prevent date rape:

- Be cautious in relationships based on dominant-male, submissive-female stereotypes. Date rapists usually have "macho" attitudes and believe women to be inferior.
- Be cautious when a date tries to control your behavior—who you can meet, where you can go, what you can do. This indicates a need to dominate and control, and it increases your vulnerability by isolating you.
- At a party, do not consume any drink that you have set down.
- Do not stay in a situation where you feel uncomfortable.
- Be very clear in your communication. If a simple "no" is not respected, leave or insist the date leave. Speak forcefully.
- Avoid giving mixed messages. For example, do not say "no" and then continue petting.
- Do not go to a place that is so private that help is not available if needed.

## Attendance Guideline

- Exclusion from school is not required.

## Medication

- No medication is required.

## Communication

- Ask adolescent about available support systems.
- If adolescent is in counseling, ask in what ways you may be most supportive.

## Resources

- Rape Treatment Center
  www.911rape.org

- Rape, Abuse, and Incest National Network
  635-B Pennsylvania Avenue, S.E.
  Washington, DC 20003
  (800) 656-4673
  www.rainn.org

# Reye's Syndrome

## Description

Reye's syndrome is a rare but serious disorder that can affect the brain, blood, and liver. An adolescent who has a viral infection may develop Reye's syndrome if specifically given aspirin or aspirin-containing medications during the infection. It can develop rapidly, so it is important to notify a health care provider if the adolescent is showing symptoms of the syndrome. It is also important that the adolescent does not take aspirin or cold remedies containing aspirin (e.g., Alka-Seltzer, Anacin, Bufferin, some Excedrin products, Pepto-Bismol) in treating chicken pox or flu-like illnesses.

## Primary Groups Affected

- Children between ages 2 and 16 years who have been given salicylates for viral infections

## Signs and Symptoms

- Usually occurs within 1 week after viral infection
- Persistent nausea or vomiting
- Decreased level of consciousness; can lead to disorientation or becoming combative—**911**
- Unusually sleepy—**911**
- Seizures or convulsions—**911**

## Classroom Guidelines

- Notify parent/caregiver if any signs or symptoms are apparent in adolescent.
- Activate local emergency medical system for transport to an emergency facility—**911**.

## Attendance Guideline

- Exclusion from school is not required once adolescent has recovered.

## Medications

- Do not administer aspirin to adolescents without specific orders from health care provider.
- Adolescent may be prescribed a variety of medications during recovery period.

## Communication

- Ask parent/caregiver to provide information regarding adolescent's prognosis and any side effects associated with disorder.
- Ask parent/caregiver/adolescent about any medications and schedule.

## Resource

- www.mayoclinic.org

# Rheumatic Fever

## Description

Rheumatic fever is an inflammatory disease that occurs approximately 2 to 3 weeks following a group A beta-hemolytic streptococcal infection, more commonly known as strep throat. Not all adolescents who suffer from this infectious organism will acquire rheumatic fever. About 1% to 5% of adolescents with a known strep infection will develop rheumatic fever. The most common sites affected by the disease are the joints and the heart. The adolescent's prognosis is dependent on the severity of the heart involvement. There is an excellent prognosis for the adolescent who does not develop heart involvement during the initial attack. Future strep infections that may occur can increase the adolescent's chances of developing heart disease.

## Primary Groups Affected

- Fewer than 2 of every 100,000 children affected
- Children of both genders equally affected
- Most common between ages 5 and 15 years
- Greater susceptibility among ethnic minorities

## Signs and Symptoms

- Past history of a streptococcal infection (sore throat, fever, possibly upper respiratory infection)
- Possibly sudden onset of symptoms
- Joint pain, usually in the larger joints such as those in the knee
- Inflammation of the heart, which can cause murmurs and chest pain with an increased heart rate—**911**
- Fever

## Classroom Guidelines

- Report fever, joint pain, or chest discomfort to parent/caregiver and school health care provider—**911**.
- Notify parents of other students that a classmate was diagnosed with a streptococcal infection.
- Dispense medications according to school regulations.
- Ensure that adolescent abides by activity restrictions.
- Allow adolescent to work at own pace if joint pain develops.
- Be aware that adolescent may initially have difficulty in tolerating a full day of school activities.

## Attendance Guidelines

- Adolescent may return to school after completing the first 24 hours of antibiotic therapy.
- Adolescent may be restricted from attending school by physician if the heart is involved. Adolescent with severe heart inflammation may require bed rest or a reduced activity level.

## Medications

- Antibiotic therapy for 10 days may be prescribed for the infection if still present.
- Aspirin or anti-inflammatory drugs to reduce inflammation in joints/heart may be prescribed.
- Steroids might be needed to control inflammation in the heart.
- Prophylactic antibiotic may be used to prevent future group A beta-hemolytic streptococcal infections.

## Communication

- Ask parent/caregiver whether adolescent has a diagnosed streptococcal infection.
- Ask the parent/caregiver/adolescent about medications to be given during school hours.
- Ask parent/caregiver whether there are any activity restrictions.
- Ask parent/caregiver whether adolescent is allowed to attend school or whether home tutoring will be required.

## Resources

- Arthritis Foundation
  www.arthritis.org

- American Heart Association National Center
  7272 Greenville Avenue
  Dallas, TX 75231
  www.americanheart.org
  *You, Your Child, and Rheumatic Fever* (brochure available at above address)

# Rocky Mountain Spotted Fever

Also known as: RMSV, *Rickettsia rickettsii*

## Description

Rocky Mountain spotted fever is the most severe and most frequently reported tick-spread illness in the United States. Bacteria that are carried by the American dog tick and the Rocky Mountain wood tick cause the disease. In general, about 1% to 5% of the tick population is infected. If the infection is not treated, the bacteria infect the cells lining blood vessels throughout the body. The bacteria may also damage the respiratory system, central nervous system, gastro-intestinal system, and/or renal system. Without prompt treatment, the infection can be fatal. As many as 3% to 5% of individuals with Rocky Mountain spotted fever die from the infection every year.

## Primary Groups Affected

- Any person bitten by an infected tick
- Children/adolescents under age 15 years (two thirds of cases)
- Peak age 5 to 9 years
- April through September (more than 90% of individuals infected)
- South-Atlantic region of United States (more than half of individuals infected)
- North Carolina and Oklahoma (highest incidences)

## Signs and Symptoms

- Symptoms that usually develop 5 to 10 days after being bitten by an infected tick

- Early symptoms:

  - Nonspecific and may resemble variety of other illnesses
  - Fever
  - Nausea or vomiting
  - Severe headache
  - Muscle pain
  - Lack of appetite

- Later symptoms:

  - Joint pain
  - Abdominal pain
  - Diarrhea
  - Characteristic red spotted rash; usually develops faster in younger persons than in older persons—**911**

## Classroom Guidelines

- When engaging in outdoor activities in high-risk areas, urge students to wear protective clothing to prevent exposure of skin and to tuck pant legs into socks.
- Urge adolescents to check for ticks after outings in high-risk areas, especially for ticks hidden in hair.
- Using tweezers or finger and wearing gloves, remove tick by gripping it gently but firmly at point where mouth parts are attached. Pull straight outward with gentle steady pressure until tick releases. Wash hands afterward.
- Do not use folklore remedies such as petroleum jelly and hot matches.
- Save tick for identification in case child becomes ill.
- Cleanse area with soap and water. If any tick parts are left under the skin, adolescent needs to see health care provider for removal.

## Attendance Guidelines

- Infected person is usually hospitalized until condition is stabilized.
- Exclusion from school is not required following acute illness.

## Medication

- Tetracycline (an antibiotic) is usually administered in two doses per day.

## Communication

- Inform parent/caregiver if tick bite occurs at school or on a school outing.
- Encourage parent/caregiver to seek medical attention promptly if parts of tick remain after removal or if symptoms develop.
- Ask whether adolescent is being treated with medications.

## Resource

- www.cdc.gov/ncidod/dvrd/rmsf/prevention

# Scabies

Also known as: mites, seven-year itch, itch mites

## Description

Scabies is skin infestation caused by a tiny mite called *Saroptes scabiei*. The pregnant female mite burrows under the skin and deposits eggs and fecal material, which causes minute, linear, thread-like lesions. The reaction causes very severe itching. The rash and itching occur after the individual becomes sensitized to the mite, usually 30 to 60 days after the initial contact. If an individual has been previously sensitized to mites, the itching will begin much sooner (48 hours after exposure). The rash is most commonly found on the wrists, on the elbows, under the arms, and between the fingers. In infants, the rash may appear anywhere but most commonly on the feet and ankles. Scabies is spread by extended skin-to-skin contact or by sharing an infected person's clothes. It takes about 45 minutes for a mite to burrow under the skin; therefore, brief contact is not likely to cause transfer of the mite.

## Primary Groups Affected

- Any age group

## Signs and Symptoms

- Intense itching
- Rash, especially common on wrists, on elbows, and between fingers

## Classroom Guidelines

- Ensure proper hand washing (*see* Procedure A).
- Discourage adolescents from sharing personal articles and clothing.

## Attendance Guideline

- Exclusion from school is required until 24 hours after treatment is completed.

## Medications

- Usually a one-time application of an over-the-counter scabicide lotion (e.g., Elimite) is used as follows. Bathe thoroughly, apply scabicide lotion liberally from head to soles of feet (not just on rash sites), and use toothpick to apply lotion under fingernails and toenails. Lotion should remain on skin for 8 to 14 hours and then be removed by bathing. Launder bed linens, towels, and clothing in very hot water and dry at high setting in dryer.
- A second treatment may be necessary 10 days later.
- It will take 2 to 3 weeks after treatment for itching and rash to subside.

## Communication

- Notify staff, school nurse, and parents/caregivers of other students, especially those with extended contact with infested adolescent.

## Resource

- www.headlice.org

# Scarlet Fever

## Description

Scarlet fever is caused by an infection with the group A streptococci bacteria (*see* Strep Throat). Some adolescents experience a rash with this illness. Scarlet fever is usually associated with a strep throat infection but infrequently can be due to a skin infection such as impetigo (*see* Impetigo). The symptoms begin suddenly, and a health care provider should see the adolescent. Incidence is highest in temperate climates, and the infection usually occurs during late winter or early spring.

## Primary Groups Affected

- Most common in children ages 6 to 12 years

## Signs and Symptoms

- High fever (103 to 104 degrees)
- Headache
- Chills or body aches
- Loss of appetite
- Nausea or vomiting
- Fatigue
- Swollen glands in the neck
- Usually a sore throat, with throat and tonsils possibly having a white covering or appearing very red
- Skin rash (that appears 12 to 48 hours after fever and sore throat) that initially resembles a bad sunburn with tiny bumps and may itch, will turn white when you press on the bumps. It usually appears first on the neck and face, but not around the

mouth; appears mainly on body trunk and skin folds and spreads to rest of the body; and usually lasts for 1 week
- Whitish or yellowish coating on the tongue initially before it turns a strawberry color
- Increased pulse

## Classroom Guidelines

- Notify parent/caregiver/school health provider if any of these symptoms appear.
- Isolate adolescent from others. Scarlet fever is contagious and can be passed through contact with the nasal or throat fluids of someone with a strep throat infection, by touching the infected skin of someone who has strep impetigo, or by sharing towels, clothing, or bed linens.
- Encourage students not to share drinking glasses and eating utensils.
- Urge proper hand washing with antibacterial soap if possible (*see* Procedure A).
- Dispense medications according to school regulations after adolescent returns to school.
- Encourage fluid intake.
- Remind adolescent to cover his or her nose and mouth for all sneezing and coughing.
- Notify caregivers/parents of any other students in classroom with a history of congenital heart defects, organ transplantation, chemotherapy treatment, or immune deficiency disorders.

## Attendance Guideline

- Exclusion from school is required. Health care provider usually will indicate return date.

## Medications

- Antibiotic treatment (usually penicillin) will reduce symptoms, minimize transmission, and reduce the likelihood of complications. Acetaminophen (Tylenol) may be used for pain and fever every 4 hours.
- Lozenges, hard candy, and warm saline gargles may soothe sore throat.

## Communication

- Ask parent/caregiver/adolescent about the schedule for medications.

## Resource

- kidshealth.org

# Schizophrenia

Also known as: acute psychosis

## Description

Schizophrenia is a devastating disorder of the brain that affects not only the individual but also family and friends. The person with schizophrenia has difficulty in thinking clearly, knowing what is real, managing feelings, making decisions, and relating to others.

## Primary Groups Affected

- The vast majority of people develop the disorder during adolescence or young adulthood.
- Childhood schizophrenia is a very severe form of the disorder and may have a stronger genetic predisposition.

## Signs and Symptoms

- Most people who develop schizophrenia appear normal at birth and during the first years of life.
- Subtle behavioral and cognitive characteristics often precede the first acute episode. These include higher than expected rates of abnormal speech and motor abnormalities such as clumsiness.
- Other preceding characteristics include social withdrawal and isolation, a decline in IQ over several years, and diminishing school performance.
- Prior to full-blown symptoms, there often is a high rate of special education placement and failed grades.
- Delusions (fixed false beliefs) are a common symptom. The content of the delusions comes from the person's experiences.

An adolescent with schizophrenia might believe that a specific
teacher is persecuting him or her.

- Hallucinations (occurrences of sounds, sights, touches, smells,
  or tastes without external stimuli to sensory organs) may be
  triggered by anxiety and changes in the brain.
- Adolescents with schizophrenia may exhibit bizarre behavior,
  hyperactivity, decreased self-care, inappropriate affect, an
  inability to experience pleasure, and disorganized thinking.
- Attention impairment and memory deficits cause severe day-
  to-day difficulties for many adolescents with schizophrenia.
  The lack of motivation often results in academic difficulties.

## Classroom Guidelines

- Accept the adolescent with schizophrenia for who he or she is
  and try to understand the student's perspective. This will help
  to empower the adolescent and assist in achieving his or her
  highest level of functioning.
- If the adolescent is having trouble in communicating, interrupt
  politely but firmly and ask a question that will help him or her
  to communicate in a more direct manner. Say something like,
  "I'm not understanding what you are saying. Could we try that
  again?"
- Put adolescent in the quietest part of the classroom to enhance
  his or her ability to listen and concentrate.
- Be aware that special education classes should include social
  skills training to improve the adolescent's level of social functioning with peers and adults.
- Look for opportunities to give positive reinforcement.
- Recognize that art class could include having all students make
  a collage that tells something about themselves and their interests. In this way, you can emphasize the positive qualities each
  collage reveals.
- Set limits on hyperactivity by providing firm direction.
- Strive toward a balance between being protective and encouraging independence.

## Attendance Guideline

- Exclusion from school is not required unless adolescent is
  acutely ill.

## Medications

- Antipsychotic medications such as Risperdal, Zyprexa, and Geodon may be prescribed.

## Communication

- Because so many people are afraid of and uninformed about schizophrenia, many families try to hide it from others. Reach out to these families and offer them support and a listening ear.
- Ask parent/caregiver for particulars of practical solutions on how to manage on a day-to-day basis.

## Resource

- American Schizophrenic Association Hotline
  (800) 847-3802
  www.schizophrenia.org

# Scoliosis

Also known as: curvature of the spine

## Description

Scoliosis is a sideways curving of more than 10 degrees of the spine. Scoliosis can occur in either the upper back or the lower back. It very rarely is seen in the neck region. The cause for most curvatures of the spine is unknown (idiopathic scoliosis). Scoliosis is usually noticed at the onset of puberty and is most frequently identified during school screenings. Some curving of the spine affects 1 of every 10 persons.

## Primary Groups Affected

- Girls, usually noticed at onset of puberty (ages 10 to 14 years)

## Signs and Symptoms

- Uneven shoulders or hips, with girls frequently complaining that the bottoms of their skirts or slacks do not hang evenly
- Shoulder blade ribs sticking out
- Rise of one side of shoulder area when bending; curve noted in spinal column

## Classroom Guidelines

- Be aware of safety concerns (e.g., falls, stairs, loss of balance) associated with adolescent who is wearing special braces or has had surgery for realignment of spine.
- Arrange for adolescent's safe exit from classroom in case of an unexpected event that requires students to leave classroom or school.

- Plan suitable activities devised to meet the needs of adolescent, but limit activity according to directions of health care provider.
- Understand that the adolescent being treated for scoliosis might need continual positive reinforcement, encouragement, and as much independence as can safely be assumed. Socialization with peers should be encouraged through group activities.

## Attendance Guideline

- Exclusion from school is not required.

## Medications

- Pain medications may be prescribed.

## Communication

- Ask parent/caregiver/adolescent about activity restrictions associated with treatment plan.

## Resource

- www.mayoclinic.org

# Self-Mutilation

Also known as: deliberate self-harm, self-injurious behavior, aggression against the self

## Description

Self-mutilation is the deliberate destruction of body tissue without conscious intent of suicide. Every year, as many as 2 million Americans deliberately cut, burn, or hurt themselves in other ways. This is 30 times the rate of suicide attempts.

## Primary Groups Affected

- Females more likely than males to self-mutilate
- Usually begins during adolescence
- Affects people of all ethnic backgrounds

## Signs and Symptoms

- Adolescents who self-mutilate often use multiple methods of self-harm such as the following:

  - Superficial to moderate behaviors, including skin cutting, skin carving (words, designs, symbols), skin burning, severe skin scratching, needle sticking, self-hitting, tearing out hair, inserting dangerous objects into the vagina or rectum, ingesting sharp objects, bone breaking, and interfering with wound healing
  - Occasional severe acts of self-mutilation such as poking out one's eye, castration, and amputation of fingers, toes, or limbs, with psychosis being a major factor in these severe forms of the behavior

- The behavior is often impulsive and linked to a stressful situation.
- The behavior has great meaning, often hidden from others, for those who do it. Some of these meanings include the following:
  - Reorienting from flashbacks
  - Reenacting childhood trauma
  - Reconnecting to a feeling of being real and alive
  - Seeking distraction from emotional pain
  - Feeling something other than despair
  - Releasing tension or rage
  - Punishing oneself
  - Requesting nurturance
  - Crying for help

## Classroom Guidelines

- Establish a trusting relationship with adolescent, who has probably experienced much criticism and little understanding regarding the self-injurious behavior.
- Recognize that the best approach is a nonjudgmental and accepting attitude and a sense of caring.
- Encourage adolescent to talk about this behavior to decrease his or her sense of isolation.
- Set limits to minimize the potential for physical injury. Have adolescent draw the "blood" or "cuts" on paper, "injure" a stuffed animal, stroke his or her own arm or leg, snap a rubber band on the wrist, or draw the feeling or memory

## Attendance Guideline

- Exclusion from school is not required.

## Medication

- No medication is required.

## Communication

- Find out the history of the self-mutilative behavior.
- Ask adolescent what helps him or her to avoid the self-harm activities.
- Ask how the family responds to the behavior when it occurs.

## Resource

- KidsPeace
  National Center for Kids Overcoming Crisis
  5300 KidsPeace Drive
  Orefield, PA 18069
  (800) 8KID-123
  www.kidspeace.org

# Sensory Integration Dysfunction

Also known as: sensory integration disorder, sensory integrative dysfunction, SI dysfunction

## Description

Sensory integration dysfunction is the inability to process information received through the senses. In this disorder, the brain has difficulty in analyzing, organizing, and connecting (integrating) sensory messages. Because of this dysfunction, the adolescent cannot respond to sensory information and behave as expected. The adolescent is frequently described as being oversensitive or undersensitive to his or her surroundings and people. Interacting and relating with others and functioning in daily life may be affected. The adolescent may also have difficulty in using sensory information to plan and organize what needs to be done and experiences learning difficulties. The adolescent in the classroom might find performing ordinary tasks and responding to everyday activities to be enormously challenging. Because of the uniqueness of every person's brain, symptoms of sensory integration disorder vary from child to child. Some adolescents may have mild dysfunction, whereas others live with moderate to severe impairment. In addition, sometimes adolescents will exhibit signs of the disorder one day and not the next.

## Primary Groups Affected

- Any child

## Signs and Symptoms

- Unusually high or low activity level, ranging from always being "on the go" and easily excited to moving slowly and showing little interest in the world
- Impulsivity: lack of self-control, unable to stop after starting an activity
- Easily distractible: short attention span, disorganized, forgetful
- Problems with muscle tone and motor coordination: awkwardness, clumsy, accident prone
- Lack of definite hand preference by age 4 or 5 years
- Poor eye-hand coordination: trouble with crayons, art projects, puzzles, tying shoes; handwriting may be sloppy or uneven
- May want to wear the same clothes over and over or to wear clothes with a specific logo or picture
- Resists new situations or experiences
- Difficulty in moving from one situation to another: may seem stubborn and uncooperative
- High level of frustration: gives up on projects easily, poor game player
- Self-regulation problems: may be unable to show emotion easily or calm down once aroused
- Academic problems: difficulty in learning new skills and concepts
- Social problems: difficulty in making friends, participating in group activities, and sharing toys
- Emotional problems: overly sensitive to change, stress, and hurt feelings; appears to be disorganized, inflexible, and irrational; low self-esteem

## Classroom Guidelines

- Be aware that this disorder is often confused with attention deficit/hyperactivity disorder. The major symptoms of SI dysfunction are unusual responses to touching and being touched and/or to moving or being moved.
- Reduce sensory overload in the classroom. You might need to seat adolescent in a spot where he or she feels safe, surrounded by others who sit quietly and pay attention. Avoid sitting adolescent by doors or windows or by fluorescent lights. Prepare worksheets with a minimum of instructions to read and problems to solve. White space around each written problem helps adolescent to focus on one at a time.

- Provide comfortable furniture if possible. Find chairs that do not tip. Adolescent's feet need to be flat on the floor. There should be a cushion on the chair.
- Keep chalkboards and worksheets clean and with a minimum of instruction.
- Attempt to develop a consistent routine. Give adolescent some time to adjust to changes.
- Encourage adolescent to be an active learner rather than a passive learner, and give him or her time to learn.
- Provide a choice of writing implements.
- Emphasize the positive, keep your voice low, and keep your expectations realistic.
- Anticipate problems and provide alternatives but not too many. Assist adolescent in making choices.
- When you want to be certain that adolescent is paying attention, get up close and look into his or her eyes.

## Attendance Guideline

- Exclusion from school is not required.

## Medication

- No medication is required.

## Communication

- Discuss with parent/caregiver the adolescent's behavior and strategies that work best.

## Resource

- www.comeunity.com/disability/sensory_integration/carol-kranowitz.html

# Sexual
# Acting Out

## Description

Sexual acting out must be distinguished from normal adolescent sexual behavior, which involves individuals of similar age and cognitive abilities engaging in behavior that is private, consensual, equal, and noncoercive. Normal behaviors in this context include sexually explicit conversations with peers, obscenities and jokes within cultural norms, sexual innuendo and flirting, interest in erotica, solitary masturbation, foreplay, mutual masturbation, oral sex, and monogamist intercourse. Adolescents who engage in inappropriate sexual behavior may be said to be acting out sexually. This behavior may range from mildly deviant to illegal behaviors. Adolescents perpetrate 50% of sex offenses against boys and perpetrate 15% to 20% of offenses against girls. Nearly 15% of all sexual offenses involving adolescent perpetrators happen on school property. Offenders may have conduct disorder.

## Primary Groups Affected

- Children who act out sexually at an earlier age are more likely to have been sexually abused themselves.
- The median age of young offenders is 14 to 15 years. The median age of victims is 7 years.
- In 90% of the cases, the offender knows the victim.

## Signs and Symptoms

- Indiscriminate sexual contact with more than one partner during the same period of time

- Verbalizes sexual aggression
- Violation of others' body space
- Pulling skirts up, pulling pants down
- Public masturbation
- Attempts to expose others' genitals
- Chronic preoccupation with aggressive pornography
- Sexually explicit talk with significantly younger children
- Touching others' genitals without permission
- Obscene phone calls, voyeurism, exhibitionism, sexual harassment
- Sexual contact with significant age difference (child sexual abuse)
- Forced sexual contact (rape)

## Classroom Guidelines

- Understand that curriculum should include facts about human reproduction, contraception, and sexually transmitted infections.
- Initiate discussions of responsible sexual behavior and commitments to relationships a number of times.
- Set immediate limits on any sexually harassing behavior.
- Give clear consistent messages about what is and is not appropriate behavior. If adolescent starts to act out, calmly interrupt the process.
- Do not leave adolescent alone with younger children.
- Locker room situations should be supervised by a responsible adult.

## Attendance Guideline

- Adolescents who have committed sex offenses need to receive specialized sex offender treatment.

## Medication

- No medication is required.

## Communication

- Discuss with parent/caregiver whether the sexually acting out behavior is limited to the school setting or whether it also occurs in other situations.
- Refer to school social worker or psychologist for further assessment.

- Inform family and adolescent that all suspected cases of child sexual abuse must be reported to legal authorities.

## Resources

- www.sexualdeviancy.com
- Safer Society Foundation
  (802) 247-5141

# Sexually Transmitted Disease: Chlamydia

Also known as: silent disease

## Description

Chlamydia is the most frequently reported infectious disease that is spread through sexual contact (vagina, oral, or anal). *Chlamydia trachomatis* is the causative bacteria and grows well in the warm moist areas of the reproductive tract, including the cervix, uterus, fallopian tubes, and urethra. The bacteria also grow well in the mouth, throat, eyes, and anus. The disease is not spread by casual contact. In women, symptoms are often so mild initially that the infection goes unrecognized (hence the term "silent disease"). If untreated, chlamydia can lead to infection and scarring of the uterus and fallopian tubes, causing pelvic inflammatory disease (*see* Pelvic Inflammatory Disease) and infertility. In men, the initial infection usually causes urinary symptoms. Untreated chlamydia in men can lead to infertility and prostate difficulties. Persons with chlamydia are more likely to contract HIV/AIDS. Chlamydia can also be spread from mother to infant during birth. The newborn can acquire eye infections and pneumonia. Chlamydia is easily diagnosed with an examination by a health care provider and is treated with antibiotics.

## Primary Groups Affected

- Any sexually active person
- Persons ages 15 to 29 years (75% of cases)

## Signs and Symptoms

- Often mild or no symptoms, especially in women
- Thick yellow discharge from the vagina or penis
- Frequent urination
- Burning and pain with urination
- Painful or swollen testicles
- Pain during intercourse

## Classroom Guidelines

- Teach the following guidelines for sexual activity:

  - Practice sexual abstinence.
  - Use a latex condom with every sexual encounter, although condoms do not totally eliminate transmission.
  - Limit the number of sexual partners.
  - If possibly infected, avoid sex and see health care provider immediately.

- Dispense medications according to school regulations.

## Attendance Guideline

- Exclusion from school is not required.

## Medications

- Usually an antibiotic is prescribed by health care provider.
- Antibiotic should be given until it is all gone.
- Acetaminophen (Tylenol) may be given for fever and pain relief with parent/caregiver permission.

## Communication

- Ask parent/caregiver about schedule of antibiotics so as to support/monitor compliance with treatment plan.

## Resource

- Centers for Disease Control and Prevention
  National STD Hotline
  (800) 227-8922 or (800) 342-2437
  In Spanish: (800) 344-7432
  www.cdc.gov

# Sexually Transmitted Disease: Crab Louse

Also known as: pubic lice, pediculus phthirus pubis

## Description

The crab louse is a parasitic insect that is generally found in pubic hair but has been known to live on other coarse body hair such as the chest, underarms, beards, legs, mustaches, eyelashes, and eyebrows. It is most often found in the genital area and is usually spread through sexual contact. It is relatively immobile when on the body, remaining attached and feeding for hours or days on one spot without removing its mouthparts from the skin. The mature adult louse lives for about 15 to 25 days. A common misbelief is that sitting on a toilet seat can spread crabs to other persons. This is highly unlikely given that this insect cannot live long away from a warm human body. In addition, the louse cannot attach itself to smooth surfaces such as a toilet seat. Animals do not get or spread crabs. Infestation with crabs frequently is noted by reddish brown "dust" (the excretions from the insects) that may be visible in underclothing. This is not the same insect found in head lice (*see* Head Lice).

## Primary Groups Affected

- Any adolescent who has sexual contact with an infested person

## Signs and Symptoms

- Itching that is usually an allergic reaction to the bites of the insect; the most common symptom and frequently the only symptom
- Ticklish feeling of something moving in the hair
- Irritability
- Reddish brown dust-like substance found in underclothing
- May cause a severe skin reaction

## Classroom Guideline

- If a situation exists where crabs may have been left on clothing or bedding, instruct them to machine wash those items that the infested person used 2 or 3 days before treatment. The hot water cycle should be used to wash clothes, and the hot cycle of the dryer for at least 20 minutes to dry clothes. If items are not washable, they should be dry cleaned.

## Attendance Guideline

- Exclusion from school is not required.

## Medications

- Over-the-counter or lice shampoo (Pediculicide) may be used at home. In most cases, retreatment is necessary.
- Prescription medication (Lindane) may be ordered by a health care provider. It is not recommended for pregnant or nursing adolescents or for very young children.
- For lice found on the eyelashes, a prescription petrolatum ointment may be applied to the eyelids two times a day for 10 days. Nonprescription petroleum jelly is likely to irritate the eyes if it is applied.

## Communication

- Encourage adolescents who express concern that they may be infested with pubic lice to speak to the school nurse.
- Encourage adolescents with pubic lice to notify any sexual partners since the occurrence of the infestation and to avoid any sexual activity until infestation has been cured.

## Resources

- www.cdc.gov
- www.creatures.ifas.ufl.edu/urban/crab_louse.htm
- www.mayoclinic.org

# Sexually Transmitted Disease: Genital Warts

Also known as: condylomata acuminata, venereal warts, human papillomavirus (HPV)

## Description

Genital warts are caused by a sexually transmitted disease known as human papillomavirus. There are more than 30 different strains of HPV that can affect the genital tract. Not all strains of HPV cause visible warts on the genitalia; in fact, most HPV infections have no symptoms, although they can be transmitted to a sex partner. However, some types of HPV are highly correlated with cancer of the cervix. This emphasizes the importance of yearly Pap smears for women who are sexually active or who have reached age 18 years. Genital warts are single or multiple growths that appear on the vulva, in or around the vagina or anus, on the cervix, and on the penis, scrotum, or groin. They can be quite small or large enough to take on a cauliflower-like shape. Visible warts can be removed, and the majority of infections are not dangerous, although a few types of HPV are associated with cancer of the cervix.

## Primary Groups Affected

- Any sexually active person

## Signs and Symptoms

- Often mild or no symptoms
- Visible warts ranging in size from 1 to 2 millimeters to large cauliflower-like lesions

## Classroom Guidelines

- Teach the following guidelines for sexual activity:

  - Practice sexual abstinence.
  - Use a latex condom with every sexual encounter, although condoms do not totally eliminate transmission.
  - Limit the number of sexual partners.
  - If possibly infected, avoid sex and see health care provider immediately.
  - Do not have sex with anyone with genital sores or unusual growths in the genital area or anus.
  - Be aware that adolescent girls should have yearly Pap smears if they are sexually active.

## Attendance Guideline

- Exclusion from school is not required.

## Medications

- Topical prescription medications are applied directly to the skin, usually three times per week.

## Communication

- Encourage adolescents and parents/caregivers to discuss sexual issues and practices.

## Resource

- Centers for Disease Control and Prevention
  National STD Hotline: (800) 227-8922 or (800) 342-2437
  In Spanish: (800) 344-7432
  www.cdc.gov

# Sexually Transmitted Disease: Gonorrhea

Also known as: clap, STD

## Description

Gonorrhea is a very common infectious disease that is spread through sexual contact (vagina, oral, or anal). *Neisseria gonorrhoeae* is the causative bacteria and grows well in the warm moist areas of the reproductive tract, including the cervix, uterus, fallopian tubes, and urethra. The bacteria also grow well in the mouth, throat, eyes, and anus. The disease is not spread by casual contact. In women, symptoms are often so mild initially that the infection goes unrecognized. Untreated gonorrhea can lead to infection and scarring of the uterus and fallopian tubes, causing pelvic inflammatory disease (*see* Pelvic Inflammatory Disease) and infertility. In men, the initial infection usually causes urinary symptoms. Untreated gonorrhea in men can lead to infertility and prostate difficulties. Gonorrhea can also spread to the blood system and joints. This can be a life-threatening condition. Persons with gonorrhea are more likely to contract HIV/AIDS. Gonorrhea can also be spread from mother to infant during birth. The newborn can become blind or have joint infections and life-threatening blood infections from gonorrhea contracted from the mother. Gonorrhea is easily diagnosed with an examination by a health care provider and is treated with antibiotics.

## Primary Groups Affected

- Any sexually active person who is having unprotected inter-course
- Three fourths (75%) of cases found in persons ages 15 to 29 years
- Highest rates in women ages 15 to 19 years; highest rates in men ages 20 to 24 years
- Three fourths of cases found in African Americans (as reported to Centers for Disease Control and Prevention)

## Signs and Symptoms

- Often mild or no symptoms, especially in women
- Thick yellow discharge from the vagina or penis
- Frequent urination
- Burning and pain with urination
- Painful or swollen testicles
- Pain during intercourse

## Classroom Guidelines

- Teach the following guidelines for sexual activity:
  - Practice sexual abstinence.
  - Use a latex condom with every sexual encounter, although condoms do not totally eliminate transmission.
  - Limit the number of sexual partners.
  - If possibly infected, avoid sex and see health care provider immediately.
  - Be truthful with sexual partners about their risk of exposure.
- Dispense medications according to school regulations.

## Attendance Guideline

- Exclusion from school is not required.

## Medications

- Usually an antibiotic is prescribed by health care provider.
- Antibiotic should be taken until it is all gone.
- Acetaminophen (Tylenol) may be given for fever and pain relief with parent/caregiver permission.

## Communication

- Ask parent/caregiver about schedule of antibiotics so as to support/monitor compliance with treatment plan.
- Encourage adolescents and parents/caregivers to discuss sexual issues and practices.

## Resources

- Centers for Disease Control and Prevention
  National STD Hotline: (800) 227-8922 or (800) 342-2437
  In Spanish: (800) 344-7432
  www.cdc.gov

- www.mayoclinic.org

# Sexually Transmitted Disease: Herpes

Also known as: genital herpes, HSV-1, HSV-2, herpes simplex virus

## Description

Herpes is a very contagious sexually transmitted disease caused by the herpes simplex virus type 1 or 2. Often there are no symptoms, but when signs do occur they include painful blisters around the genitals and rectum. The first outbreak of herpes tends to be the most painful one and can last 2 to 4 weeks. The outbreak usually occurs 2 to 7 days after exposure to the virus. The infection is spread from blisters but can also be spread between outbreaks when the skin appears to be healthy. The infection can also be spread to an infant during birth if the mother is experiencing an outbreak. The infection can be very serious to the newborn. Repeated outbreaks of herpes can occur weeks or months after the initial one but tend to be less severe and last a shorter amount of time. Gradually, the outbreaks will be reduced so long as the adolescent remains healthy. Various factors that may trigger later outbreaks include stress, fatigue, illness, skin irritation, menstruation, surgery, and vigorous sexual intercourse. There is no cure for the virus, but symptoms can be helped with medications prescribed by a health care provider.

## Primary Groups Affected

- Any sexually active person

## Signs and Symptoms

- Pain or itching in the skin around the genital area
- Initially, small painful red bumps
- Blisters or open sores
- Burning or pain with urination
- Flu-like symptoms that include the following:
  - Headache
  - Fever
  - Swollen glands (lymph nodes) in the groin area

## Classroom Guidelines

- Teach the following guidelines for sexual activity:
  - Practice sexual abstinence.
  - Use a latex condom with every sexual encounter, although condoms do not totally eliminate shedding of the herpes virus.
  - Limit the number of sexual partners.
  - If possibly infected, avoid sex and see health care provider immediately.
  - Be truthful with sexual partners about their risk of exposure.
- Dispense medications according to school regulations.

## Attendance Guideline

- Exclusion from school is not required.

## Medications

- An antiviral medication may be prescribed by health care provider.
- Acetaminophen (Tylenol) may be given for fever and pain relief with parent/caregiver permission.

## Communication

- Ask parent/caregiver about schedule of antibiotics so as to support/monitor compliance with treatment plan.
- Encourage adolescents and parents/caregivers to discuss sexual issues and practices.

## Resources

- National Herpes Hotline
  (919) 361-8488
- Centers for Disease Control and Prevention
  National STD Hotline
  (800) 227-8922 or (800) 342-2437
  In Spanish: (800) 344-7432
  www.cdc.gov
- www.ashastd.org/hrc
- www.mayoclinic.org
- E-mail: herpesnet@ashastd.org

# Sexually Transmitted Disease: Syphilis

Also known as: VD, syph

## Description

Syphilis is a sexually transmitted disease caused by *Treponema pallidum*. The disease can also be transmitted to a person through infected blood, to a fetus through the placenta, or to an infant during birth. The initial symptom is a localized chancre (sore), but the disease actually becomes systemic almost right from its onset. Treatments that eradicate the local lesion and stop sexual transmission might not necessarily stop the spread of syphilis systemically into the central nervous system. Syphilis is diagnosed with a blood test and is treated with antibiotics. Blood tests are done periodically to assess the effectiveness of treatment.

## Primary Groups Affected

- Any sexually active person who is having unprotected intercourse
- Risk groups include the following:
  - Homosexual and bisexual males
  - African American males
  - Hispanics
  - Those living in urban areas
  - Users of crack and cocaine

## Signs and Symptoms

### Primary Disease: Chancre

- Chancre at the site of infection (usually genitals) that appears 10 to 90 days after exposure
- Usually painless
- Varies in size from 3 millimeters to 2 centimeters
- May persist for 2 to 6 weeks
- Nearby lymph nodes may be enlarged
- Often goes unnoticed

### Secondary Disease

- Begins 6 to 8 weeks after chancre heals
- Low-grade fever
- Headaches
- Malaise
- Weight loss
- Aching in joints
- Rash, skin lesions
- Loss of hair

### Latent Disease

- Signs of secondary disease gone, but still contagious to partners and fetus

### Tertiary (Late) Disease

- Occurs in one third of those not treated
- Develops 2 to 20 years after initial infection

## Classroom Guidelines

- Teach the following guidelines for sexual activity:
  - Practice sexual abstinence.
  - Use a latex condom with every sexual encounter, although condoms do not totally eliminate transmission.
  - Limit the number of sexual partners.
  - If possibly infected, avoid sex and see health care provider immediately.
  - Be truthful with sexual partners about their risk of exposure.
- Dispense medications according to school regulations.

## Attendance Guideline

- Exclusion from school is not required.

## Medications

- Usually an antibiotic is prescribed by health care provider.
- Antibiotic should be taken until it is all gone.
- Acetaminophen (Tylenol) may be given for fever and pain relief with parent/caregiver permission.

## Communication

- Ask parent/caregiver about schedule of antibiotics so as to support/monitor compliance with treatment plan.
- Encourage adolescents and parents/caregivers to discuss sexual issues and practices.

## Resources

- Centers for Disease Control and Prevention
  National STD Hotline
  (800) 227-8922 or (800) 342-2437
  In Spanish: (800) 344-7432
  www.cdc.gov

- www.mayoclinic.org

# Sexually Transmitted Disease: Trichomoniasis

Also known as: trich, STD

## Description

Trichomoniasis is a common sexually transmitted disease that affects men and women. It is caused by the protozoa *Trichomonas vaginalis.* If symptoms do occur, they usually are seen 1 to 4 weeks after exposure. The diagnosis needs to be made by a health care provider, and the infection can be cured with a prescription medication. As with all sexually transmitted diseases, both partners need to be treated to prevent reinfection of each other or someone else. Untreated trichomoniasis can increase the risk of acquiring HIV and can also increase the risk of preterm birth in pregnant women.

## Primary Groups Affected

- Any sexually active person who is having unprotected intercourse

## Signs and Symptoms

- If the man has symptoms, they include the following:
  - Irritation inside the penis
  - Mild urethral discharge
  - Slight burning after urination or ejaculation

- If the woman has symptoms, they include the following:
  - Frothy, yellow-green vaginal discharge
  - Strong odor to vaginal discharge
  - Discomfort with intercourse
  - Irritation and itching in the vaginal area
  - Lower abdominal pain

## Classroom Guidelines

- Teach the following guidelines for sexual activity:
  - Practice sexual abstinence.
  - Use a latex condom with every sexual encounter, although condoms do not totally eliminate transmission.
  - Limit the number of sexual partners.
  - If possibly infected, avoid sex and see health care provider immediately.
  - Be truthful with sexual partners about their risk of exposure.
- Dispense medications according to school regulations.

## Attendance Guideline

- Exclusion from school is not required.

## Medications

- Usually an antibiotic is prescribed by health care provider.
- Antibiotic should be given until it is all gone.
- Acetaminophen (Tylenol) may be given for fever and pain relief with parent/caregiver permission.

## Communication

- Ask parent/caregiver about schedule of antibiotics so as to support/monitor compliance with treatment plan.
- Encourage adolescents and parents/caregivers to discuss sexual issues and practices.

## Resource

- Centers for Disease Control and Prevention
  National STD Hotline
  (800) 227-8922 or (800) 342-2437
  In Spanish: (800) 344-7432
  www.cdc.gov

# Sickle
# Cell Anemia

## Description

Sickle cell anemia is a genetic disorder in which normal hemoglobin is replaced by sickle hemoglobin (Hg S). If the adolescent carries only one of these recessive genes, he or she is labeled as sickle cell trait and shows no symptoms. The Hg S causes the red blood cells to become elongated in shape. This impairs the cells' ability to flow freely through blood vessels and causes small obstructions known as a vaso-occlusive crisis. When this occurs, pain results due to the lack of circulation. Conditions that can cause such a crisis include low oxygen supply (e.g., at high altitude), lack of fluids, infection, and exposure to cold temperatures, which causes the small blood vessels to vaso-constrict. Over time, the adolescent may experience damage to many body systems. Common areas affected include the eyes, stomach, intestines, and kidneys. In addition, there are two more serious types of crises. Sequestration crisis occurs when there is an excessive pooling of blood in the liver and spleen. This significantly reduces the total blood volume. The adolescent appears to be in shock, and it can be fatal if not treated promptly. Aplastic crisis occurs when the production of red blood cells is markedly reduced, and the adolescent will suffer from severe anemia.

## Primary Groups Affected

- Most common among those with ancestors from Sub-Saharan Africa, South America, Cuba, Central America, Saudi Arabia, India, and the Mediterranean countries
- In the United States, occurs in 1 of every 1,000 to 1,400 Hispanic American births and 1 of every 500 African American births

## Signs and Symptoms

- Pain during an acute crisis
- Pale color, fatigue, and shortness of breath during activities with anemia—**911**
- Decreased vision, abdominal pain, and urinary incontinence in long-standing disease

## Classroom Guidelines

- Dispense medications according to school regulations.
- Ensure that adolescent abides by activity restrictions.
- Refer adolescent to school health professional if pain or fever develops.
- Allow adolescent to drink fluids and use washroom facilities as needed.
- Be sure that adolescent dresses warmly on cold days, especially with gloves and boots.
- Assist adolescent if the pain interferes with his or her ability to walk.
- Arrange for adolescent's safe exit from classroom in case of an unexpected event that requires students to leave classroom or school.
- Notify parents/caregivers of students if infectious/contagious illness is present in the classroom.

## Attendance Guidelines

- Exclusion from school is not required because this is not a contagious disease.
- Adolescent may have multiple absences if frequent pain crises occur.

## Medications

- Pain medications may be used.
- Prophylactic antibiotic use is sometimes employed in the younger population to prevent infections that might cause a crisis.

## Communication

- Ask parent/caregiver/adolescent how often the student experiences a pain crisis.

- Ask how much fluid adolescent should drink each day and whether he or she follows this plan independently.
- Ask whether medications are to be given during school hours.
- Ask parent/caregiver whether pain medication will interfere with adolescent's ability to function in school.
- Ask the parent/caregiver/adolescent whether there are any activity restrictions, especially regarding contact sports.
- Ask about participation in outdoor activities on cold days.

## Resources

- Midwest Association for Sickle Cell Anemia
  65 E. Wacker Place
  Chicago, IL 60601-7203
  (312) 663-5700

- Sickle Cell Disease Association of Illinois
  200 N. Michigan Avenue, Suite 605
  Chicago, IL 60601-5980
  (312) 345-1100
  *Sickle Cell Trait* (brochure available at above address)

- www.sicklecelldisease.org

# Skin Disorder: Acne

Also known as: pimples, zits

## Description

Acne is a common skin disorder associated with changes that take place as adolescents mature from childhood to puberty. The hormones (androgens that are present in both genders) responsible for the physical changes in the body cause the sebaceous (oil) glands of the skin to produce more sebum (oil). This oil can lead to plugged pores and the outbreak of lesions called pimples or zits. Acne is also a general term for blackheads (open comedones), whiteheads (closed comedones), pimples, and even deeper lumps that can occur on the face, neck, chest, back, shoulders, and upper arms. Severity of acne "outbreak" varies among adolescents from mild to severe. Scarring can result from both severe and mild cases. Acne generally disappears by the early 20s in males and somewhat later in females.

## Primary Groups Affected

- Any adolescents; incidence of 30% to 85% of all teenagers, usually starting between ages 10 and 13 years and lasting 5 to 10 years
- Severe cases: Boys 10 times more frequently than girls
- Family history of acne
- Adolescents taking medications for extreme stress or depression (side effect of drugs)

## Signs and Symptoms

- "Bumps," blackheads, whiteheads, pimples, cysts, scarring
- Pain when pressure is applied

- In girls, premenstrual outbreak frequent (2 to 7 days before period)
- Frequently oily hair

## Classroom Guidelines

- Be aware that sensitivity toward adolescent with acne, social relationships, self-confidence, body image, and self-esteem may be affected. Observe for signs of depression (*see* Depression).
- Encourage adolescent to use stress management techniques.
- Teach adolescents to avoid "acne irritants" such as oily or greasy cosmetics and sunscreens and instead to use products labeled "oil free," "water based," or "noncomedongenic."
- Understand that it may be normal for some adolescents with acne to have increased redness, peeling of the skin, and flare-ups after certain treatments.
- Arrange for outdoor activities with limited sun exposure for adolescent using acne products. Some products increase the skin's sensitivity to sunlight and ultraviolet light from tanning booths.
- Encourage adolescent not to squeeze or pick at acne and to wash face with mild soap and pat dry. Hard scrubbing of the skin can cause further irritation. Dispel the common myth that acne is a result of poor hygiene practices.

## Attendance Guideline

- Exclusion from school is not required. Adolescent may be absent for appointments/treatments with health care provider.

## Medications

- Topical creams, antibiotics, birth control pills, and/or Accutane may be prescribed depending on the severity of the acne.

## Communication

- Ask parent/caregiver for information regarding any medications/treatments adolescent may be taking for acne.
- Discuss with parent/caregiver/school nurse whether adolescent with acne appears more withdrawn, angry, or frustrated and suggest seeking advice from health care provider. A common myth regarding acne is that nothing can be done and that it is just part of growing up.

## Resources

- www.skincarephysicians.com/acnenet/acne.html
- www.mayoclinic.org
- www.niams.nih.gov/hi/topics/acne/acne.htm
- American Academy of Dermatology
  P.O. Box 4014
  Schaumburg, IL 60168
  (888) 462-3376
  www.aad.org

# Skin Infection: Fungal

Also known as: tinea pedis (athlete's foot), tinea cruris (jock itch), tinea capitis (ringworm of the scalp)

## Description

Tinea is the medical word for a group of related fungal infections. Fungal infections, caused by several types of mold-like organisms called dermatophytes, live on the dead tissue of skin, hair, and nails. The infection can be passed from shared clothing, combs, and pets. All fungi grow best in a warm moist environment. Athlete's foot, the most commonly occurring fungal infection, affects the soles of the feet and between the toes. Jock itch causes itch and burning in the groin area, including the inner thighs, buttocks, and anal area. Ringworm often occurs over the scalp and neck area, and as the name implies, there is a ring appearance; however, it is not caused by a worm.

## Primary Groups Affected

- Any age group

## Signs and Symptoms

- Ringworm of scalp: patchy areas with dandruff-like scaling, hair loss and broken stubbles of hair
- Jock itch: itching or redness on inner thighs, buttocks, and anal area
- Athlete's foot: itching, burning, and redness on soles of feet; stinging on soles of feet; skin that may peel, flake, and/or crack; nails discolored and thick

## Classroom Guidelines

- Ensure proper hand washing (*see* Procedure A).
- Encourage good hygiene.
- Eliminate the use of any shared articles such as towels, hats, and personal items.
- Minimize close contact with infected adolescents until they are treated.
- Urge adolescents to dry well after showering or swimming.
- Recommend that adolescents wear waterproof shoes to protect feet in shower and gym areas.
- Discourage adolescents from wearing same shoes all the time and from wearing synthetic-material shoes.
- Urge adolescents to wear cotton socks.

## Attendance Guideline

- Exclusion from school is not required once treatment has begun; however, adolescent should avoid touching affected area.

## Medications

- A fungicidal medication (lotion, shampoo, cream, spray, or powder) may be applied to affected area.
- Oral medications may also be prescribed.
- Treatment may be prolonged (weeks or months).

## Communication

- Advise parent/caregiver and school nurse about adolescent's fungal skin infection.
- Ask parent/caregiver about schedule of medications.

## Resource

- www.mayoclinic.org

# Sleep Disorders

Also known as: sleepwalking, sleep deprivation, narcolepsy, sleep apnea

## Description

Getting enough sleep gives adolescents energy and motivation for the day. During adolescence, there is a delay in the secretion of melatonin, a hormone that induces sleepiness. That is why adolescents do not become sleepy until 10:30 p.m. or later. Adolescents require 8½ to 9½ hours of sleep each night. Studies show that many adolescents do not get sufficient sleep given the high demands on their time due to homework, extracurricular activities, socializing, and after-school jobs. Excessive daytime sleepiness may cause serious academic and personal problems. Adolescents sometimes may be perceived as lazy, lethargic, or rude. There is an increased risk of car accidents related to falling asleep or delayed reaction time.

## Primary Groups Affected

- Sleepwalking is most common between ages 5 and 12 years. Most children outgrow sleepwalking by age 15 years.
- The first symptoms of narcolepsy usually appear during adolescence or the early 20s.

## Signs and Symptoms

- Sleepwalking:
  - Partial waking
  - Eyes open, dazed expression
  - Walking or other activities
  - Confusion or disorientation if awakened

- Sleep deprivation:
  - Habitually takes a 1- to 2-hour nap after school
  - Is unable to fall asleep prior to 1 or 2 a.m. and has difficulty in getting up in the morning because sleep deprivation interferes with the biological sleep cycle
  - Has problems in concentrating and paying attention that interfere with learning
  - Falls asleep in the classroom regularly
  - Is moody and irritable
  - May be at higher risk for substance abuse with the use of stimulants to stay awake

- Narcolepsy:
  - Overwhelmed by daytime drowsiness and sleep attacks, regardless of how much sleep adolescent got the night before
  - Possible sudden loss of muscle tone that can cause changes from slurred speech to total physical collapse, lasting from a few seconds to a few minutes

## Classroom Guidelines

- Work with teachers, administration, school board, and school district to delay school's start time to 8:30 a.m.
- Suggest to adolescent that his or her bed be used only for sleeping—not for homework, playing, or watching television.
- Encourage adolescent to avoid stimulants, such as caffeine, at around bedtime.
- If there is a diagnosis of narcolepsy, try to ignore the episodes of sleepiness.

## Attendance Guideline

- Exclusion from school is not required.

## Medication

- Adolescent may take a central nervous system stimulant if narcolepsy persists for a period of time.

## Communication

- Discuss normal adolescent patterns of sleep with parent/caregiver.

- Discuss how demands on adolescent's time may be decreased or modified to improve sleep patterns.

## Resources

- National Sleep Foundation
  1522 K Street, N.W., Suite 500
  Washington, DC 20005
  (202) 347-3471
  www.sleepfoundation.org

- www.narcolepsynetwork.org

# Slipped Capital Femoral Epiphysis

Also known as: coxa vera

## Description

Slipped capital femoral epiphysis is a disorder of the hip in adolescents. It is identified as a disease of puberty. Slipped capital femoral epiphysis is a slipping of the thigh bone head (femur—the longest and strongest bone in the body) in relation to the neck of the thigh bone at a certain point (epiphyseal line). The covering (cartilage) of the femoral head may be destroyed and result in permanent loss of motion of the femur head. Some adolescents experience "stable" slipped capital femoral epiphysis and can bear weight on the side of the body where they are having pain. Those with "unstable" slipped capital femoral epiphysis are not able to bear any weight on the affected side, either with or without crutches. The cause of this disorder is not known in the majority of cases. Some adolescents with this disorder also have known endocrine disorders such as hypothyroidism, certain types of renal failure, or a history of having prior radiation therapy. A small percentage of adolescents experience this disorder in both hips.

## Primary Groups Affected

- Preadolescent and adolescent children, with at least 50% having a weight exceeding the 95th percentile according to age
- Adolescents who grow rapidly
- Twice as frequent in African Americans
- Twice as frequent in boys as in girls, usually diagnosed between ages 12 and 14 years

## Signs and Symptoms

- Pre-slip stage (may last for 1 to 3 months):

  - Complains of pain in the groin or knee on exertion
  - Complains of leg weakness
  - Symptoms produced by prolonged standing or walking
  - Limping

- Acute stage:

  - Restricted movement of the affected leg
  - Complains of pain in the groin, thigh, and/or knee
  - May experience periods of time without any symptoms
  - Severe cases: lower leg spontaneously rotates outward when adolescent flexes hip
  - May need crutches to walk

## Classroom Guidelines

- Arrange for adolescent's safe exit from classroom in case of an unexpected event that requires students to leave classroom or school.
- Be aware that adolescent might have activity restrictions and might need alternative activities when classmates are on field trips requiring excessive walking, climbing, running, and/or jumping.
- Understand that adolescent might need to be encouraged to use crutches.
- Recognize that adolescent might need additional time and assistance to get to classes on time.
- Be aware of safety concerns with use of crutches such as falls, stairs, loss of balance, and icy/wet weather conditions.

## Attendance Guideline

- Exclusion from school is not required; however, adolescent may have extended absence due to surgery or immobilization as a treatment plan.

## Medications

- Anti-inflammatory medications may be ordered by health care provider.

## Communication

- Ask parent/caregiver/adolescent about activity abilities and restrictions.
- Ask about schedule of any medications to be given at school.
- Notify parent/caretaker of any complaints of increased pain noted in the classroom.

## Resource

- http://orthoinfo.aaos.org

# Snake Bite

## Description

Adolescents need to be taught that even though most snakes are not poisonous, they should not pick up or play with snakes. Infections or allergic reactions from the bite of a "harmless" snake can occur. Moreover, there are snakes whose venom is poisonous and requires activation of the local emergency medical system or immediate treatment by a health care provider. The appropriate antivenin given within a specific time may save a life. Adolescents who frequent wilderness areas or who camp, hike, picnic, or reside in snake-inhabited areas should be observant of the dangers posed by some snakes. Rattlesnakes, copperheads, cottonmouth water moccasins, and coral snakes are considered to have poisonous bites.

## Primary Groups Affected

- Any adolescent in contact with snakes

## Signs and Symptoms

- Open bloody wound on skin with surrounding fang marks—**911**
- Swelling at site of bite
- Severe localized pain
- Burning at site of bite
- Blurred vision—**911**
- Excessive sweating
- Convulsions—**911**
- Diarrhea
- Dizziness—**911**
- Weakness—**911**
- Fainting—**911**

- Fever—**911**
- Increased thirst
- Loss of muscle coordination, inability to walk—**911**
- Nausea or vomiting
- Numbness and tingling—**911**
- Difficulty in breathing—**911**
- Increased salivation—**911**
- Rapid pulse—**911**
- Skin discoloration—**911**

## Classroom Guidelines

- Carry adolescent to safety. Do not allow adolescent to walk or perform any type of exercise.
- Activate local emergency medical system immediately. Either you or emergency medical responders should call ahead to emergency room so that antivenin can be ready when adolescent arrives. Inform emergency medical responders and/or emergency room personnel if adolescent is allergic to horse products. (Antivenin is obtained from horses, so snake bite victims sensitive to horse products must be managed carefully.)
- Speak calmly to adolescent so as to decrease his or her anxiety.
- Wash bite site gently with soap and water.
- Remove any rings or constricting items on affected extremity.
- Assist adolescent in sitting or lying down, immobilize bitten area, and keep it *lower* than heart.
- Apply clean moist bandage.
- Immobilize area using padding and binder.
- Monitor breathing and pulse.
- Notify parent/caregiver.
- Be aware that American Red Cross guidelines recommend that if adolescent cannot receive medical care within 30 minutes, a bandage should be applied and wrapped 2 to 4 inches above the bite site to help slow venom. The bandage should not be constricting and should be loose enough to slip a finger under it. If a suction device is available, apply it over bite to help draw venom out of wound without making a cut. (This device is often included in commercial snake bite kits.)
- Follow school guidelines on reporting and documenting snake bites.

- Do not apply a tourniquet, do not cut into snake bite, do not give adolescent anything by mouth, do not raise site of bite above level of adolescent's heart, and do not try to suction venom.
- Discuss with students the following ways in which to protect themselves from snake bites. Avoid picking up or playing with any snake. Do not put hands or feet into any area if you cannot see the area. Tap ahead of you with walking stick before entering an area you cannot see; most snakes will attempt to avoid people if given a warning. Wear thick boots and remain on hiking paths as much as possible. Stay out of tall grassy areas. Do not pick up rocks or firewood unless you are out of a snake's striking distance. Be cautious and alert when climbing rocks and leave snakes alone. Do not get too close to a snake.

## Attendance Guideline

- Exclusion from school is not required, but observe adolescent for signs/symptoms of infection and notify parent/caregiver if any are seen.

## Medication

- Antivenin may be used.

## Communication

- Notify parent/caregiver immediately and urge to see health care provider.
- If adolescent is receiving a series of rabies vaccine and antiserum injections, ask parent/caregiver for information concerning reactions.

## Resource

- www.healthcentral.com

# Spider Bite

## Description

Most spiders are harmless, with the exception of the black widow and the brown recluse (violin spider). These spiders are usually found in warm climates. A bite from either of these spiders necessitates prompt medical attention and activation of the local emergency medical system.

## Primary Groups Affected

- Children of any age, especially if in or around basements, closets, or attics

## Signs and Symptoms

- Bite marks (black widow spider—double fang marks)—**911**
- Pain and swelling
- Nausea or vomiting—**911**
- Difficulty in breathing and swallowing—**911**
- Redness at site—**911**
- Brown recluse spider symptoms: deep blue or purple area around the bite surrounded by white-colored ring and large red outer ring (sometimes described as a bull's eye), blister that turns black, headache, body aches, rash, fever, nausea or vomiting—**911**
- Black widow spider symptoms: immediate pain, burning, swelling, and redness at site of the bite; cramping pain and muscle rigidity in stomach, chest, shoulder and back; headache; dizziness; rash; itching; restlessness; anxiety; sweating; nausea or vomiting; tearing of eyes; eyelid swelling; increased saliva; weakness; tremors; unable to move (especially legs)—**911**

## Classroom Guidelines

- For any spider bite, wash area well with soap and water, apply a cold or ice pack to the bite site, and elevate bite site if possible. Notify parent/caregiver and urge to see health care provider.
- For a brown recluse spider bite, do all of the above *plus* activate local emergency medical system—**911**.
- For a black widow spider bite, do all of the above *plus* apply an antibiotic cream (if available) to protect against infection—**911**.

## Attendance Guideline

- Exclusion from school is not required.

## Medications

- Acetaminophen (Tylenol) may be given for pain with parent/caregiver permission.
- Depending on severity of the bite, health care provider may prescribe a variety of medications.

## Communication

- Notify parent/caregiver of spider bite.
- Ask parent/caregiver/adolescent for information regarding prescribed medications.

## Resources

- American Red Cross
  See local chapter

- www.umm.edu/non_trauma/spider.htm

# Spinal Cord Injury: Acute Care

Also known as: paraplegia, quadriplegia

## Description

Most traumas to the spinal cord in adolescents are the result of being involved in motor vehicle accidents, suffering blows to the head, falling on one's back, or being injured in other athletic activities. A spinal cord injury may affect any of the spinal nerves; the higher the injury in the spinal column, the more severe the damages. Adolescents who live with complete or partial loss of movement of the lower extremities are said to have paraplegia, whereas those who cannot function or who have limited functional abilities of the four extremities live with quadriplegia. A high cervical cord injury can result in the adolescent being dependent on a ventilator to breathe. The care of an adolescent living with spinal cord injury is complex and challenging. In the classroom, the adolescent may experience many physical and psychological barriers.

## Primary Groups Affected

- Boys more often than girls

## Signs and Symptoms

- Blunt force or indirect trauma to head or spinal cord
- Inability to move at least one extremity
- Loss of consciousness

## Classroom Guidelines

- In any event where spinal cord injury is suspected or possible and the adolescent is conscious, speak calmly and tell adolescent not to move. Adolescent should be moved only by trained personnel who have the ability to immobilize the head and trunk and move adolescent onto a backboard.
- Assess adolescent's breathing and be prepared to administer CPR—**911.**
- Activate local emergency medical system and notify parent/caregiver.

## Attendance Guideline

- Adolescent should be transported to the nearest hospital emergency room.

## Medication

- No medication is necessary.

## Communication

- Notify parent/caregiver as soon as possible regarding the injury and give name and location of hospital so that parent/caregiver can go directly to emergency room.

## Resources

- www.spinalcord.org
- www.spinalinjury.net

# Spinal Cord Injury: Long-Term Care

## Description

Recent advances in emergency care and rehabilitation now permit many adolescents with spinal cord injury to survive and be present in the classroom. The types of disability associated with a spinal cord injury vary depending on the severity, nerve fiber damage, and level of the injury. Adolescents with higher level spinal cord injury will be more challenged in participating in classroom activities. In addition, adolescents with long-term spinal cord injury are prone to develop bladder infections, lung infections, and bed sores (pressure ulcers and decubitus ulcers). Other symptoms, such as pain, sensitivity to stimuli, and muscle spasms, may develop over time.

## Primary Groups Affected

- Boys more often than girls

## Signs and Symptoms

- Inability to move one or more extremities normally

## Classroom Guidelines

- Arrange for adolescent's safe exit from classroom in case of an unexpected event that requires students to leave the classroom or school.

- Be familiar with school policy regarding any ventilator or oxygen equipment safety concerns and procedures.
- Allow adolescent to maintain adequate fluid intake to prevent dehydration.
- Plan classroom schedule to allow adolescent to participate in a successful bladder/bowel management program. (Depending on the level of injury, many adolescents learn to catheterize themselves at a very early age.)
- Be aware that adolescents with injuries at the thoracic 6 or above are at risk for the medical emergency of autonomic dysreflexia. Signs of autonomic dysreflexia include the following:
  - Sudden headache
  - Sweating
  - Increased blood pressure
  - Flushed reddened skin
  - Goosebumps
  - Blurry vision or seeing spots
  - Anxiety
  - Difficulty in breathing
  - Tightness in chest

- Understand that adolescents having any of the above signs or symptoms should be placed in a sitting position or have their heads raised 90 degrees. Loosen anything tight (e.g., belt, pants/slacks, tight underwear), check blood pressure if possible, check to make sure any catheter tube is not kinked (the most common cause seems to be overfilling of the bladder), and call—**911**.
- Be aware that environmental temperature controls, such as air conditioning, can affect adolescent's body temperature, especially if injury is high on the spinal cord. Be sure that adolescent avoids sunburns; have adolescent use sunscreen when outside (*see* Procedure I).
- Assist or permit adolescent to change position frequently (every 2 hours) to avoid pressure ulcers. Make sure that adolescent is positioned in wheelchair correctly. If assisting adolescent with positioning, be sure to lift and not pull him or her so as to decrease potential pressure ulcer injury. Pressure relief may be obtained by leaning adolescent forward, with chest toward thighs, and carefully tipping the wheelchair back 65 degrees.
- Understand that adolescent might need to be in a lying down position for part of the school day to decrease the risk of pressure ulcers.

- Encourage adolescent to be independent and to participate in activities with nondisabled classmates within the limits of safety and health.
- Observe adolescent for signs of depression (*see* Depression).

## Attendance Guideline

- Exclusion from school is not required unless adolescent is recovering from complications related to spinal cord injury.

## Medications

- A combination of medications tailored to adolescent's needs may be prescribed.

## Communication

- Ask parent/caregiver/adolescent about activity abilities and restrictions.
- Ask about special procedures, extra equipment, and specific instructions regarding equipment.
- Ask parent/caregiver/adolescent about schedule of any medications to be given at school
- Ask whether adolescent desires to inform classmates of what it is like to live with a spinal cord injury.
- Notify parent/caregiver of any health problems noted in the classroom.

## Resources

- www.spinalcord.org
- www.spinalinjury.net
- www.northeastrehab.com/articles/dysreflexia.htm

# Splinters

## Description

Small wooden splinters can usually be successfully removed without much difficulty. However, large items such as a fishhook, a piece of glass, a deeply embedded object, or a difficult-to-see object might need the attention of a health care provider.

## Primary Groups Affected

- Any adolescents

## Signs and Symptoms

- Small object protruding near surface of skin

## Classroom Guidelines

- Wash hands (*see* Procedure A) and use disposable gloves if available.
- Clean area around splinter with soap and water, being careful not to break splinter.
- Gently remove splinter with tweezers that have been cleaned with alcohol or with a flame if available. Allow tweezers to cool before using.
- Squeeze wound to encourage bleeding that will flush out dirt.
- Wash area again, pat dry, and apply sterile bandage over site.
- Be aware that cactus spines may be removed by placing a piece of cellophane tape (sticky side down) over the spine and lifting off.
- If the splinter breaks or will not come out, ensure that adolescent sees a health care provider for removal.

## Attendance Guideline

- Exclusion from school is not required.

## Medication

- No medication is required.

## Communication

- Notify parent/caregiver if splinter breaks.

## Resources

- www.med.jhu.edu/peds
- www.choa.org/first_aid/splinter

# Sports-Related Injury: Achilles Tendonitis/Achilles Tendon Tear

## Description

Achilles tendonitis is an inflammation of the tendon behind the ankle that connects the leg and ankle to the heel bone. The Achilles tendon serves as the power source for pushing off with the foot. Long-standing Achilles tendonitis (inflammation) can lead to tendonitis, which is a degeneration of the tendon fibers. This is caused by excessive running or jumping without proper stretching. An Achilles tendon tear is a tearing of the tendon behind the ankle that connects the leg and ankle to the heel bone. These tears typically occur during cutting and jumping sports, are the result of violent contractions of the large calf muscles, and usually do not involve any contact with other players. In some cases, the tendon rupture can produce the inflammation Achilles tendonitis.

## Primary Groups Affected

- Adolescent uphill runners
- Adolescents engaged in running and jumping sports such as basketball, tennis, and football

## Signs and Symptoms

- Achilles tendon tear: a "pop" felt behind the ankle after an injury

- Achilles tendonitis: pain behind the ankle when engaging in running or jumping
- Tenderness over the Achilles tendon and weakness when testing the calf muscle

## Classroom Guidelines

- Encourage all adolescents to participate in warming up before exercising.
- Encourage all adolescents to participate in proper stretching before exercising for prevention of Achilles tendon tears.
- Adolescent should be encouraged to wear shoe inserts if provided for Achilles tendonitis.
- Be aware of safety concerns associated with adolescent who is wearing cast for Achilles tendon repair.
- Arrange for adolescent's safe exit from classroom in case of an unexpected event that requires students to leave the classroom or school.
- Plan suitable activities devised to meet the needs of adolescent, but limit his or her activity according to directions of health care provider.
- Be aware that casting may be ordered for Achilles tendon tears.

## Attendance Guideline

- Exclusion from school might not be required unless bed rest is ordered by the health care provider. Adolescent may be absent due to physical therapy or if surgery is recommended for Achilles tear.

## Medications

- Anti-inflammatory medications may be used.

## Communication

- Ask parent/caregiver/adolescent about any activity restrictions.
- Ask about medication and treatment schedule.

## Resource

- www.emedx.com

# Sports-Related Injury: Anterior Cruciate Ligament or Medial Collateral Ligament Tear

Also known as: ACL injury, MCL sprain

## Description

An ACL injury is a partial or complete rupture of the anterior cruciate (located by the knee ligament). The ACL is a strong band of tissue that prevents the shin bone (tibia) from extending excessively beyond the thigh bone (femur). An ACL injury results from a violent twisting motion of the knee that can occur when the adolescent athlete lands on his or her feet and then changes directions. The ACL can tear if the knee is hyperextended (bent backward). The MCL is a strong band of tissue on the inside part of the knee. This ligament helps to prevent outward movement of the leg at the knee. Any motion that forcefully moves the leg outward at the knee can cause an MCL sprain. In addition, a hard blow to the outside part of the lower thigh can buckle a knee and injure the MCL.

## Primary Groups Affected

- ACL injury: adolescent athletes involved in basketball, football, soccer, or skiing

- Adolescent athletes involved in any sport that involves jumping, cutting, or twisting movement
- MCL sprain: adolescent athletes involved in football or skiing

## Signs and Symptoms

- Pain, stiffness, tenderness, swelling
- ACL injury: an audible "pop" and "giving way" sensation
- Excessive fluid inside the knee
- Limited range of motion
- MCL sprain: mild to moderate pain, swelling on the inside part of the knee

## Classroom Guidelines

- Encourage appropriate warm-up and cool-down exercises prior to physical activity.
- Arrange for adolescent's safe exit from classroom in case of an unexpected event that requires students to leave the classroom or school.
- Plan suitable activities devised to meet the needs of adolescent, but limit activity according to directions of health care provider.

## Attendance Guideline

- Exclusion from school is not required unless adolescent is required to undergo surgery.

## Medications

- Pain medications may be ordered by health care provider.

## Communication

- Ask parent/caregiver/adolescent about any activity restrictions.
- Ask about medication and treatment schedule.

## Resources

- www.emedx.com
- American Academy of Pediatrics
  www.aap.org
- American Academy of Orthopedic Surgeons
  Prevent Injuries America
  (800) 824-BONES (2663)

# Sports-Related Injury: Elbow Pain

Also known as: tennis elbow (lateral epicondylitis), golfer's elbow (medial epicondylitis)

## Description

Tennis elbow is a painful condition on and around the bony prominence on the outside of the elbow. It is an inflammation of the tendons and muscles of the forearm. These muscles are located above the elbow joint and control wrist and hand movement. Inflammation or a partial tear may occur if these muscles are subjected to excess or repetitive stress. Pain from this inflammation may occur and progress suddenly or gradually. Golfer's elbow is a painful condition on the inside part of the forearm. It is an inflammation of the tendons and muscles that control wrist and hand movement. It usually arises from using the tendons and muscles too much. Occasionally, it may begin after a sudden traumatic movement of the elbow or wrist. Pain from inflammation may occur and progress suddenly or gradually.

## Primary Groups Affected

- Tennis elbow: adolescent athletes who are involved in tennis, racquet sports, bowling, or weight training
- Adolescents who use improper technique or handle size in racquet sports
- Golfer's elbow: adolescent athletes who are involved in golf or who use improper lifting techniques

## Signs and Symptoms

- Tennis elbow: pain and tenderness on the outside part of the elbow

  - Increased pain with any attempt to either play racquet sports or lift heavy objects with the wrist or hand

- Golfer's elbow: pain and tenderness on the inside part of the elbow

  - Pain produced by direct pressure over the muscle group that controls the wrist and hand

## Classroom Guidelines

- Emphasize the American Academy of Orthopedic Surgeons' recommendations when adolescent is playing tennis:

  - Always take time to warm up and stretch.
  - Try to avoid playing tennis on hard surfaces with no "give" such as cement, asphalt, and synthetic courts.
  - Wear heel inserts to absorb the shock and help prevent lower back injuries.
  - Wear tennis shoes with good support to prevent ankle injuries.

- Be knowledgeable about first aid and administer first aid for minor injuries, such as facial cuts and bruises, or for minor tendonitis, strains, or sprains.
- Make sure that the equipment and techniques are used correctly when adolescent is playing tennis or golf.
- Encourage adolescent to avoid overusing the forearm and wrist muscles.
- Encourage adolescent to maintain strong and flexible forearm and wrist muscles.
- Be prepared for emergency situations and have a plan to reach medical personnel in an emergency.

## Attendance Guidelines

- Exclusion from school is not required unless adolescent is to undergo surgery.
- Adolescent may be excluded from tennis, racquetball, weight training, bowling, or golf for a limited time according to health care provider guidelines.

## Medication

- A steroid injection may be ordered if the pain and inflammation continue.

## Communication

- Ask parent/caregiver/adolescent about any activity restrictions.
- Ask about medication and treatment schedule.

## Resources

- www.emedx.com
- American Academy of Pediatrics
  www.aap.org
- American Academy of Orthopedic Surgeons
  Prevent Injuries America
  (800) 824-BONES (2663)

# Sports-Related Injury: "Jumper's Knee"

Also know as: patellar tendonitis

## Description

"Jumper's knee" may occur when there is overuse of the knee. The patellar tendon is a structure that connects the kneecap (patella) to the tibia (shin bone). The patellar tendon becomes inflamed and may be altered in appearance. Some of the more common factors associated with this condition are a rapid increase in the frequency of training, a sudden increase in the intensity of training, a transition from one training method to another, repeated training on a rigid surface, improper mechanics during training, genetic abnormalities of the knee joint, and poor base strength of the quadriceps muscles.

## Primary Groups Affected

- Adolescent athletes who play basketball
- Adolescent athletes who engage in running and jumping sports such as volleyball
- Adolescent athletes who make the transition from football to basketball given that these two sports place different stresses on the knee joint

## Signs and Symptoms

- Pain in the area of the tendon

- Complains of knee feeling "tight":
  - Pain experienced early in workout and after workout is completed
  - Some swelling of the tendon
  - Tendon that feels like it is "squeaking"

## Classroom Guidelines

- Encourage practice as well as rehabilitation and rest. Adolescent athletes are often ordered by health care providers to remain active in their sports.
- Encourage adolescent athletes to avoid overusing the knee through cross-training.
- Encourage adolescent athletes to maintain maximum flexibility and to always warm up before sports.
- Apply ice intermittently to the knee if adolescent complains of pain.

## Attendance Guideline

- Exclusion from school is not required.

## Medications

- Anti-inflammatory and/or pain medications may be ordered.

## Communication

- Ask parent/caregiver/adolescent about any activity restrictions.
- Ask about medication and treatment schedule.

## Resources

- www.emedx.com
- American Academy of Pediatrics
  www.aap.org
- www.athleticadvisor.com
- American Academy of Orthopedic Surgeons
  Preventing Injuries America
  (800) 824-BONES (2663)

# Sports-Related Injury: Shin Splints

Also known as: medial tibial stress syndrome

## Description

Shin splints cause lower leg pain. They are caused by very small tears in the leg muscles at their point of attachment to the shin. There are two types. Anterior shin splints occur in the front portion of the shin (tibia), whereas posterior shin splints occur on the inside (medial) part of the leg along the tibia. Anterior shin splints are due to muscle imbalances, insufficient shock absorption, or toe running. Shin splint injuries may be caused by tightness in the muscles, hard surface running, improper athletic shoes, and/or rapidly increasing the speed or distance of running. It is a typical overuse injury.

## Primary Groups Affected

- Adolescent athletes who engage in exercise and are not properly conditioned
- Adolescents who do not warm up properly or who run on hard or uneven surfaces, wear improper shoes, or have anatomical abnormalities
- Adolescent athletes who are runners, sprinters, figure skaters, or gymnasts

## Signs and Symptoms

- Sometimes produce same signs and symptoms as a stress fracture in the tibia (*see* Sports-Related Injury: Stress Fracture); can progress to stress fracture if not treated properly

- Pain located on the medial (inside) part of the lower leg
- Pain often worse with running or other weight-bearing exercise
- Pain that may be related to training on exceptionally hard surfaces or on tight turns
- Pain that may still occur after stopping the activity
- May complain of tight calf muscles

## Classroom Guidelines

- Encourage adolescent to decrease the pounding force when running.
- Encourage adolescent to use ice for shin splints. Ice area immediately *after* running (never before running).
- Encourage adolescent to participate in proper warm-up and cool-down exercises:
  - Gentle stretching of the posterior leg and thigh muscles
  - Strengthening and flexibility programs that may be ordered to correct muscle imbalances
- Encourage adolescent to wear proper footwear for running activities or to wear a special orthopedic device if ordered by health care provider.
- Be aware that running surfaces should be chosen carefully. Hardest to softest surfaces are as follows: steel, concrete, asphalt, packed dirt, grass, treadmill, bark chips.
- Be aware that when adolescent is recovering from shin splints, the following progression may be followed before returning to road running: water running, cycling, going up stairs repeatedly, using a treadmill (and then road running).

## Attendance Guideline

- Exclusion from school is not required unless adolescent is to attend physical therapy as ordered by health care provider.

## Medications

- Anti-inflammatory medications may be ordered to reduce inflammation and relieve pain.

## Communication

- Ask parent/caregiver/adolescent about any activity restrictions.
- Ask about medication and treatment schedule.

## Resources

- www.ucls.uchicago.edu/activities/sports/girls
- www.spinalhealth.net

# Sport Related Injury: Shoulder Pain

Also known as: rotator cuff tendonitis, rotator cuff tear, impingement syndrome

## Description

The shoulder is prone to a great many injuries from trauma. Acute (sudden) shoulder pain is commonly caused by fractures, sprains, or strains. Sprains of the shoulder are most often due to falls on the point of the shoulder. Because of the shoulder's shallow socket and lack of ligaments, any weakness of the small rotator cuff muscles makes it easy for the head of the shoulder to slide part-way out of the socket, which is a partial dislocation (subluxation). Chronic shoulder pain (pain over time) is often known as rotator cuff tendonitis or a rotator cuff tear. Rotator cuff injuries may also be called impingement syndrome. Impingement occurs when inflammation or bony spurs narrow the space available for the rotator cuff tendons. Rotator cuff tendonitis and tears occur either from a sudden violent movement of the shoulder or from chronic overuse that damages the four muscles that stabilize the shoulder and allow the arm to move through a full range of motion.

## Primary Groups Affected

- Adolescents who participate in sports associated with repetitious and constant overhead positioning such as tennis, basketball, baseball, softball, and football
- Adolescents who participate in long-distance competitive swimming

- Adolescents who participate in gymnastics (usually more severe rotator cuff muscle injuries)
- Adolescents who golf (external rotation of the shoulder)

## Signs and Symptoms

- Pain and tenderness in the shoulders when engaged in over-head arm activities
- Weakness and decreased range of motion
- Swelling in the shoulder
- Displaced fracture may be obvious with swelling and bone protrusion
- Noticeable deformity at the shoulder joint

## Classroom Guidelines

- Make sure that all adolescents with sudden shoulder pain seek medical attention immediately. Seek help according to school policy.
- Do not move adolescent's shoulder if pain began suddenly.
- Apply ice if swelling is observed.
- Encourage adolescent to avoid repetitive overhead activity and to improve flexibility of the shoulder muscles.
- Encourage adolescent to participate in warm-up and cool-down exercises prior to sporting events.
- Encourage adolescent not to overuse the shoulder. Have adolescent start out slowly with any new physical activity and to gradually increase the training program.
- Adolescent should never be allowed to "work through the pain."
- Teach adolescent that prevention of rotator cuff tears is best accomplished by maintaining a strong and stable shoulder through a prescribed exercise regimen. Avoiding repetitive over-head activity and improving flexibility of the shoulder may help.
- Adolescent should refrain from activities that contributed to the injury and should adhere to health care provider's instructions.

## Attendance Guideline

- Exclusion from school is not required unless adolescent undergoes surgery or is ordered to attend physical therapy.

## Medications

- Anti-inflammatory medication or steroid injections may be ordered.

## Communication

- Notify parent/caregiver of injury and urge to seek medical care from health care provider.
- Request information from parent/caregiver/adolescent about any restrictions, medications, or special accommodations.
- Request release to participate in sports/physical activity from health care provider.

## Resources

- www.emedx.com
- www.aap.org

# Sports Related Injury: Stress Fracture

Also known as: tibial and fibular stress fractures

## Description

Stress fractures are very common in adolescent athletes. A stress fracture of the tibia is a crack that develops in the shin bone over time from repetitive stress on the bone. Normally, muscles absorb the shock put on the legs during activity. When there is continuous pounding of the legs during an activity, the muscles tire and lose much of their ability to absorb shock. When the muscles do not absorb the shock very well, there is increased stress on the bone. The bone cannot endure the increased stress, so it begins to crack. X rays or bone scans may be ordered to detect stress fractures. Stress fractures may be very difficult to diagnose because they might not show up on X rays when they first develop. Fractures often heal without casting or surgery.

## Primary Groups Affected

- Adolescent athletes who engage in exercises and are not properly conditioned
- Adolescent athletes who do not warm up or cool down properly
- Athletes who are runners, sprinters, figure skaters, or gymnasts

## Signs and Symptoms

- Pain at the start of running activity
- Pain reproduced by jumping on affected leg

- Generalized tenderness over the medial part of the tibia or lateral aspect of the fibula
- Pain that suddenly increases
- Pain that can be felt not only when running but also when walking

## Classroom Guidelines

- Encourage adolescent to decrease the pounding force when running. Otherwise, adolescent might need to refrain from running for 6 to 8 weeks.
- Be aware of safety concerns associated with an adolescent who is wearing a cast (*see* Procedure C) or using crutches.
- Arrange for adolescent's safe exit from classroom in case of an unexpected event that requires students to leave the classroom or school.
- Plan suitable activities devised to meet the needs of adolescent, but limit activity according to directions of health care provider.
- Encourage adolescent to rest and prop up the extremity until there is no longer any tenderness.
- Encourage adolescent to ice the affected area.
- Encourage adolescent to participate in biking or swimming or to engage in other activities that do not produce pain (with approval from health care provider).
- Encourage adolescent to wear proper footwear and/or to use arch supports for running activities.

## Attendance Guideline

- Exclusion from school is generally not required unless adolescent is to undergo surgery.

## Medications

- Anti-inflammatory medications may be used to decrease inflammation and reduce pain.

## Communication

- Ask parent/caregiver/adolescent about any activity restrictions.
- Ask about medication and treatment schedule.

## Resources

- www.ucls.uchicago.edu/activities/sports/girls
- www.spinalhealth.net
- www.aap.org/advocacy/releases/sportsinjury.htm

# Staph Infection

Also known as: *Staphylococcus aureus* infection, impetigo, pyoderma, folliculitis, cellulitis, scalded skin syndrome

## Description

*Staphylococcus aureus* is a bacterial organism that is normally found on the skin; therefore, it is the organism most commonly involved in skin infections. Many different kinds of infections, such as impetigo, pyoderma, boils, cellulitis, and scalded skin syndrome, are caused by *S. aureus.* Impetigo frequently is found around the nose and mouth of toddlers and preschoolers and is more commonly seen during the summer months. It begins with a reddened area that becomes full of fluid (vesicle) and eventually opens and oozes, leaving a heavy, honey-colored crust that causes itching. Pyoderma involves a deeper infection from *S. aureus* into the skin leading to fever and inflammation and pus at the affected area. Folliculitis means that a hair follicle becomes infected and can cause a pimple, a boil (furuncle), or multiple boils (carbuncle). It can be caused when hair is pulled back tightly with barrettes or rubber bands. Folliculitis can range from a mild inflammation at one hair follicle site to multiple sites that can be very inflamed and cause fever and extreme tiredness. More severe folliculitis might need to be opened, drained, and treated with antibiotics. Cellulitis involves tissue beneath the skin leading to inflammation of tissue and local lymph nodes. With cellulitis, an abscess, fever, and extreme tiredness are common and often require hospitalization and antibiotics. The skin has a "sandpaper" reddened appearance, with areas of fluid-filled pockets that may require hospitalization and antibiotic treatment.

## Primary Groups Affected

- Any age group

## Signs and Symptoms

- Fluid-filled areas of skin called vesicles
- Reddened inflamed skin
- Honey-colored crusted areas
- Itching
- Pus-filled lesions/hair follicles
- Fever
- Extreme tiredness
- Swollen lymph nodes (glands)
- "Sandpaper" reddened skin

## Classroom Guidelines

- Ensure proper hand washing (*see* Procedure A).
- Remind adolescent not to scratch or rub affected area given that infection is found under the fingernails.

## Attendance Guideline

- Exclusion from school is required until areas are crusted over.

## Medications

- Antibiotics, medications, or ointments may be prescribed.

## Communication

- Ask parent/caregiver how medication should be given to adolescent.

## Resource

- www.kidshealth.org

# Stomachache

## Description

Stomachaches are a common complaint of children. Some adolescents experience lactose intolerance and complain of a "hurting" stomach 30 minutes to 1 hour after eating a lunch that includes milk and/or other dairy products. In addition, some adolescents complain of stomachaches as a response to stress. It is important that stomachaches be taken seriously given that they may be a symptom of a more serious health problem.

## Primary Groups Affected

- Adolescents of any age

## Signs and Symptoms

- Pain in stomach
- Nausea or vomiting

## Classroom Guidelines

- Notify parent/caregiver and urge to see health care provider if adolescent complains of severe stomach pain, if pain does not go away after 30 minutes, or if adolescent is experiencing difficulty in breathing.
- Allow adolescent to lie down. Provide a receptacle in case of vomiting.
- Do not give adolescent anything to eat.
- If adolescent has acute pain in middle of abdomen that settles in lower right abdomen, increased temperature, nausea or vomiting, and diarrhea, notify parent/caregiver and urge to seek emergency care (*see* Procedure F)—**911**.

- If adolescent is diagnosed as lactose intolerant, adhere to restrictions and inform cafeteria personnel so that they do not encourage adolescent to drink milk and other dairy products with lactose.

## Attendance Guideline

- Exclusion from school is not required unless complaints of pain are for an extended period of time.

## Medications

- Over-the-counter stomach relief medications may be administered with parent/caregiver permission or per school policy.

## Communication

- Notify parent/caregiver if adolescent is exhibiting symptoms of stomachaches.
- Ask about possibility of adolescent being lactose intolerant. (A higher incidence is found in Asian, Southern European, Arab, Israeli, and African American children.)

## Resource

- www.cdc.gov

# Strep Throat

Also known as: tonsillitis, pharyngitis

## Description

Strep throat is one of the most common bacterial infections of the throat. The infection is caused by group A streptococcus bacteria. This infection can be confirmed only by a throat culture. This illness is spread by direct close contact with other people via respiratory droplets (coughing or sneezing). Untreated people are most infectious for 2 to 3 weeks after the onset of the infection. Symptoms appear 1 to 5 days after exposure to the infection. People are no longer infectious within 24 hours after treatment begins. Without treatment, serious complications can occur such as scarlet fever, rheumatic fever, abscesses, and kidney problems.

## Primary Groups Affected

- Most common between ages 2 and 14 years

## Signs and Symptoms

- Sudden onset of sore throat
- Fever of 102 to 104 degrees
- Vomiting
- Tiredness
- Difficulty in swallowing
- Unable to eat
- Muffled voice
- Skin rash

## Classroom Guidelines

- Dispense medications according to school regulations.
- Allow adolescent to drink plenty of fluids.
- Remind adolescent not to share drinking glasses, straws, or eating utensils.
- Encourage proper hand washing (*see* Part III, Procedure A).
- Remind adolescent to cover nose and mouth when sneezing or coughing.
- Notify caregivers/parents of all adolescents in classroom with a history of congenital heart defects, organ transplantation, chemotherapy treatment, or immune deficiency disorders.

## Attendance Guideline

- May return to school after being on antibiotics for a full 24 hours and fever has resolved.

## Communication

- Ask parent/caregiver/adolescent about the schedule for medications.

## Resources

- www.kidshealth.org
- www.naid.nih.gov/factsheets

# Suicide

Also known as: taking one's life

## Description

Suicidal behavior is defined as either the behavior and thoughts leading up to the act of suicide or the act of taking one's own life. The end result—survival or death—is described as either attempted or completed suicide. Suicide is not a random act. It is a way out of a problem, a dilemma, or an unbearable situation.

## Primary Groups Affected

- Suicide is the third leading cause of death among young people ages 15 to 24 years. This rate has tripled since 1950.
- Approximately one fifth (20.5%) of students in the 9th through 12th grades have seriously thought about attempting suicide, 16% have made a specific suicide plan, and 8% have actually attempted suicide in any given recent year.
- The risk is highest for Euro-American male adolescents.

## Signs and Symptoms

- Suicide is often associated with a diagnosis of bipolar disorder (manic-depressive disorder).
- Verbal cues may include statements such as "It won't matter much longer," "I won't be here when you come back on Monday," and "Will you miss me when I'm gone?"
- Behavioral cues may include a change in school performance, an increased tendency toward accidents, and a desire to give away personal belongings.

- Suicidal intentions may show up in writing, drawings, or doodling.
- A pervading sense of hopelessness has a very strong association with suicide.
- A suicidal adolescent often experiences thoughts of self-blame, negative self-evaluation, and dire expectations for the future.
- Adolescents who commit suicide often do so during periods of high stress in their lives.
- Lesbian and gay adolescents are six times more likely to commit suicide than are heterosexual adolescents.
- When adolescent suicides are publicized by the news media or when there are television dramas about suicide, the rate of adolescent suicide increases for several weeks following the event. Suicides that are inspired by suicides in this way are called copycat suicides.

## Classroom Guidelines

- Remember that adolescents who are suicidal are afraid. They fear that no one cares.
- Understand that adolescents who are suicidal might not introduce the topic because they fear being judged or considered weak or "crazy."
- Introduce the topic by asking, "Often, when adolescents are feeling very upset or depressed, they have thoughts of killing themselves. Have you had any thoughts of wanting to kill yourself?"
- Take all adolescent suicidal thoughts very seriously.
- If adolescent is actively suicidal—having both a plan and the means—someone must remain with the person at all times until he or she can be moved to a safe environment. Immediate evaluation at a hospital is mandatory. A parent/caregiver can be called for transport, or if all else fails an ambulance can be used to transport the suicidal adolescent to the emergency room.

## Attendance Guideline

- Exclusion from school is not required unless adolescent is acutely suicidal.

## Medication

- No medication is required.

## Communication

- Inform parent/caregiver immediately when there are any signs of suicidal thoughts or behaviors.

## Resources

- Crisis Line
  (800) 521-4000

- Suicide Hotline
  (888) SUICIDE (784-2433)

- Light for Life Foundation for the Prevention of Youth Suicide
  P.O. Box 644
  Westminster, CO 80030-0644
  (303) 429-3530
  www.yellowribbon.org

# Swimmer's Ear/Foreign Object in Ear

Also known as: external otitis, otitis externa

## Description

Swimmer's ear is an inflammation or infection in the ear canal. The inflammation occurs because the environment in the ear canal has been changed by swimming or bathing, increased humidity, decreased earwax, trauma, or even a foreign body such as an eraser, a peanut, or a bean. In rare situations, the infection may lead to hearing loss.

## Primary Groups Affected

- Anyone spending long periods of time in water
- Preschool and school-age children who might place foreign bodies in their ears

## Signs and Symptoms

- Severe ear pain that increases when outer ear is touched or moved
- May experience itching in ear canal
- Greenish-yellowish discharge or pus from ear
- Hearing loss
- Fever
- Swollen ear canal

## Classroom Guidelines

*Swimmer's Ear*

- Prevention includes spending less than 1 hour in water; allowing ears to completely dry (1 to 2 hours) before returning to water; shaking head and using corner of towel to dry ears; and placing a 50/50 combination of alcohol and white vinegar (SwimEar) in both ears in morning, at bedtime, and after each swimming session, leaving in ears for 5 minutes (avoid cotton-tipped applicators or bobby pins).

*Foreign Body*

- Soft objects, such as paper and insects, can be removed with a forceps/tweezers.
- Small hard objects, such as pebbles, can be removed with water irrigation.
- Vegetative matter, such as beans and pasta, should not be removed with irrigation because this will cause the object to swell and become more difficult to remove.

## Attendance Guideline

- Exclusion from school is not required.

## Medications

- An analgesic such as acetaminophen (Tylenol) or ibuprofen (Motrin) may be taken for pain.
- Antibacterial and corticosteroid preparations may be instilled into ear canal for 7 to 10 days.

## Communication

- Ask parent/caregiver about schedule of medications.
- Ask how long to keep adolescent out of water (usually 10 to 14 days).

## Resource

- www.kidshealth.org

# Tattooing Infection/Reaction

## Description

Tattooing infection/reaction is a response of the body to any indelible design, letter, scroll, figure, symbol, or other mark placed with the aid of needles or other instruments and done by scarring on or under the skin.

## Primary Groups Affected

- Any adolescents with tattoos

## Signs and Symptoms

- Infection reactions to a tattoo may include pain, redness, swelling, increased body temperature (above 99 degrees), drainage that has a foul smell, fatigue, and nausea or vomiting.
- Allergic reactions can occur due to dyes and pigments. Nodules may form around tattoo.
- Extensive scarring may occur.
- Skin reactions are increased with red and yellow dyes. In rare cases, hepatitis B and C can be contracted from the tattooing process.

## Classroom Guidelines

- Notify parent/caregiver/school health provider if adolescent complains of any of any symptoms after getting tattoo.
- Wash tattoo using warm soapy water, rinse with cold water, and pat dry. Do not rub with towel.

- Because tattoo should not be directly exposed to sunlight for 4 weeks, you might need to restrict outdoor activity for adolescent.
- Instruct adolescent to avoid school (public) pools until infection is healed.

## Attendance Guideline

- Exclusion from school is required when adolescent has increased temperature.

## Medications

- Antibiotics and analgesics may be ordered for adolescent, and the schedule of medications must be followed.

## Communication

- Ask parent/caregiver/adolescent about any special restrictions or medications due to the tattoo.

## Resource

- www.mayoclinic.org

# Testicular Cancer

Also known as: TC

## Description

Cancer is a disease of the body's cells. Too many cells are produced that form tumors that can invade and destroy nearby health tissues and organs. Cancerous cells can also spread, or metastasize, to other parts of the body and form new tumors.

## Primary Groups Affected

- Testicular cancer is the most common cancer in young men between ages 15 and 35 years.
- Children born with an undescended testicle have an increased risk of getting testicular cancer regardless of whether surgery is done to correct the problem.
- Euro-Americans are at higher risk for getting testicular cancer than are Hispanic Americans, African Americans, and Asian Americans.

## Signs and Symptoms

- A lump the size of a pea or marble that may or may not be painful
- A hardening or change in size of the testicle
- A feeling of heaviness in the scrotum
- A dull ache in the lower abdomen or in the groin
- A sudden collection of fluid in the scrotum

## Classroom Guidelines

- Recognize that all adolescent males should be given information about testicular self-exam (*see* Procedure H).

- Understand that it is natural that an adolescent with testicular cancer will have many different emotions such as fear, anger, despair, hope, and courage. Do not force adolescent to talk about his feelings, but be available if he asks you to be a confidant.
- Realize that concerns about the future are common, including concerns about medical tests and treatments, sexuality, and fertility.

## Attendance Guideline

- Exclusion from school is not required.

## Medication

- No medication is required.

## Communication

- Recognize that parent/caregiver should be involved in providing information about testicular self-exam. This may be new information for parent/caregiver.
- Stress that it is just as important for boys to do testicular self-exams as it is for girls to do breast self-exams.
- Explain that testicular cancer is a disease that primarily affects young men and has a good prognosis if caught during the early stages.

## Resources

- American Cancer Society
  1599 Clifton Road, N.E.
  Atlanta, GA 30329
  (800) ACS-2345

- Testicular Cancer Resource Center
  www.acor.org/diseases/tc

# Thyroid Disorder

Also known as: thyroiditis, Hashimoto's disease

## Description

Hashimoto's disease is the most frequent cause of thyroid enlargement in adolescents. This disorder accounts for the largest percentage of juvenile hypothyroidism (low levels of thyroid hormone). Hashimoto's disease affects body growth and results in childhood obesity.

## Primary Groups Affected

- Found more frequently in girls after age 6 years, peaking during adolescence
- Occurs more frequently in Euro-American adolescents than in African American adolescents
- Adolescents living with diabetes mellitus, Down syndrome, or Turner syndrome

## Signs and Symptoms

- Short stature
- Weight gain
- Enlarged thyroid gland that may be noticeable when swallowing
- Fatigue
- Falls asleep easily
- Puffy face
- Cold extremities, discolored patchy skin
- Change in activity level

## Classroom Guidelines

- Understand that adolescents with long-standing hypothyroidism may experience marked changes in classroom behavior and may have difficulty in concentrating, complain of feeling cold and having a lack of energy, and appear tired even when awake.
- Be aware that an adolescent living with this disease may wear a sweater even in warm weather and complain of being cold.

## Attendance Guideline

- Exclusion from school is not required.

## Medications

- Synthetic thyroid hormone usually must be taken daily on a time schedule.

## Communication

- Ask parent/caregiver/adolescent about schedule of medications to be given at school.
- Discuss any ongoing medical recommendations.

## Resources

- www.mayoclinic.org
- www.thyroid.ca
- www.thyroid.about.com

# Tooth Abscess

Also known as: oral abscess

## Description

A tooth abscess is an accumulation of pus near the tooth root that causes the gum to be swollen and reddened and that causes moderate to severe pain. One side of the face may appear to be swollen. It occurs more frequently in primary teeth and sometimes follows a filling fracture or tooth fracture.

## Primary Groups Affected

- Adolescents of any age

## Signs and Symptoms

- Pain with pressure
- Pain with extremely hot or cold fluids
- Swollen gum
- Swollen jaw
- Irritability
- Holding hand to area

## Classroom Guidelines

- Place a cold compress on affected side of face to decrease pain.
- Notify parent/caregiver and urge immediate care by a dentist.

## Attendance Guideline

- Exclusion from school is not required.

## Medications

- Pain, anti-inflammatory, and antibiotic medications may be prescribed and administered as directed by health care provider. Antibiotic therapy is usually for 7 to 14 days as ordered by health care provider.

## Communication

- Notify parent/caregiver and urge immediate follow-up with a dentist.
- Ask parent/caregiver/adolescent about treatment given.
- Ask about medication schedule.

## Resource

- www.vh.org/pediatric/patient/pediatrics/cqqa/toothinjury. html

# Toothache

Also known as: dental caries, cavities

## Description

Toothache usually refers to pain around the teeth or jaw. Toothaches are one of the most common problems that affect children at all ages. It is the leading mouth problem in children. Toothaches due to cavities must be taken seriously because if they are left untreated, they can cause the loss of the involved teeth. However, a cracked tooth (fractured tooth), an exposed tooth root, gum disease, and diseases of the jaw can also cause toothaches. Sometimes a toothache in an adolescent has nothing to do with the teeth and is a symptom of an earache, a sinus infection, or (in more serious cases) a heart problem.

## Primary Groups Affected

- Adolescents of any age

## Signs and Symptoms

- Adolescent complains of a throbbing sensation that can be either continuous or intermittent in mouth.
- Jaw may be swollen.
- Adolescent complains of pain when eating sweets and extremes of hot and cold liquids.
- Adolescent with toothach due to cracked tooth may complain of pain after chewing or biting hard objects such as hard candies, pencils, and nuts.

## Classroom Guidelines

- Place a warm cloth over side of face affected by pain.
- Urge adolescent not to bite or chew on pencils, pens, and the like.

## Attendance Guideline

- Exclusion from school is not required.

## Medications

- Pain medications may be prescribed and administered as directed by health care provider.

## Communication

- Notify parent/caregiver and urge care and follow-up with a dentist.
- Ask parent/caregiver/adolescent about medication schedule.

## Resources

- www.vh.org/pediatric/patient/pediatrics/cqqa/toothinjury.html
- www.medicinenet.com
- www.floss.com
- www.tsa.mgh.harvard.edu

# Tooth Injury

Also known as: knocked out tooth, fractured tooth, broken tooth, dental emergency

## Description

Any injury to the head and neck region in adolescents can cause a fracture or even knock out a tooth. A child's front upper teeth are most at risk for being injured. A dentist may restore baby teeth that are broken. However, baby teeth that are knocked out completely are not usually reimplanted. If an adolescent has a permanent tooth knocked out, the teacher must respond *quickly* for the best chance of saving the tooth.

## Primary Groups Affected

- Adolescents who are active or who engage in physical contact sports

## Signs and Symptoms

- Missing tooth or teeth
- Bleeding gums

## Classroom Guidelines

- Be aware that a knocked out tooth may cause a large amount of bleeding and frighten adolescent.
- Use a calm approach and provide gentle reassurance to reduce adolescent's anxiety.
- Wash hands and put on disposable gloves (*see* Procedure A).

- Locate tooth after instructing students who are assisting in this process not to touch tooth but rather to notify you if it is found.
- Pick up tooth by the crown (white part), as opposed to the root, and rinse gently with milk, contact lens solution, child's saliva, or saline (a last resort is water if the tooth is dirty). Do not scrub or scrape tooth clean, even if the tooth has been found outdoors. Be sure to insert plug in sink or basin to avoid dropping tooth down drain.
- Insert tooth into socket and have adolescent maintain tooth in place. If adolescent is reluctant to have tooth put into socket, or if you fear that adolescent may swallow tooth, place tooth in a commercially available Tooth Saver or Save-A-Tooth jar. These jars contain an ideal medium for transport of a tooth. If these products are not available, use milk; if milk is not available, place tooth in water. (A tooth that is left to dry must be replanted within 30 minutes; whereas a tooth that is kept in milk must be reimplanted within 30 minutes to 1 hour; after 90 minutes, there is little chance for successful replanting of tooth.) If broken tooth fragment is found, it should be taken to the dentist for bonding. Tooth fragments should also be kept moist.
- Place clean gauze over tooth socket, making sure that the dressing allows adolescent to bite on the gauze and not the other teeth.
- Remove gloves and wash hands.
- Notify parent/caregiver and urge immediate care by dentist.
- Encourage adolescents to use mouth guards when participating in sports.

## Attendance Guideline

- Exclusion from school is not required.

## Medications

- Pain and antibiotic medications may be prescribed and administered as directed by health care provider.

## Communication

- Notify parent/caregiver as soon as possible of injury and urge immediate follow-up with dentist.

- Ask parent/caregiver/adolescent about any activity restrictions.
- Ask about medication schedule.

## Resources

- www.vh.org/pediatric/patient/pediatrics/cqqa/toothinjury.html
- www.schoolnurse.com

# Tourette's Syndrome

Also known as: tic disorder

## Description

Tourette's is a disorder of the brain characterized by sudden, rapid, recurrent motor and vocal tics.

## Primary Groups Affected

- Usually starts between ages 5 and 9 years
- Can begin as early as age 1 year and as late as adolescence
- More frequent among males

## Signs and Symptoms

- Motor tics include eye blinking, facial grimacing, head jerking, neck movements, shoulder shrugging, hand movements, hopping, touching people, and pulling on clothing.
- Common vocal tics include throat clearing, grunting, coughing, sniffing, stuttering, yelling, screaming, and making animal sounds.
- A small minority exhibit copralalia (the involuntary use of obscene words).
- Fully 80% also have ADHD (*see* Attention Deficit/Hyperactivity Disorder).
- The majority (50% to 70%) exhibit obsessive and compulsive symptoms (*see* Obsessive-Compulsive Disorder).

## Classroom Guidelines

- Understand that adolescents with Tourette's syndrome need assistance to maintain healthy self-esteem in the face of their seemingly "strange" behavior.
- Create a classroom climate of acceptance, belonging, and security. Do not allow teasing or bullying of adolescent with Tourette's syndrome.
- Explain to all students the basic concepts of this disorder and the involuntary nature of the various tics.
- Celebrate adolescent's achievements, no matter how small.
- Encourage positive self-talk such as "I can do this" and "I am a worthwhile person."
- At the end of the day, have adolescent review the following questions:

  - What have I tried that was new today?
  - What have I done today better than before?
  - Who are the people I have helped today?
  - Who has helped me today?
  - What gave me the most pleasure today?

## Attendance Guideline

- Exclusion from school is not required.

## Medications

- Clonidine (Catapres), an antihypertensive medication, reduces motor tics in many individuals with Tourette's syndrome.
- A nicotine patch may have a beneficial effect in relieving some of the symptoms.

## Communication

- Ask parent/caregiver what coping mechanisms adolescent has developed to cope with or disguise the motor and vocal tics.
- Communicate significant social problems with adolescent's peers.

## Resource

- Tourette Syndrome Association
  42-40 Bell Boulevard
  Bayside, NY 11361-2820
  (800) 237-0717
  www.tsa.mgh.harvard.edu

# Toxic Shock Syndrome

Also known as: TSS

## Description

Toxic shock syndrome, first identified about 20 years ago, is caused by toxins produced by *Staphylococcus aureus*. Most TSS cases have been associated with tampon use. It is postulated that the tampon (especially the super absorbent types) cause small tears in the vagina and allow the bacteria toxin to enter the body. It is also suggested that stagnating blood in the tampon encourages bacteria growth. For these reasons, super absorbent tampons are no longer sold. Also, women who use tampons are encouraged to alternate tampons with sanitary pads and to use pads during sleep hours. There have been some cases of TSS reported with the contraceptive sponge and diaphragm use. TSS is a systemic infection (all through the body) and can cause death (5% of cases). If TSS symptoms are suspected, the tampon should be removed immediately because this stops bacteria growth in 80% of cases. Treatment for TSS usually involves hospitalization with intravenous antibiotics. An adolescent with TSS has a 30% chance of experiencing a second episode in the future.

## Primary Groups Affected

- Menstruating women
- Women using barrier contraception (diaphragm)
- Persons who have had nasal surgery

## Signs and Symptoms

- High fever (101 degrees or higher)
- Diarrhea
- Nausea or vomiting
- Red, sunburn-like rash (develops after 1 or 2 days)
- Peeling skin
- Severe muscle aching
- Disorientation
- Sudden fall in blood pressure
- Fainting
- Sore throat
- Redness of eyes, mouth, throat, and vagina

## Classroom Guidelines

- Include the following information about TSS when discussing menstruation with adolescents:

  - Wash hands before tampon insertion.
  - Change tampons frequently.
  - Use sanitary pads during sleep hours.
  - Do not leave diaphragm in place longer than recommended time.
  - Avoid use of diaphragm during menstruation and childbirth.

## Attendance Guideline

- Exclusion from school is not required.

## Medications

- Usually an antibiotic is prescribed by health care provider.
- Antibiotic should be given until it is all gone.
- Acetaminophen (Tylenol) may be given for fever and pain relief with parent/caregiver permission.

## Communication

- Ask parent/caregiver about schedule of antibiotics so as to support/monitor compliance with treatment plan.

## Resources

- www.cdc.gov
- www.womens-health.com
- www.findarticles.com

# Tuberculosis

Also known as: TB

## Description

Tuberculosis is a highly contagious, chronic bacterial infection that affects the lungs, although in some cases other organs of the body are involved. The tubercle bacillus (responsible germ) is found in air droplets from someone infected with the tubercle bacillus when that person coughs or sneezes. All adolescents should be screened annually for TB if they live in high-risk situations such as overcrowded living conditions and homeless shelters. Adolescents who have emigrated from another country with many cases of TB are also at risk. It is important for teachers to be aware that there is a difference between being infected with tubercle bacillus and having "active" TB disease. Tuberculosis infection occurs when a person has the TB bacteria in his or her body, has no symptoms, and is not contagious. The risk of developing the disease for such a person is highest during the first 1 to 2 years after infection. Having active TB means that the person has symptoms and is contagious.

## Primary Groups Affected

- Minority children seemingly more susceptible than Euro-American children
- Adolescents who are malnourished
- Adolescents living with HIV/AIDS
- Adolescents who have lived in, who emigrated from, or traveled to other countries where TB is prevalent such as Latin America and the Caribbean, Africa, Asia, Eastern Europe, and Russia
- Adolescents living in poverty, migrant camps, or homeless shelters

- Adolescents living in medically underserved communities
- Adolescents with family members diagnosed with TB

## Signs and Symptoms

- Fatigue
- Fever
- Loss of weight
- Night sweats
- Coughing
- Chills
- Enlarged lymph nodes (rarely)
- Positive tuberculin test
- Positive chest X ray

## Classroom Guidelines

- Explain to other students in classroom the need to be tested.
- Be sensitive to the emotional needs of adolescent living with tuberculosis.
- Explain that adolescent may be tested again in 10 to 12 weeks.
- Explain to adolescent that TB can almost always be cured with medicine.
- Plan suitable activities devised to meet the needs of adolescent living with tuberculosis, but limit activity according to directions of health care provider.
- If possible, open windows or place a fan in windows to pull in fresh air.

## Attendance Guidelines

- Exclusion from school is required for adolescent with active TB of the lungs or throat; however, once treatment begins, adolescent is not usually considered contagious provided that the treatment regimen is followed as prescribed by health care provider.
- Exclusion from school is not required for adolescent who tests positive but does not have symptoms.
- Health care provider or local health department will determine when adolescent can safely return to school.

## Medications

- Several different drugs are prescribed for adolescents with active TB to kill all bacteria.

## Communication

- Ask parent/caregiver/adolescent about any activity restrictions.
- Ask about schedule of medications to be given and side effects. It takes about 6 to 12 months of medication to kill all of the TB bacteria.
- Ask for suggestions as to how adolescent may devise a drug reminder schedule for medications that need to be taken during school hours.

## Resources

- www.mayoclinic.org
- www.cdc.gov

# Urinary Tract Infection

Also known as: UTI, bladder infection (cystitis), urethra infection (urethritis), kidney infection (pyelonephritis)

## Description

A urinary tract infection may involve the bladder, urethra, or kidneys and is caused by bacteria (germs) that get into the urinary tract. The causes of UTI include bubble baths, wearing tight-fitting clothing, wearing nylon underwear, holding urine too long, and (girls) wiping from back to front (which brings bacteria from the bowel toward the urethra/bladder).

## Primary Groups Affected

- Females more likely than males
- Most common between ages 4 and 8 years

## Signs and Symptoms

- Complains of pain or burning when urinating
- Complains of stomach or lower back pain
- Urine that smells bad and/or looks cloudy or reddish from blood
- Needs to go to bathroom more often than usual
- May have fever
- May vomit

## Classroom Guidelines

- Dispense medications according to school regulations.
- Reinforce instructions for girls to wipe from front to back after they urinate.
- Reinforce instructions to urinate regularly and not to hold urine for long time.
- Be aware that in the case of repeated UTIs, you might need to encourage urination every 30 minutes to 2 hours.
- Provide opportunities for drinking plenty of water (8 to 10 glasses per day).
- Encourage adolescent to go to the bathroom frequently.

## Attendance Guideline

- Exclusion from school is not required.

## Medications

- Usually an antibiotic is prescribed by health care provider.
- Antibiotic should be given until it is all gone.
- Acetaminophen (Tylenol) may be given for fever and pain relief with parent/caregiver permission.

## Communication

- Ask parent/caregiver about schedule of antibiotics so as to support/monitor compliance with treatment plan.

## Resource

- www.familydoctor.org

# Vaginitis

Also known as: yeast infection, candidiasis, fungal infection, bacterial vaginosis (BV), gardnerella

## Description

Vaginitis occurs when the normal vaginal flora and pH level have been disturbed. This disturbance can be caused by antibiotics, hormones, contraceptives, douches, vaginal medications, sexual intercourse, sexually transmitted diseases, stress, and changes in sexual partners. Bacterial vaginosis (BV) is the most commonly occurring vaginitis and is caused by an overgrowth of bacteria. Candidal vaginitis (yeast infection) is the second most common type of vaginitis and is caused by any overgrowth of yeast. Both share some common symptoms, such as itching, irritation, and discharge, but have different medications used for treatment. For this reason, women who self-treat with over-the-counter medications often do not receive satisfactory relief or have reoccurrence of symptoms due to misdiagnosis. It is paramount to have the initial diagnosis made by a health care provider to get the proper medication. Bacterial vaginosis is not a sexually transmitted disease, although it is more common in women who are sexually active. Male partners do not need to be treated if the diagnosis is bacterial vaginosis. Partners might need some treatment if they are experiencing symptoms of candidal vaginitis such as itching and irritation.

## Primary Groups Affected

- Bacterial vaginosis: females (generally those who are sexually active)
- Candidal vaginitis: anyone (especially after receiving antibiotics, diabetic or immunocompromised conditions)

## Signs and Symptoms

### *Bacterial Vaginosis*

- Malodorous "fishy" discharge, especially after intercourse or around menstrual cycle
- White or gray thin discharge
- Itching and irritation of the vulva and vagina

### *Candidal Vaginitis*

- Itching and irritation of the vulva and vagina
- Thick white discharge without odor

## Classroom Guidelines

- Reinforce the importance of being diagnosed by a health care provider.
- Reinforce that hygiene practices that decrease development of vaginitis include the following:

  - Wear cotton underwear. Remove at bedtime.
  - Limit use of tampons.
  - Limit tub baths, especially with scented soaps.
  - Do not douche for any reason.

## Attendance Guideline

- Exclusion from school is not required.

## Medications

- Prescription medications for both bacterial vaginosis (antibiotic) and candidal vaginitis (antifungal) are available in oral medications and in vaginal creams generally used at bedtime.
- Over-the-counter vaginal creams are available for candidal vaginitis, but only after proper diagnosis.

## Communication

- Ask parent/caregiver about schedule of medications so as to support/monitor compliance with treatment plan.

## Resource

- www.vaginalinfections.com

# PART III

## Health Policies and Procedures

# Procedure A

## Hand Washing

Hand washing is the single most effective practice that prevents the spread of germs that can cause colds, flu, pneumonia, diarrhea, and sometimes even more serious diseases. You can stop the spread of germs by washing your hands and teaching your students good hand-washing practices.

### Steps to Good Hand Washing

**Step 1:** Wet both hands with warm running water.

**Step 2:** Apply a liquid soap (dime to quarter size) or bar soap (antibacterial soaps may be used but are not required) to hands and rub hands together for 15 to 20 seconds. Wash all surfaces thoroughly, including wrists, palms, backs of hands, fingers, and under fingernails. (It takes approximately 20 seconds to say the Pledge of Allegiance, sing the *Happy Birthday* song, or recite the poem *Twinkle, Twinkle, Little Star*.) Rub longer if hands are visibly soiled. This is the most important step of washing away germs.

**Step 3:** Rinse hands thoroughly under running water. Leave the water running until after drying hands.

**Step 4:** Dry hands with a single-use paper towel. Pat your skin to avoid cracking or chapping. Activate hand dryer with your elbow.

**Step 5:** Turn off water with a different dry paper towel to prevent the germs from the faucet from getting back on your hands.

**Step 6:** Consider applying a hand lotion after washing to prevent and soothe dry skin.

## When You Should Wash Your Hands

- *Before* you eat food, treat a cut or sore, tend to a sick child, or insert or remove contact lenses
- *After* you go to the bathroom, help a child with toileting, help a child who is vomiting or has diarrhea, touch an animal or pet cages, take off plastic or vinyl gloves, handle garbage, blow your nose, cough or sneeze, or handle money (or when your hands are visibly dirty and handle uncooked foods)

## When to Wear Gloves

Disposable gloves should be worn to provide a protective barrier and to prevent contamination of hands when touching blood, body fluids, mucus membranes (inside mouth), and nonintact skin (e.g., cuts, sores).

*Remember:* The wearing of disposable gloves does *not* replace the need to wash your hands. Gloves may have very small defects or may be torn during use, both of which can lead to hands becoming contaminated when taking off the gloves. Wash hands immediately after disposing of gloves. Hands are to be washed even if not visibly contaminated.

## When Water Is Not Available

When running water is not available, towelettes may be used as a temporary measure until hands can be cleaned under running water. Water basins should not be used as an alternative to running water. If there are no alternatives to a water basin as a temporary measure, clean and disinfect the basin between each use. The Centers for Disease Control and Prevention has stated that disease outbreaks have been linked with sharing wash water and wash basins.

## Spills Cleanup

The Occupational Safety and Health Administration has addressed concerns about transmission of certain diseases through contact with blood or body fluids. Each school system should have accessible to staff its policies and procedures related to these concerns. Specific procedures related to cleanup and the appropriate current solutions of a mixture of chlorine bleach and water should be readily available.

## Resources

- www.gphealthsmart.com/teaching/index.asp
- www.asmusa.org (can download a free poster about the importance of hand washing)
- www.cdc.gov
- www.mayoclinic.org

# Procedure B

## Bleeding

### Bleeding From Minor Cuts or Abrasions

Small wounds and abrasions (scrapes) do not pose any serious threat to adolescents. In the event of a minor injury that results in a small amount of bleeding, do the following:

- Rinse the area with warm water to clean away dirt.
- Wash with a mild soap and water.
- Cover the area with a sterile bandage/gauze.
- If the dressing becomes wet or soiled, remove and replace with a new sterile dressing.
- Be aware that once a scab has formed, the wound no longer needs a dressing.
- Recognize that signs of improper healing include increasing redness, swelling, heat, and drainage (pus).

### Bleeding From Larger Cuts or Lacerations

Large wounds require more immediate attention. Do the following:

- Rinse the area with warm water to clean away dirt.
- Wash with a mild soap and water.
- Cover the area with a sterile bandage/gauze.
- Protect yourself by wearing latex gloves.
- If the wound is bleeding, raise the bleeding area above the level of adolescent's heart.
- Apply pressure over the wound with the palm of your hand for 5 minutes.
- Do not apply a tourniquet or lift pressure to check the wound.
- If the dressing becomes soaked with blood, leave in place and put another dressing over the first one. Continue to apply pressure.

- Call **911** in the following instances:
  - Adolescent does not seem alert or responsive
  - Bleeding does not stop after 5 minutes of pressure
  - Wound is on the face, neck, or head
  - There is something stuck in the wound (do not remove protruding objects)
  - Wound is caused by a knife or gunshot
  - Cut seems to be deep

## Resource

- www.kidshealth.org

# Procedure C

## Care of Casts

There are basically two types of casts that are used for adolescents in immobilizing specific body parts. Instructions regarding cast care are based on the type of cast that is applied: either synthetic (fiberglass) or plaster. Synthetic casting material is lighter, dries in 30 minutes, has a rough exterior, and is water resistant. Plaster casts take 10 to 72 hours to dry and have a smooth exterior.

### Guidelines for Synthetic Casts

- Be aware that weight may be placed on a newly casted leg or arm 30 minutes after it is applied unless you are otherwise informed by the parent/caregiver or health care provider.
- Be aware that the rough surface makes the cast harder to autograph.
- If the cast becomes damp, dry thoroughly with a blow dryer on a cool setting. Failure to dry the cast may cause sores under the cast.
- Follow guidelines for plaster casts.

### Guidelines for Plaster Casts

- Check with parent/caregiver/adolescent about any restrictions of activity. Adolescent might need to avoid strenuous activities for the first few days.
- Be aware that weight may be placed on the newly casted leg after 48 hours unless you are otherwise informed by the parent/caregiver or health care provider.
- Be aware that adolescent should use crutches with a leg cast.
- Elevate adolescent's casted extremity if possible. Avoid allowing the casted extremity to hang down for any length of time.

Restrict adolescent's standing for too long, even with the use of crutches.

- Place a wet cast on a pillow or soft pad. (Avoid using fingers to move a wet cast; use the palm of the hand to avoid indentations. Avoid placing a wet cast on a hard surface because this may dent wet plaster.)
- Do not allow adolescent to scratch under the cast or to put any objects inside the cast because this may irritate the skin and cause a sore.
- If adolescent has a boot for the cast, make sure that adolescent wears it whenever he or she is walking. Not doing so, even for short periods of time, can cause the cast to crack and soften.
- Keep the cast dry. If adolescent needs to walk in the rain or snow, the cast should be protected with a plastic or waterproof covering or a cast shoe.
- Notify school health care personnel and parent/caregiver immediately if adolescent complains of the cast feeling too tight or too loose; if the cast becomes broken or cracked; if adolescent feels painful pressure areas or increased swelling; if adolescent complains of tingling, pain, or numbness that is not relieved by elevating the casted extremity; if you notice an excessive odor (some perspiration odor from the cast is normal); if the skin becomes darker or lighter than the comparable extremity; if you notice reddened skin or bleeding around the edges or on the cast itself; or if adolescent has a temperature above 101.3 degrees.
- Arrange for adolescent's safe exit from classroom in case of an unexpected event that requires students to leave the classroom or school.

## Resource

- www.vh.org/patients/ihb/ortho/castwear.html

# Procedure D

## Care of Tracheostomy

Tracheotomy or tracheostomy is a procedure where a cut (incision) is made into the windpipe (trachea) that forms either a temporary or permanent opening (ostomy). The opening or hole (stoma) allows for the insertion of a short tube that permits the adolescent to get air and remove mucus. Instead of breathing through the nose and mouth, the adolescent will now breathe through the tracheostomy opening. In the school setting, the adolescent might need to be suctioned (remove secretions) to keep the tube clear of mucus that can block the tracheostomy and hinder breathing. Some adolescents require suctioning prior to eating. In some cases, adolescents might be able to perform this procedure without assistance.

### Guidelines for Tracheostomy Suctioning

- Ask parent/caregiver the reason for adolescent having a tracheostomy. Request any specific instructions from health care provider regarding the procedure such as when suctioning should be performed, whether sterile saline drops should be instilled in the tracheostomy opening prior to suctioning, length of catheter insertion, disposal of used equipment, and care of the suction machine and connecting tube. Ask whether the suctioning technique should be following clean or sterile procedure. Ask parent/caregiver about any activity restrictions due to the tube (e.g., swimming, showers). Request that parent/caregiver demonstrate the tracheostomy suctioning initially.
- Wash hands prior to suctioning (*see* Procedure A). Put on protective eyewear.
- Remove the suction catheter (tube) from the package. Do not touch the part of the catheter that goes directly into adolescent's tracheostomy. Put a sterile glove on the hand that will be touching the catheter.

- Attach the suction catheter to the suction machine tubing.
- Turn on the suction machine with the nongloved hand.
- If saline drops are to be instilled, put in the drops at this time.
- With your thumb *off* the opening, insert the catheter without touching the part of the tube that goes into the opening. Never apply suction when inserting the catheter. Insert the catheter just beyond the length of the tracheostomy tube. Ask parent/caregiver the specific length of catheter insertion.
- Stand to the side of adolescent when suctioning. This procedure may produce a cough reflex, and the mucus may propel out of the stoma on you if you are standing directly in front of adolescent.
- With your thumb *on* the opening *intermittently,* withdraw the catheter with a rotating or twisting motion. When first inserting the catheter, it is helpful to count "1-one thousand, 2-one thousand, 3-one thousand, 4-one thousand." Or, you may choose to take a breath and hold it when you start inserting the tube and then remove it when you are no longer able to hold your breath. Remember that suctioning can cause adolescent to be anxious because he or she cannot breath during suctioning and that adolescent might need time to rest afterward. If you need to suction again, wait at least 30 to 60 seconds before suctioning and rinse the catheter by putting the tip in the water and applying suction until the catheter is free of any mucus.
- Note any changes in color, thickness, or smell of the mucus, and report such changes to parent/caregiver.
- Turn off the suction machine. Dispose of equipment per procedure without letting the tip touch anything else.
- Offer comfort to adolescent as needed.
- Remove gloves and wash hands.

## Communication

- Share with parent/caregiver how suctioning is progressing.
- Notify parent/caregiver of any changes in color, thickness, or smell of the mucus.
- Ask parent/caregiver to list specific activity restrictions and how stoma is to be protected on the playground. Ask to list specific safety concerns associated with adolescent having a tracheostomy such as avoiding swimming pools or streams. Parent/caregiver may request that adolescent remain indoors on very windy days to prevent small items from entering stoma.

## Resources

- www.childrens-mercy.org
- http://tracheostomy.com
- http://wellness.ucdavis.edu/general_health/family_practice/ tracheostomy

# Procedure E

## Tube Feedings

This procedure is also referred to as gastric gavage, nasogastric gavage, or gastrostomy. An adolescent who is unable to take nourishment or medications by mouth for a variety of health problems may have a tube inserted through his or her nose (NG-tube), mouth (OG-tube), or stomach (G-tube) or into the intestines (J-tube). Most adolescents will have a gastrostomy (stomach) tube or a gastrostomy button. Usually, adolescents receive commercially prepared feedings continuously (bag and pump) or intermittently (bolus or bag) designated at certain times of the day. The health care provider and/or dietitian determine the type and amount of nourishment. Depending on the health care provider's instructions, adolescents with tube feedings may also be taking some nourishment by mouth. Initially, the thought of tube feeding a student in your classroom might seem frightening, but it can be done with the proper instruction.

### Guidelines for Intermittent G-Tube Feedings

- Ask parent/caregiver the reason for adolescent having a tube feeding and for any specific instructions from health care provider such as feeding schedule, amount of feeding and any special preparations, rate of flow of the feeding, and about how long it should take to feed adolescent. Ask parent/caregiver whether adolescent is to eat or drink fluids by mouth as well. Ask for any activity restrictions due to the tube (e.g., swimming, showers). Request that parent/caregiver/school nurse demonstrate the tube feeding initially.
- Wash hands prior to tube feeding (*see* Procedure A). Put on disposable gloves.
- Gather equipment: large syringe (30 to 50 milliliters) without plunger or needle or funnel, tap water (unless otherwise

indicated), and formula or medications usually given at room temperature.

- Be aware that most children are fed in a semi-reclining or sitting position. Position adolescent with his or her head higher than the stomach. It is important to have contact with adolescent during the feeding time. Interact with and talk to adolescent.
- *Bolus Feeding:* Attach funnel or syringe without plunger to feeding tube, pour tap water (usually 1 to 2 ounces unless otherwise instructed) and then feeding into a syringe, not allowing air into the tubing or syringe. Raising or lowering the funnel/syringe controls the rate of feeding. When nourishment is completed, add tap water to clear tube and clamp or kink tubing. Disconnect syringe/funnel from the tube. Clamp/cap and secure tubing unless otherwise instructed. Be aware that, depending on adolescent and tube/button, some adolescents will need a decompression tube to vent air after the feeding.
- *Feeding Bag:* Clamp tubing. Fill bag and tubing with feeding. Hang bag from a pole or hook about 12 inches above adolescent's stomach. Open the clamp and regulate the drip according to instructions. You might initially need to squeeze the bag to start the feeding. Control rate of flow with the clamp. The feeding should take 15 to 30 minutes. If given too fast, adolescent may complain of sweating, nausea, vomiting, or diarrhea.
- Keep adolescent in sitting position for 30 to 60 minutes after feeding to prevent reflux (backward or return flow).
- Remove gloves and wash hands.
- Wash feeding equipment with hot soapy water, rinse well, and air dry. Feeding supplies may be reused.

## Communication

- Share with parent/caregiver how feedings are going, including any problems or changes. Ask for a written feeding plan to keep track of the schedule, amount, and type of feeding. Revise and update plan as necessary.
- Notify parent/caregiver if skin around the G-tube is warm, tender, bright red, swollen, or bleeding. Notify immediately if site is red and sore or has green or white liquid where the tube enters the skin and the child has a fever or is vomiting.
- Notify parent/caregiver if there is excess leaking around the tube or opening (soaking a gauze) or if adolescent is vomiting or has diarrhea or constipation.

- Notify parent/caregiver if the tube is blocked and you cannot remove blockage or if the tube is pulled out. With a blocked tube, try to *slowly* push water into the tube with a syringe. Use very slow and easy pushing. Never try to push any object into the tube to unclog it.
- Notify parent/caregiver if adolescent has a temperature above 101 degrees.

## Resources

- www.hs.state.az.us/cfhs/ons/pchance/spec-d.htm
- www.pedisurg.com
- www.cincinnatichildrens.org
- staff.washington.edu/growing/nourish/tubecare.htm

# Procedure F

## Medical Emergencies

Examples of medical emergencies in adolescents that may warrant immediate medical attention include the following:

- Experiencing chest or abdominal pain or pressure
- Difficulty in breathing or shortness of breath
- Large puncture wounds (including human bites)
- Bite from an unknown animal, snake, or insect
- Fall that results in a loss of consciousness
- Fall where adolescent ends up on his or her back
- Hitting the head or suffering a head injury
- Burns
- Suspected of inhaling, swallowing, or touching poisonous substances
- Suspected of taking an overdose of drugs
- Bleeding that does not stop after applying pressure
- Difficulty with movement or difficulty in feeling someone touching body after a fall or an injury
- Sudden slurred speech
- Hitting head and bleeding or drainage apparent from the ears, nose, and/or eyes
- Injection with the EpiPen (*see* Part III, Procedure K)
- Broken bones
- Severe asthmatic episode
- Severe allergic reaction
- Severe pain in any part of body
- Cannot stop vomiting, bleeding from the face, or having diarrhea episodes
- Sudden dizziness, weakness, or change in vision
- Expression of suicidal or homicidal feelings

- Victim of abuse
- Experiencing hallucinations and being incoherent in thoughts
- Stiff neck along with fever or headache
- Having pupils that are unequal or experiencing sudden blindness
- Inability to walk without staggering
- Experiencing persistent seizure activity
- Stopped breathing

---

Anytime you are not comfortable with a medical situation, call for assistance by activating the local emergency medical system in your area. You may save a young person's life!

Be ready to give the following information:

- Your location, including cross-streets and landmarks
- The telephone number you are calling from in case you become disconnected
- Your name
- What happened
- Who is injured and how many are injured
- Condition of adolescent needing assistance (e.g., conscious or unconscious, location of any bleeding, whether breathing on own, whether complaining of pain)
- What is being done to help adolescent

**Do not hang up first. Let the dispatcher hang up first!**

# Procedure G

## Pets in the Classroom

### Classroom Guidelines for Pets in the Classroom

- Be aware that pets/reptiles kept in classrooms should not be handled unless appropriate hand-washing and cleanup facilities are available and made accessible.
- Be aware that after any handling of pets/reptiles, hands should be washed with soap (antibacterial preferred) and water (*see* Part III, Procedure A).
- Keep pets/reptiles away from areas where food is stored, prepared, or eaten.
- Do not use the same sink to clean pet/reptile accessories or caging material where food is prepared.
- Do not allow adolescents to touch food or eating utensils after touching pets/reptiles.
- Keep pet/reptile cages as clean as possible.
- Do not permit unsupervised handling of pets/reptiles by adolescents.
- Clean caging material with rubber gloves.
- When washing pet/reptile cages or accessories, avoid splashes to the face or wear goggles.
- Do not use bathroom facilities for pet/reptile-related activities unless they are thoroughly disinfected.
- Consult veterinarian or pet care professional for recommendations on soaps and other products useful for disinfecting hands and surfaces.
- Be aware that disinfectant lotions, sprays, or similar products should be carried whenever reptiles are going to be handled and hand-washing facilities might be absent such as on field trip events.

## Infectious Diseases Related to Pets

| Infectious Disease | Pets | Susceptibility |
| --- | --- | --- |
| Cryptococcus (krip-toe-kok'us) | Birds (especially pigeons) | Adolescents with immune disorders |
| Psittacosis (sit-uh-ko'sis) | Birds (especially parrots and parakeets) | Bird owners |
| Cat scratch disease | Cat | Cat owner, youth with immune disorders |
| Cryptosporidium (krip-toe-spor-id'ee-um) | Cat | Adolescents with immune disorders |
| Dipylidium | Dog and cat flea tapeworm | Children of women who were infected during pregnancy and adolescents with immune system disorders |
| Hookworm | Puppies and kittens | Owners of puppies and kittens, adolescents, pregnant women, and persons who are malnourished |
| Rabies | Unvaccinated dogs, cats, skunks, foxes, raccoons, coyotes, and bats | Adolescents who have been bitten by animals with rabies |
| Hantavirus | Rodent droppings, urine, and saliva; virus can spread to the air and on dust particles | Adolescents who are camping, hiking, or participating in outdoor hobbies |
| Ringworm | Cats and dogs | Adolescents and owners of cats and dogs |
| Toxocariasis (roundworms) (tox-o-car-i'a-sis) | Dogs (especially puppies) and cats | Adolescents |
| Salmonellosis | Small animals/reptiles (e.g., hamsters, gerbils, pet mice, pet rats, guinea pigs, rabbits, lizards, snakes, turtles, iguanas) | Adolescents, owners of these pets/reptiles, adolescents with immune disorders or organ transplants, and adolescents who are receiving radiation |
| Lymphocytic choriomeningitis (lim-fo-sit'ik kor-ee-o-men-in-jie'tiss) | Pet mice or hamsters | Owners of pet mice or hamsters and adolescents whose mothers became infected during pregnancy |

# Procedure H

## Testicular Self-Exam

Starting at age 14 or 15 years, monthly self-examination of the testicles is an effective way in which to detect testicular cancer at an early stage. The self-exam is best performed after a warm bath or shower, when the scrotum is most relaxed. Instruct adolescent boys how to conduct a testicular self-exam as follows:

- Stand in front of a mirror. Check for any swelling on the scrotal skin.
- Find the epididymis (the soft, tube-like structure behind the testicle that carries sperm). Become familiar with this structure so that you do not mistake it for a lump.
- Examine each testicle with both hands. Place the index and middle fingers under the testicle with the thumbs placed on top. Roll the testicle gently between the thumbs and fingers. You should not feel any pain when doing the exam.
- Cancerous lumps usually are found on the sides of the testicle but can also show up on the front.
- If you find a lump, see a urologist (a doctor specializing in the urinary tract and male genitals).
- Other signs of testicular cancer include the following:
  - A lump the size of a pea or marble that may or may not be painful
  - A hardening or change in size of the testicle
  - A feeling of heaviness in the scrotum
  - A dull ache in the lower abdomen or in the groin
  - A sudden collection of fluid in the scrotum

# Procedure I

## Skin Cancer Prevention

### Guidelines for Adolescents

Skin cancer is the most common type of cancer, as well as the most rapidly increasing form of cancer, in the United States. More than 1 million cases of basal cell or squamous cell carcinoma (the most common types of skin cancer) occur annually in the United States. The third most common type of skin cancer is melanoma. It causes more deaths than basal or squamous cell combined.

Skin cancer was estimated to result in an estimated 9,600 deaths in 2002. Of these deaths, melanoma was estimated to account for 7,400 lives lost, whereas the other types of skin cancer was estimated to result in only 2,200 deaths. Ultraviolet radiation (sunlight) causes between 65% and 90% of melanomas. Children or adolescents who have a history of one or more sunburns have been found to be at increased risk for developing basal cell carcinoma or melanoma as adults. In addition, children or adolescents frequently develop moles, an important risk factor for skin cancer.

More than half of a person's lifetime exposure to ultraviolet rays is obtained during childhood and adolescence. Alarmingly, less than one third of American adolescents practice safe sun protection routines. According to the Mayo Clinic, nearly half of all Americans will develop a cancerous skin lesion at least once by age 65 years.

### Primary Groups Affected

| Skin Type | Tanning and Sunburn History |
| --- | --- |
| I | Always burns, never tans, is sensitive to sun exposure |
| II | Burns easily, tans minimally |
| III | Burns moderately, tans gradually to light brown |

| IV | Burns minimally, always tans well to moderately brown |
| V | Rarely burns, tans profusely to dark |
| VI | Never burns, is deeply pigmented, is least sensitive |

SOURCE: Centers for Disease Control and Prevention. (2002). *Guidelines to prevent cancer among young people: Questions and answers on skin cancer prevention.* [Online.] Retrieved January 20, 2003, from www.cdc.gov

NOTE: Persons with skin types I and II are at the highest risk for damage as a result of sun exposure.

*Any person can get skin cancer regardless of skin type.* However, there is greater risk among those who sunburn readily and tan poorly, namely those with red or blond hair and fair skin that freckles or burns easily. All persons, regardless of skin types, need to adopt habits to decrease their risk.

Following are Centers for Disease Control and Prevention recommendations for schools to encourage skin cancer prevention on school property and elsewhere:

- When possible, encourage scheduling of outdoor activities during times when the sun is not at peak intensity. Peak times are typically between 10 a.m. and 4 p.m. during Daylight Savings Time or between 9 a.m. and 3 p.m. during Standard Time. These are the most hazardous times for ultraviolet (UV) ray exposure in the United States and are greatest during the late spring and early summer. Teach students that UV rays can affect their bodies on cloudy and hazy days as well as on sunny days and that rays will reflect off surfaces such as water, cement, sand, and snow.
- Request administration to modify building and grounds codes to increase the availability of shade in frequently used outdoor spaces.
- Encourage or require students to wear protective clothing, hats, and sunglasses when outdoors. Wide-brimmed hats, dry (as opposed to wet) tightly woven clothes, and darker colors are preferred. Long-sleeved shirts and long pants and wrap-around sunglasses provide for increased UV ray protection. If wearing baseball caps, students should also protect ears and neck area from sun.
- Establish sunscreen use routines before going outside (sunscreen and lip screen with at least SPF 15, applied generously 30 minutes before going outside and reapplied after swimming or sweating). Remind students to check expiration date of

sunscreen. Exposure to high temperatures can shorten the expiration date. Sunscreens without expiration dates usually are effective for no more than 3 years.

- Support health education activities needed for skin cancer prevention.
- Disseminate skin cancer prevention information to adolescents' families.
- Develop guidance for allocation of resources for skin cancer prevention.

## Resources

- cancerinfo@cdc.gov
- healthyyouth@cdc.gov/choose_your_cover
- Centers for Disease Control and Prevention
  *Guidelines for School Programs to Prevent Skin Cancer*
  (888) 842-6355 or (888) 231-6405
  www.cdc.gov/mmwr/preview/mmwrhtml/rr5104a1.htm
- mayoclinic.org

# Procedure J

## Immunizations

The Advisory Committee on Immunization Practices (ACIP) is a national advisory group made up of experts from the Centers for Disease Control and Prevention (www.cdc.gov), the American Academy of Pediatrics (www.aap.org), and the American Academy of Family Physicians (www.aafp.org). Each year, the ACIP issues an updated Recommended Childhood Immunization Schedule (www.cdc.gov/ nip/acip). Its Web site also features fact sheets, statistics, a glossary, and links to organizations offering additional information.

State-by-state school entry vaccination requirements may be found at the National Network for Immunization Information (NNii) Web site (www.immunizationinfo.org). The NNii is a partnership of the American Academy of Pediatrics, the American Academy of Family Physicians, the American Nurses Association, and several other medical societies concerned with school health.

# Recommended Childhood and Adolescent Immunization Schedule -- United States, 2003

| Vaccine ▼  Age ► | Birth | 1 mo | 2 mos | 4 mos | 6 mos | 12 mos | 15 mos | 18 mos | 24 mos | 4-6 yrs | 11-12 yrs | 13-18 yrs |
|---|---|---|---|---|---|---|---|---|---|---|---|---|
| Hepatitis B[1] | HepB #1 | HepB #2 (only if mother HBsAg (-)) | | | HepB #3 | | | | | | HepB series | |
| Diphtheria, Tetanus, Pertussis[2] | | | DTaP | DTaP | DTaP | | DTaP | DTaP | | DTaP | Td | |
| Haemophilus influenzae Type b[3] | | | Hib | Hib | Hib | Hib | | | | | | |
| Inactivated Polio | | | IPV | IPV | | IPV | | | | IPV | | |
| Measles, Mumps, Rubella[4] | | | | | | MMR #1 | | | | MMR #2 | MMR #2 | |
| Varicella[5] | | | | | | Varicella | | | | | Varicella | |
| Pneumococcal[6] | | | PCV | PCV | PCV | PCV | | | PCV | PPV | | |
| Hepatitis A[7] | | | | | | | | | | Hepatitis A series | | |
| Influenza[8] | | | | | | | Influenza (yearly) | | | | | |

range of recommended ages  |  catch-up vaccination  |  preadolescent assessment

Vaccines below this line are for selected populations

This schedule indicates the recommended ages for routine administration of currently licensed childhood vaccines, as of December 1, 2002, for children through age 18 years. Any dose not given at the recommended age should be given at any subsequent visit when indicated and feasible. Indicates age groups that warrant special effort to administer those vaccines not previously given. Additional vaccines may be licensed and recommended during the year. Licensed combination vaccines may be used whenever any components of the combination are indicated and the vaccine's other components are not contraindicated. Providers should consult the manufacturers' package inserts for detailed recommendations.

**Approved by the Advisory Committee on Immunization Practices (www.cdc.gov/nip/acip), the American Academy of Pediatrics (www.aap.org), and the American Academy of Family Physicians (www.aafp.org).**

**Footnotes: Recommended Childhood Immunization Schedule
United States, 2002**

**1. Hepatitis B vaccine (Hep B).** All infants should receive the first dose of hepatitis B vaccine soon after birth and before hospital discharge; the first dose may also be given by age 2 months if the infant's mother is HBsAg-negative. Only monovalent hepatitis B vaccine can be used for the birth dose. Monovalent or combination vaccine containing Hep B may be used to complete the series; four doses of vaccine may be administered if combination vaccine is used. The second dose should be given at least 4 weeks after the first dose, except for Hib-containing vaccine which cannot be administered before age 6 weeks. The third dose should be given at least 16 weeks after the first dose and at least 8 weeks after the second dose. The last dose in the vaccination series (third or fourth dose) should not be administered before age 6 months.

Infants born to HBsAg-positive mothers should receive hepatitis B vaccine and 0.5 mL hepatitis B immune globulin (HBIG) within 12 hours of birth at separate sites. The second dose is recommended at age 1-2 months and the vaccination series should be completed (third or fourth dose) at age 6 months.

Infants born to mothers whose HBsAg status is unknown should receive the first dose of the hepatitis B vaccine series within 12 hours of birth. Maternal blood should be drawn at the time of delivery to determine the mother's HBsAg status; if the HBsAg test is positive, the infant should receive HBIG as soon as possible (no later than age 1 week).

**2. Diphtheria and tetanus toxoids and acellular pertussis vaccine (DTaP).** The fourth dose of DTaP may be administered as early as age 12 months, provided 6 months have elapsed since the third dose and the child is unlikely to return at age 15-18 months. **Tetanus and diphtheria toxoids (Td)** is recommended at age 11-12 years if at least 5 years have elapsed since the last dose of tetanus and diphtheria toxoid-containing vaccine. Subsequent routine Td boosters are recommended every 10 years.

**3. _Haemophilus influenzae_ type b (Hib) conjugate vaccine.** Three Hib conjugate vaccines are licensed for infant use. If PRP-OMP (PedvaxHIB® or ComVax® [Merck]) is administered at ages 2 and 4 months, a dose at age 6 months is not required. DTaP/Hib combination products should not be used for primary immunization in infants at age 2, 4 or 6 months, but can be used as boosters following any Hib vaccine.

**4. Inactivated poliovirus vaccine (IPV).** An all-IPV schedule is recommended for routine childhood poliovirus vaccination in the United States. All children should receive four doses of IPV at age 2 months, 4 months, 6-18 months, and 4-6 years.

**5. Measles, mumps, and rubella vaccine (MMR).** The second dose of MMR is recommended routinely at age 4-6 years but may be administered during any visit, provided at least 4 weeks have elapsed since the first dose and that both doses are administered beginning at or after age 12 months. Those who have not previously received the second dose should complete the schedule by the visit at age 11-12 years.

**6. Varicella vaccine.** Varicella vaccine is recommended at any visit at or after age 12 months for susceptible children (i.e. those who lack a reliable history of chickenpox). Susceptible persons aged ! 13 years should receive two doses, given at least 4 weeks apart.

**7. Pneumococcal vaccine.** The heptavalent **pneumococcal conjugate vaccine (PCV)** is recommended for all children aged 2-23 months and for certain children aged 24-59 months. **Pneumococcal polysaccharide vaccine (PPV)** is recommended in addition to PCV for certain high-risk groups. See *MMWR* 2000;49(RR-9);1-37.

**8. Hepatitis A vaccine.** Hepatitis A vaccine is recommended for use in selected states and regions, and for certain high-risk groups; consult your local public health authority. See *MMWR* 1999;48(RR-12);1-37.

**9. Influenza vaccine.** Influenza vaccine is recommended annually for children age ! 6 months with certain risk factors (including but not limited to asthma, cardiac disease, sickle cell disease, HIV and diabetes; see *MMWR* 2001;50(RR-4);1-44), and can be administered to all others wishing to obtain immunity. Children aged ∀12 years should receive vaccine in a dosage appropriate for their age (0.25 mL if age 6-35 months or 0.5 mL if aged # 3 years). Children aged ∀ 8 years who are receiving influenza vaccine for the first time should receive two doses separated by at least 4 weeks.

Additional information about vaccines, vaccine supply, and contraindications for immunization, is available at www.cdc.gov/nip or at the National Immunization Hotline, 800-232-2522 (English) or 800-232-0233 (Spanish).

# Procedure K

## EpiPen

EpiPen is a portable auto-injecting device available from Dey, L. P. (Napa, CA). EpiPen can be used in an emergency to administer epinephrine in response to a severe allergic reaction (anaphylaxis). A complete guide to using EpiPen can be found at Dey's Allergic Reaction Central Web site (www.allergic-reactions.com).

NDC 49502-500-01 (EPIPEN)
NDC 49502-500-02 (EPIPEN 2-PAK)
NDC 49502-501-01 (EPIPEN JR)
NDC 49502-501-02 (EPIPEN JR 2-PAK)

| EPIPEN® & EPIPEN® JR |
| --- |
| (epinephrine) Auto-Injectors |
| *For allergic emergencies (anaphylaxis)* |

### IMPORTANT INFORMATION

### Both EPIPEN® & EPIPEN® JR

-- are disposable, prefilled automatic injection devices
-- are for allergic emergencies
-- contain a single dose of epinephrine (intramuscular)
-- are available by prescription only (Rx)
-- contain **no latex**

### Amount of epinephrine delivered

**EPIPEN®**   = one dose of **0.30mg** epinephrine *(USP, 1:1000, 0.3mL)*

**EPIPEN® JR** = one dose of **0.15 mg** epinephrine *(USP, 1:2000, 0.3mL)*

-- *Note:* most of the liquid (about 90%) stays in the auto-injector after use and cannot be reused

## When to Use

Use the EPIPEN®/EPIPEN® JR auto-injector *only* if you are a hypersensitive (allergic) person and your doctor has prescribed it for allergic emergencies. Such emergencies may occur from insect stings or bites, foods, drugs, latex, other allergens, exercise-induced anaphylaxis, or unknown causes (idiopathic).

## Emergency Treatment of Allergic Reaction (Anaphylaxis)

-- If you experience the signs and symptoms described by your physician:
   -- Use the EPIPEN®/EPIPEN® JR auto-injector immediately, **through clothing if necessary.**
   -- Repeat injection with an additional EPIPEN® or EPIPEN® JR may be necessary- consult your physician.
   -- Follow "Directions for Use" section carefully.
   -- Then follow steps in "Immediately After Use" section.
   -- Avoid exertion.
-- If you have been stung by an insect:
   -- Remove insect stinger with your fingernails if possible.
   -- Do not squeeze, pinch, or push it deeper into the skin.
   -- If available, apply ice packs or sodium bicarbonate soaks to the stung area.

## Care & Storage

-- Keep the EPIPEN®/EPIPEN® JR auto-injector ready for use at all times.
-- Store:
   -- in a dark place at room temperature (59-86°F)
   -- plastic carrying tube provides added UV light protection
   -- do NOT refrigerate
   -- do NOT expose to extreme cold or heat
-- Note expiration date on the unit (month & year)
   -- example: "Aug. 02" = Aug. 31, 2002
   -- replace it before the expiration date
   -- see below to enroll in the Expiration Reminder Program
   -- always have at least one unexpired unit on hand
-- Examine contents in clear window of auto-injector periodically
   -- replace the unit if the solution is discolored or contains solid particles (precipitate)
   -- the physician may recommend emergency use of an auto-injector with discolored contents rather than to postpone treatment

## WARNING

-- **Never put thumb, fingers, or hand over black tip.** Needle comes out of black tip. Accidental injection into hands or feet may result in loss of blood flow to these areas. If this happens, go immediately to the nearest emergency room.
-- EPIPEN®/EPIPEN® JR should be injected *only* into the outer thigh (see "Directions for Use").
-- **Do NOT remove gray activation cap until ready to use.**

## DIRECTIONS FOR USE

--Follow these directions *only* when ready to use.
--**Never put thumb, fingers, or hand over black tip.**
--**Do NOT remove gray activation cap until ready to use.**

1) Familiarize yourself with the unit.

Black Tip (needle comes out during use) — Clear Window — Gray Activation Cap (do **NOT** remove until ready to use)

EPIPEN® EPINEPHRINE AUTO-INJECTOR

<--- - - - Auto-Injector - - - -->

2) Grasp unit, with the black tip pointing downward.
3) Form a fist around the auto-injector (black tip down).
4) With your other hand, pull off the gray activation cap.

5) Hold black tip near outer thigh.
6) Swing and **jab firmly** into outer thigh so that auto-injector is perpendicular (at a 90° angle) to the thigh.

7) Hold **firmly in thigh** for several seconds.

8) Remove unit, massage injection area for several seconds.
9) Check black tip:
   -- if needle is exposed, you received the dose
   -- if not, repeat steps #5-8
10) *Note:* most of the liquid (about 90%) stays in the auto-injector and cannot be reused.

11) Bend the needle back against a hard surface.
12) Carefully put the unit (needle first) back into the carrying tube (*without* the gray activation cap)
13) Recap the carrying tube.
14) See "Immediately After Use" box on right side.

**IMMEDIATELY AFTER USE**
-- **Go immediately to the nearest hospital emergency room.**
You may need further medical attention.
-- Tell the physician that you have received an injection of epinephrine (show your thigh).
-- Give your used **EPIPEN®/EPIPEN® JR** to the physician for inspection and proper disposal.

MANUFACTURED FOR DEY,
NAPA, CALIFORNIA 94558, U.S.A.
by Meridian Medical Technologies, Inc.
Columbia, MD 21046, U.S.A.
U.S. Patent No. 4,031,893
03 535 00A 12/00

# Bibliography

Allison, G. T., Weston, R., Shaw, R., Longhurst, J., James, L., Kyle, K., Nehyba, K., Low, S. M., & May, M. (1996). The reliability of quadriceps muscle stiffness in individuals with Osgood-Schlatter disease. *Journal of Sport Rehabilitation, 7,* 258–266.

American Dental Association, Council on Scientific Affairs. (1999). The dental team and latex hypersensitivity. *Journal of the American Dental Association, 130,* 257–264.

Anderson, J. A. (1997). Milk, eggs, and peanuts: Food allergies in children. *American Family Physician, 56,* 1365–1374.

Ball, J., & Bindler, R. (1999). *Pediatric nursing: Caring for children.* Upper Saddle River, NJ: Appleton & Lange.

Ball, J. W., & Bindler, R. C. (2003). *Pediatric nursing: Caring for children* (3rd ed.). Upper Saddle River, NJ: Prentice Hall.

Behrman, R., & Kleigman, R. (1998). *Nelson's essentials of pediatrics.* Philadelphia: W. B. Saunders.

Bernardo, L. M., & Bove, M. (1993). *Pediatric emergency nursing procedures.* Boston: Jones & Bartlett.

Boskner, G. (2002). *Textbook of adult and pediatric emergency medicine* (2nd ed.). Atlanta, GA: American Health Consultants.

Boynton, R. W., Dunn, E. S., & Stephens, C. R. (1998). *Manual of ambulatory pediatrics* (4th ed.). Philadelphia: Lippincott-Raven.

Bradley, B. J. (1996, October). Tinea capitis today: What nurses need to know about identifying and managing fungal infections of the scalp in the school setting. *Journal of School Nurses.* (Special supplement)

Bragdon, A. D., & Gamon, D. (2000). *Brains that work a little bit differently.* Cape Cod, MA: Brainwaves Center.

Brewer, E., & Angel, K. (1992). *Parenting a child with arthritis.* Los Angeles: RGA Publishing.

Burns, C., Barber, N., Brady, M., & Dunn, A. (1996). *Pediatric primary care: A handbook for the nurse practitioner.* Philadelphia: W. B. Saunders.

Burns, C. E., Brady, M. A., Dunn, E. S., & Starr, N. B. (2000). *Pediatric primary care: A handbook for nurse practitioners* (2nd ed.). Philadelphia: W. B. Saunders.

Casella, J. F., Bowers, D. C., & Pelidis, M. A. (1997). Disorders of coagulation. In K. B. Johnson & F. A. Oski (Eds.), *Oski's essential pediatrics* (pp. 1472–1491). Philadelphia: Lippincott-Raven.

Cassidy, J., & Petty, R. (1990) *Textbook of pediatric rheumatology* (2nd ed.). New York: Churchill Livingstone.

Chandra, R. K. (1997). Food hypersensitivity and allergic disease: A selective review. *American Journal of Clinical Nutrition, 66,* S526–S529.

Cherry, J. D. (1999). Parvovirus infections in children and adults. *Advances in Pediatrics, 46,* 245–269.

Coakley-Maller, C., & Shea, M. (1997). Respiratory infections in children: Preparing for the fall and winter. *Advances for Nurse Practitioner, 5*(9), 20–27.

Delfico, A. J., Dormans, J. P., Craythorne, C. B., & Templeton, J. J. (1997). Intraoperative anaphylaxis due to allergy to latex in children who have cerebral palsy: A report of six cases. *Developmental Medicine & Child Neurology, 39,* 194–197.

DeStefanol Lewis, K., & Thomson, H. B. (1986). *Manual of school health.* Menlo Park, CA: Addison-Wesley.

Duggan, C. (1996). HIV infection in children. *Pediatric Nursing, 8*(10), 32.

Epstein, J. L., & Kiryk, P. K. (2002). Adolescent health. *Nursing Clinics of North America, 37,* 373–382.

Faust, K., Shrewsbury, C., Zaglaniczny, K., & Jarrett, M. (1999). A comparative analysis of latex allergy in the healthy versus high-risk pediatric population. *ANA Journal, 67,* 461–466.

Flannery, R. B. (1999). *Preventing youth violence: A guide for parents, teachers, and counselors.* New York: Continuum.

Fox, J. A. (2002). *Primary health care of infants, children, and adolescents* (2nd ed.). St. Louis, MO: C. V. Mosby.

Gilden, J. H. (1998). Human parvovirus B19: Flushing in face though healthy (fifth disease and more). *Pediatric Nursing, 24,* 325–329.

Globus, S. (2002). Osgood-Schlatter: More than growing pains. *Current Health, 28*(5), 20–21.

Graham, M. V., & Uphold, C. R. (1999). *Clinical guidelines in child health.* Gainesville, FL: Barmarrae Books.

Greene, C. (Ed.). (1995). *Johns Hopkins Children's Center First Aid for Children Fast: Emergency procedures for all parents and caregivers.* New York: Dorling Kindersley.

Grose, C. (1997). Varicella-zoster virus infection. In K. B. Johnson & F. A. Oski (Eds.), *Oski's essential pediatrics* (pp. 1127–1130). Philadelphia: Lippincott-Raven.

Hale, C. M., & Polder, J. A. (1997). *The ABC's of safe and healthy child care: A handbook for child care providers.* Washington, DC: U.S. Department of Health and Human Services, Public Health Service.

Hoeman, S. P. (2002). *Rehabilitation nursing: Process, application, and outcomes* (3rd ed.). St. Louis, MO: C. V. Mosby.

Jackson, P. L., & Vessey, J. A. (1996). *Primary care of the child with a chronic condition* (2nd ed.). St. Louis, MO: C. V. Mosby.

Kerr, J. R., & Preston, N. M. (2001). Current pharmacotherapy of pertussis. *Expert Opinions in Pharmacotherapy, 2,* 1275–1282.

Kline, M. W. (1997). Otitis media. In K. B. Johnson & F. A. Oski (Eds.), *Oski's essential pediatrics* (pp. 1301–1303). Philadelphia: Lippincott-Raven.

Klippel, J., & Weyand, C. (1997). *Primer on the rheumatic diseases* (11th ed.). Atlanta, GA: Arthritis Foundation.

Kranowitz, C. S. (1998). *The out-of-sync child: Recognizing and coping with sensory integration dysfunction.* New York: Skylight Press.

Lee, M. H., & Kim, K. T. (1998). Latex allergy: A relevant issue in the general pediatric population. *Journal of Pediatric Health Care, 12,* 242–246.

Leung, A. K., & Robson, W. L. (1996). Evaluating the child with chronic diarrhea. *American Family Physician, 53,* 635–643.

Levy, A. M., & Fuerst, M. L. (1993). *Sports injury handbook: Professional advice for amateur athletes.* New York: John Wiley.

Loder, R. T., Aronsson, D. D., Dobbs, M. B., & Weinstein, S. L. (2000). Slipped capital femoral epiphysis. *Journal of Bone and Joint Surgery, 82A,* 1170–1187.

Lubkin, I. M., & Larsen, P. D. (2002). *Chronic illness: Impact and interventions* (5th ed.). Boston: Jones & Bartlett.

Matson, D. O. (1994). Viral gastroenteritis in day-care settings: Epidemiology and new developments. *Pediatrics, 94,* 999–1001.

McCarthy, A. M., Williams, J. K., & Eidal, L. (1996). Children with chronic conditions: Educators' views. *Journal of Pediatric Health Care, 10,* 272–279.

Meeropol, E. V. (1998). The R.U.B.B.E.R. tool: Screening children for latex allergy. *Journal of Pediatric Health Care, 12,* 320–323.

Mudd, K. M., & Noone, S. A. (1995). Management of severe food allergy in the school setting. *Journal of School Nursing, 11*(3), 30–32.

Nowicki, M., & Balistreri, W. (1992). Hepatitis A to E: Building up the alphabet. *Contemporary Pediatrics, 9*(11), 118–128.

Oski, F. (1994*). Principles and practice of pediatrics.* Philadelphia: J. B. Lippincott.

Petty, S. (1997). *Piercing: A guide to safety.* Waco, TX: Health EDCO.

Pillitteri, A. (1999). Nursing care of the child with an infectious disorder. In A. Pillitteri (Ed.), *Child health nursing* (pp. 667–697). Philadelphia: Lippincott, Williams, & Walkins.

Potts, N., & Mandelco, B. (2002). *Pediatric nursing: Caring for children and their families.* Clifton Park, NY: Delmar.

Sampson, H. A., & Burks, A. W. (1996). Mechanisms of food allergy. *Annual Review of Nutrition, 16,* 161–177.

Santen, S. A., & Altieri, M. F. (2001). Pediatric urinary tract infection. *Emergency Medicine Clinics of North America, 19,* 675–690.

Schmitt, B. D. (1993). When your child has an eye infection with pus. *Contemporary Pediatrics, 10*(3), 117–118.

Silverman, P. R. (2000). *Never too young to know: Death in children's lives.* New York: Oxford University Press.

Stiefel, L. (1995). Erythemia infectiosum (fifth disease). *Pediatric Review, 16,* 474–475.

Tipsord-Klinkhammer, B., & Andreoni, C. P. (1998). *Quick reference for emergency nursing.* Philadelphia: W. B. Saunders.

Votroubek, W. L., & Townsend, J. L. (1997). *Pediatric home care* (2nd ed.). Gaithersburg, MD: Aspen.

Waley, L. F., & Wong, D. L. (2000). *Nursing care of infants and children.* St. Louis, MO: C. V. Mosby.

Ward, R. G. (2001). Tourette syndrome. *Nursing Spectrum, 14,* 22–24.

Wilkinson, B. (1998). *Coping with the dangers of tattooing, body piercing, and branding.* New York: Rosen Publishing.

Wong, D. L., & Hockenberry-Eaton, M. (2001). *Wong's essentials of pediatric nursing.* St. Louis, MO: C. V. Mosby.

# Index

**CORWIN
PRESS**

The Corwin Press logo—a raven striding across an open book—represents the happy union of courage and learning. We are a professional-level publisher of books and journals for K-12 educators, and we are committed to creating and providing resources that embody these qualities. Corwin's motto is "Success for All Learners."